Radiant Aspiration

Radiant Aspiration

The Butterlamp Prayer
Lamp of Aspiration
By
Chimed Rigdzin Rinpoche

With commentary by
James Low

Published by Simply Being www.simplybeing.co.uk

A catalogue record of this book is available from the British Library.

ISBN: 978-0-9569239-0-5

Typeset in Tibetan unicode font: Jomolhari-ID-a3d.ttf; headings: Baskerville Old Face; body of text: Palatino Linotype; transliteration from Tibetan: Arial; Translation lines: Times New Roman, Palatino Linotype, Book Antiqua.

Printed and bound in Great Britain by Lightning Source, Chapter House, Pitfield Kiln Farm, Milton Keynes, MK11 3LW.

Dedicated
to all those oppressed
by the darkness of others

Our nature is radiant
yet hidden from us.
May the light of non-duality
illuminate this paradox.

Contents

Preface

The Butterlamp Prayer which is the heart of this book arose from the aspiration to benefit one person and all beings. The one person was Tulku Tsorlo who was living in Tibet. His closest disciple, Chimed Rigdzin, was living in India, in retreat in Tsopema, the site of one of Padmasambhava's great miracles. Chimed Rigdzin, also known as Lamaji, C.R. Lama and Zilnon Lingpa, would never see his teacher again due to the Chinese invasion of Tibet. However, he felt his presence and often met him in his dreams. This prayer of aspiration was written by him in one sitting in order to ward off difficulties for Tulku Tsorlo who was then sixty-one, an age of transition linked with problems.

The link between student and teacher is infinite, without limits. Neither time nor space can interrupt the flow of connection. This is because the very function of that link is to illuminate the nature of our existence. In experiencing the inseparability that continues through all the changes that occur, we awaken to the ground of our being, the openness which is the source of everything. The teacher returns us to ourself, and through that we start to be a bit useful to others. Devotion, aspiration, wishing the best for others – these are the great vehicles to carry us on the journey home.

I first translated *The Butterlamp Prayer* with C.R. Lama thirty-five years ago and have revised the translation many times since then. For C.R. Lama this was a vital text which, in a very precise, condensed way, reminds us of the key points of the dharma path. For many years until his death in 2002 he would host an annual offering of one hundred thousand butterlamps and this prayer of aspiration was the central practice at these events. These offering retreats still continue in Poland and India.

The texts in this book can be read as part of dharma practice by anyone who is interested. The key point is to engage with an open heart intent on the benefit of others. When I was a small child the lights in our street still ran on gas. Every evening the lamplighter would come with his ladder and light each lamp in turn with a spark from the pole he carried. How fortunate we are in our lives if someone lights our lamp through the spark of theirs. Lineage, the transmission of the lamp, is vital. Luckily there are many bright ones moving in our world who can ignite our flame in the midst of our darkness. We all have the fuel, the basic capacity – our task is to break out of our self-enclosure and avail ourselves of the passing flame. Even a book can serve this function.

When the texts in this book were first translated and printed in India the work was done in the small courtyard of C. R. Lama's house in Shanti-niketan. This was simple accommodation provided by the university where he worked. The English was typed onto waxed paper and the Tibetan text was then written in the wax with a metal pen. The sheet was then put on an inked drum and used to print about a hundred copies before it started to break up. Over the years many people have contributed to the reprinting and translating into new languages of this Butterlamp Prayer. Working in dharma sweetly allows us to be connected with the heart energy of many people. This is a real delight and sustenance.

This edition appears due to the help of Sarah Allen, Gordon Ellis, Ruth Rickard, Johanna Stoll and Barbara Terris. The printing has been generously sponsored by Hans-Jörg Burkhart.

May the light in our hearts lighten our load and guide us home.

Introduction

Aspiring for the benefit of all beings is the heart of dharma practice. The expansive and inclusive wish for universal wellbeing illuminates the web of interconnectedness within which we live. Light connects us and is the basis for our existence. We talk of enlightenment, of wanting all beings to be forever in the light of awakening, to be both enlightened and enlightening.

This book is an exploration of an aspiration which is recited while butterlamps are being offered. The key text is popularly called *The Butterlamp Prayer*. It was written by Chimed Rigdzin Rinpoche (C.R. Lama, 1922-2002) as a way to remove obstacles in the life of his teacher, Tulku Tsorlo. In addition to this prayer there is a section from *The Aspiration of Good Deeds* (*bZang sPyod sMon Lam*) which sets out a path of infinite multiplication of virtuous activity as our means of transcending our customary limited, rational perception. There is a third short text, *The Sutra of the Story of King Golden Hand and his Aspiration*, which tells the story of a noble sacrifice, the benefits of which continue to manifest in our time.

These texts unite in an aspiration to benefit sentient beings by means of an actual activity, a practice, which directly impacts all beings, bringing illumination and benefit. As long as we imagine that the limited sense we have of ourselves is an accurate description of our nature, our potential, our capacity, we are likely to feel overwhelmed by the difficulties of this world. There are so many beings, with so much suffering, living in such complicated circumstances – what could we possibly do? Yet due to the kindness of the Buddha and the teachers of the many lineages of practice there are many, many effective and compassionate methods which we can learn and use.

One central method is the practice of making offerings. Offering can be done with actual substances – food, wealth, butterlamps, flowers and so on, which are offered up to the Buddha and then given to poor people who are in need, as well as to holy people to honour them and aid their work. Offerings can be made to stupas and other sacred objects as a way of honouring them. This also allows the symbolism they manifest to resonate in our being. Offerings can be made with the imagination whereby we offer the contents of the world and all that might be pleasing to beings in the different realms of existence and to buddhas, bodhisattvas and all those residing in the pure realms. We can offer our body, as in the practice of Chod, so that its transformation pleases the four orders of guests, from the highest to the lowest. This offering also frees us from identification with our own ordinary illusory body to which we are so attached. In tantric practice, light is radiated as an offering to all the buddhas who in turn send back light to purify and liberate all beings.

Making offerings is a way of connecting to all that seems separate and other. It helps us to awaken to the truth of dependent co-origination; to directly experience the ceaseless flow of the mutual influencing of all that manifests. From this we can experience the absence of inherent self-nature, the absence of individual, personal essence, in all beings and in all phenomena. Infinite openness, infinite emptiness is the actuality of all that manifests; illusory forms moving together, neither essentially separate nor merged. This luminous display offers no basis for attachment nor for fantasies of control.

Offering butterlamps, offering light, is a particularly effective way of awakening to the radiance of our own natural condition. The activity of preparing the lamps, filling them, lighting them, and afterwards cleaning them helps us to live with impermanence – this is especially powerful when we set out to burn 100,000 lamps! These activities and the work of reciting and visualising are part of movement, the ceaseless flow of manifestation. However, if we are only attentive to the aspect of flow we can turn dharma into just another way of being busy, so we must integrate these many kinds of movement with the stillness of the unchanging nature of our own mind.

Thus before we commence the offerings we sit in an alert yet relaxed way, and with the presence of all the teachers at the centre of our body we open ourselves to our natural state, through the slow, deep outbreath. Resting in that open, unchanging awareness we are inseparable from the source and ground of everything. Then from, and within, that state we commence the recitation, experiencing it as the flow of energy of the dharmakaya, the experience of the nature of our mind.

Maintaining our presence in the integration of stillness and movement we remain alert and mindful. This provides protection from the habitual tendency to slip into automatic pilot, going through the motions but not being fully here. Each moment of existence is fresh but the power of our dulling habits and assumptions is great. This practice, any practice, can easily become just another way of passing time, of being asleep to the full potential of the situation. This is where faith is vital. Without faith in the transmission, in the vital life of the teaching, we can slip back into our limited self-concerns. Faith brings us back into the living presence of the dharma within us. The teachings are not abstract theory – they are about who and what we are. When the dharma becomes just another thing that we do, it loses its power to awaken us from our limiting assumptions. Something really is at stake! Samsara may be an illusion but it is not a joke when intense suffering comes. So every moment of practice, and that means every moment of life, is vital.

The Aspiration of Good Deeds of Bodhisattva Samantabhadra shows us the truth of the Buddha's statement in the *Dharmapada* that 'mind is chief, the ruler of all things'. Our minds are always busy ascribing significance to phenomena and then reacting to these projections as if the object truly had the value, positive or negative, we have placed on it. This habitual activity is taken for granted and so becomes invisible. Being focused on our own likes and dislikes we paint the world with the colours of our mind, the tones of our conditioning and limitations. This not only cuts us off from seeing the lively potential of what is there, but also keeps us trapped in the primacy of our self-reference. There are no truly self-existing entities. Whatever we see, hear or touch is devoid of any internal essence, being an illusion, an appearance arising due to causes but without any substantial existence. We ourselves can decide whether we will inhabit a small world of self-interest or a vast universe of loving connection. Other people are neither other than us nor the same as us; we are each unique and yet inseparable, for our own connectedness is actual, while our sense of having a separate individual essence is an illusion.

When the bodhisattva Samantabhadra made his great aspiration he liberated and transformed the power of imagination. His focus is universal, on the wellbeing of all that lives. By developing a vision of countless buddhas and bodhisattvas he goes beyond the usual market transaction of: I give this to you and in return you give that to me. He imagines the whole of space to be filled with enlightened beings who each radiate love and compassion to all. This is inconceivable, beyond the totalizing arithmetic of our daily concern with winning and losing, fairness and balance. And if we also imagine this field of radiance we will experience a dissolution of our ordinary ego identity. The accountant in our head will dissolve and our innate generosity, the radiance of our open heart, will be freed to move beyond computation. The infinity of the vision reveals the infinite nature of the one who entertains that vision. As with all profound dharma practice, compassion towards others opens wisdom in oneself, and the arising of wisdom feeds the gentle flame of compassion. Samantabhadra's text is so clear and beautiful it requires no commentary, only a heartfelt engagement.

The Sutra of the Story of the Lamp of King Golden Hand and his Aspiration is a very powerful short text that exemplifies the spirit of heroic mahayana practice. The story tells how King Golden Hand asked the Buddha Dipamkara, 'The One Who Became a Butterlamp', how he generated the virtue that led to him radiating infinite light from his body. This Buddha describes how he placed one thousand buttered wicks on his body and ignited them as an offering to all the buddhas. This might seem to be a horrifying thing to do if our mind focuses on the pain we imagine him suffering. But Buddha Dipamkara says the offering was made calmly, 'without hope or expectation'. It was not part of a trade or a deal, it was an open offering of love. It is not about punishing the body but is a way of shifting the centre of our own concerns. The wish to honour the enlightened ones transcends our ordinary fixation on the comfort of the body. By focusing on the good qualities of the other, of the buddhas, an alchemical transformation occurs. Faith transforms self-referential limitation into infinite connectivity, and this gives rise to the light that radiates from Buddha Dipamkara's body. Inspired by the Buddha's action the King develops an expansive intention of his own. The King's aspiration is vast, transforming a specific act occurring at a finite point in space and time into an infinite gesture for the wellbeing of all sentient beings. The selflessness of Buddha Dipamkara evokes a similar altruistic turn in the King, allowing him to transcend his limitations, his fear of pain, his self-pity and all the other habits of self-cherishing that keep our intentions small and self-serving. A virtuous act is magnified by the intention which drives it. It is not the act in and of itself which determines its value but the purpose it serves. Burning his hand becomes a means to an end: the illumination of all beings in the six realms of samsara.

Sacrifice can be perverse when it is part of a delayed gratification which never arrives. If one is sacrificing for life in heaven, for the success of the revolution etc., then one is a hostage to fortune, for the 'great idea' has captured one's life. In this buddhist context, however, the sacrifice and its result arise together, for the act of giving to the other brings the simultaneous releasing of the self. Only openheartedness can support such a sacrifice – and in making the sacrifice one finds that one's heart is opened! This is not a concept but a lived experience as we become lighter, more connected to everything and more free to participate in the non-dual co-emergence beyond trading, bargaining, gaining and losing.

When the King transforms his hand into a butterlamp, he prays that its light will reach every part of the universe. Many different environments and people are described, pointing to the way the simple intention to benefit all manifests as many diverse gestures which meet the specific needs of particular groups. Compassion is not about recruiting others to our dogma but, rather, about becoming what they need us to be. In order to do this without feeling overwhelmed and put upon, we need to relax into our own nature, the spacious, hospitable presence of awareness inseparable from emptiness. The one who can offer everything to all is not a limited person, but the emergence of the radiant energy of the source which is not an entity. The ground of our being is ungraspable, unknowable yet revealed through our participation in the non-dual flow of becoming. This becoming, although diverse and ever changing, never leaves its ground, just as a reflection never leaves the mirror.

Some practices focus on the aspect of wisdom, of seeing how things are, while others focus on compassion, on selflessly connecting with all beings. Both lead to the falling away of the conditioning which obscures the natural state. Both are more likely to flourish if one has faith. Faith is not a thing to be gained or lost. It is a quality of the integrated heart, of a person at peace with themselves, able to abide in the presence of the practice without the conflict generated by doubt and uncertainty.

The Butterlamp Prayer was written in a form that can be recited by people practicing in any of the Tibetan buddhist traditions. Indeed, it can be recited by anyone who is moved to do so. It does not require any initiation. It is usual to begin practice with taking refuge and developing bodhicitta and to conclude it with the dedication of merit. These are offered here in well known, general formats. Readers can of course use the forms they are most familiar with. C.R. Lama, who wrote *The Butterlamp Prayer*, lived as a married lama, as is common in the Nyingmapa tradition. He lived very simply and worked as a teacher in a university in Bengal, India. Rinpoche, as he was called, emphasised the importance of using the best ingredients possible when making offerings, since even small offerings done with care and attention to detail promote a calm, meditative mood. In respecting the buddhas we respect our own buddha-nature and that of all beings.

It is reported in the buddhist tradition that the final statement of Buddha Shakyamuni was an encouragement to his followers to make use of his teaching and 'to be a lamp to yourself'. Each of us has to ignite the lamps of study, reflection and meditation so that the teaching becomes alive in us. This involves the interaction between the dharma that we learn and our own experience. The middle way involves a respectful conversation between both aspects. Not mixing dharma with other systems or our own ideas is important so that we can reflect on the teachings themselves. Yet they can only become fully alive through application in our daily life and that involves developing and trusting our own clarity and discernment.

The natural light of awareness is always present, although usually unnoticed, in the minds of all sentient beings. Through the recitation of this *Aspiration* and reflection on its meaning, we can move from the dualistic relative light, arising from study and reflection, to awakening in the unchanging natural light revealed through meditation.

The final part of this volume is my brief commentary on *The Butterlamp Prayer*. I hope it encourages a deeper engagement with this marvellous text and sheds some light on our unchanging integration with the natural radiance of our being.

Part 1

The Butterlamp Prayer
by Chimed Rigdzin, Zilnon Lingpa

with

The Sutra of the Story of the Lamp of King Golden Hand and his Aspiration

Text in English

PRELIMINARIES

My awareness is the red dakini holding a curved knife and a skull cup. From my heart emanates a radiant white dakini who has the most wonderful face with three eyes looking at the sky. The palms of her two hands are joined together at her heart and hold the wish-fulfilling jewel, Source of all Satisfaction, from which numberless rays of light radiate out endlessly spreading countless offering goddesses.

These goddesses have the most beautiful ornaments and each holds one of the outer, inner and secret lamps in her hands. The lamp pots are the size of the ring of iron mountains that contains the world. Their quantity of oil equals a great ocean. Their wicks are the size of Mt. Meru and their flames reach the top of the world. Their light is brighter than a million million suns. By their power all outer and inner darkness is cleared away and thus the fuel of samsara belonging to all beings is completely burned up.

Salutation to the Three Jewels. Salutation to the Perfect Ones. Vajra essence. Great gift. All Tathagatas, Arhats, Samyak Sambuddhas are like that.

Om. Vajra, vajra, great vajra, great shining vajra. Great vidya vajra. Great bodhicitta vajra. Great enlightenment's meaning. Coming out by stages, all deeds like vajras. Experience becomes very pure and strong.

Om. Vajradharma jewel. Long life. Excellent life. All buddha realms. Knowledge. Transcendent wisdom. Sound naturally has vajra dharma essence. Satisfying all, they rise out endlessly filling the sky.

OFFERING THE LAMPS

Wonderful! In the pot of all-pervading hospitable space swirls the oil of non-dual awareness. On the wick of absorbed contemplation free of dualistic thought, the flame of the self-existing clarity of awareness burns bright. Thoughts arising from the affliction of stupidity are liberated in their own place. Without being rejected they dissolve in the vastness of the actuality of what is. Original knowing as hospitable space manifests as shining rays of light. In order to dispel the darkness of ignorance of all sentient beings we offer this to the guru and the gods of the Buddha clan. Please accept and then bestow supreme and general accomplishments.

Wonderful!   In the pot free of bias, without centre or circumference, swirls the oil of liberating attachment on the natural ground. On the wick of knowing one's own nature of happiness and clarity the flame of the arising of the natural clarity of awareness burns bright. Thoughts arising from the affliction of anger are liberated in their own place. Without being rejected they dissolve in the vastness of the non-duality of clarity and emptiness. Original knowing as mirroring manifests as shining rays of light. In order to dispel the darkness of ignorance of all sentient beings we offer this to the guru and the gods of the Vajra clan. Please accept and then bestow supreme and general accomplishments.

Wonderful!   In the pot of hospitable space that is the same everywhere swirls the oil of dualistic altruism. On the wick of the union of appearance and emptiness the flame of actualising naked awareness burns bright. Thoughts arising from the affliction of pride are liberated in their own place. Without being rejected they dissolve in the vastness of perfect equality. Original knowing as identity manifests as shining rays of light. In order to dispel the darkness of ignorance of all sentient beings we offer this to the guru and the gods of the Ratna clan. Please accept and then bestow supreme and general accomplishments.

Wonderful!   In the pot of attention to the distinct features of all phenomena swirls the oil of undeclining great happiness. On the wick of the union of happiness and emptiness, the flame of the energy of awareness revealing each appearance as it is burns bright. Thoughts arising from the affliction of desire are liberated in their own place. Without being rejected they dissolve in the vastness of non-dual great happiness. Original knowing as precise discernment manifests as shining rays of light. In order to dispel the darkness of ignorance of all sentient beings we offer this to the guru and the gods of Padma clan. Please accept and bestow supreme and general accomplishments.

Wonderful!   In the pot of the wheel of continuous activity swirls the oil of effortless accomplishment free of striving. On the wick of the union of clarity and emptiness the flame of awareness free of beginning and end burns bright. Thoughts arising from the affliction of jealousy are liberated in their own place. Without being rejected they dissolve in the vastness of freedom from work and effort. Original knowing as effective action manifests as shining rays of light. In order to dispel the darkness of ignorance of all sentient beings we offer this to the guru and the gods of the Karma clan. Please accept and then bestow supreme and general accomplishments.

Wonderful! In the pot of the ground of all bound by delusion swirls the oil of the many thoughts arising from the minor afflictions. On the wick of belief in self-existing entities that arises from ignoring, the flame of the great original knowing free of reification burns bright. The obscuration arising from the afflictions is liberated in its own place. Without being rejected it dissolves in the vastness of the absence of inherent self-nature in all phenomena. The great impartial original knowing manifests its own shining light. In order to dispel the darkness of ignorance of all sentient beings we offer this to the guru, the three jewels, the three roots and all the deities. Please accept and then bestow supreme and general accomplishments.

Wonderful! In the pot of infinite hospitable space swirls the oil of the many small thoughts that appear ceaselessly. On the wick of the radiant natural light of knowing, the flame of the traceless destruction of the five poisons burns bright. Obscuration by and to knowledge is liberated in its own place without residue. Without being rejected it dissolves in the vastness of the absence of inherent self-nature in all beings. The all-pervading natural clarity manifests as the purity of its own shining light. In order to dispel the darkness of ignorance of all sentient beings we offer this to the guru, the three jewels, the three roots and all the deities. Please accept and then bestow supreme and general accomplishments.

Wonderful! In the pot of samsaric objects of knowledge swirls the oil of dualistic confusion which generates karma and the afflictions. On the wick of the non-duality of happiness and sorrow the flame that arises from original knowing burns bright. All confused sentient beings are liberated in their own place. Without being rejected they dissolve in the vastness of the non-duality of graspable object and grasping mind. The great original knowing free of grasping manifests its own shining light. In order to dispel the darkness of ignorance of all sentient beings we offer this to the guru, the three jewels, the three roots and all the deities. Please accept and then bestow supreme and general accomplishments.

Wonderful! In the pot of inconceivable measureless love swirls the oil of immeasurable compassion. On the wick of very pure immeasurable equanimity the flame of spreading immeasurable joy burns bright. Thoughts arising from the five afflicting poisons are liberated in their own place. They dissolve in the vastness of the great infinitude of the immeasurable. Inconceivable non-duality manifests its own shining light. In order to dispel the darkness of ignorance of all sentient beings we offer this to the guru, the three jewels, the three roots and all the deities. Please accept and then bestow supreme and general accomplishments.

Wonderful. In the pot of knowing all beings to be my parents swirls the oil of remembrance of the kindness with which they have held me. On the stick of the desire to repay their kindness the cotton of very beautiful love is wound well with the power of tender compassion. The flame of the most excellent purity burns bright. Thoughts of the absence of connection between myself and others are liberated in their own place and dissolve in the vastness of great compassion with and without an object. The light of our own result of unsurpassed complete enlightenment is shining. In order to dispel the darkness of ignorance of all sentient beings we offer this to the guru, the three jewels, the three roots and all the deities. Please accept and then bestow supreme and general accomplishments.

Wonderful! In the pot of very pure morality swirls the inexhaustible oil of very pure generosity. On the stick of very pure concentration, with the very pure attitude of diligence, the cotton of very pure patience is tied. The flame of very pure true knowing burns bright. The desire to privilege one's own welfare dissolves in the vastness of benefiting others. With the increase of power, compassionate method and aspiration, transcendent original knowing manifests its own shining light. In order to dispel the darkness of ignorance of all sentient beings we offer this to the guru, the three jewels, the three roots and all the deities. Please accept and then bestow supreme and general accomplishments.

Wonderful! In the pot of the finest pure morality, swirls the oil of the noble eightfold path. On the wick stick of unwavering, steady absorbed contemplation the nine methods of mind control and the four aspects of mental development are tied. With the result of the perfect attainment of the six powers, the flame of true knowing arising from study, reflection and meditation burns bright. Judgemental thoughts dissolve in the vastness of complete freedom from thoughts. The completely pure three trainings manifest their own shining light. In order to dispel the darkness of ignorance of all sentient beings we offer this to the guru, the three jewels, the three roots and all the deities. Please accept and bestow supreme and general accomplishments.

Wonderful!   In the pot of the outer vessel of an entire human skin swirls the inner contents of flesh, blood and bones. On the wick stick of the shining heart and channels is wound the cotton of the organs and entrails made from the five elements. The flame of all the radiant components of existence burns bright. The debased illusory body dissolves in the vastness of a mass of light. The diversifying energy of the original knowing of natural presence manifests as shining rays of light. In order to dispel the darkness of ignorance of all sentient beings we offer this to the guru, the three jewels, the three roots and all the deities. Please accept and bestow supreme and general accomplishments.

Wonderful! In the pot of the pervasive ground of all swirls the oil of simultaneous, discriminating and complaisant ignorance. On the wick stick of the ignorant belief in inherent self-nature is wound the cotton of the obscurations arising from afflictions and false knowledge. The flame of the natural radiance of all-pervading awareness burns bright. Simultaneous and discriminating ignorance dissolve in the vastness of hospitable space. Original knowing of natural presence free of reification manifests as shining rays of light. In order to dispel the darkness of ignorance of all sentient beings we offer this to the guru, the three jewels, the three roots and all the deities. Please accept and then bestow supreme and general accomplishments.

Wonderful!   In the pot of the five sense organs, the eyes and so on, swirls the oil of the five desirable qualities of form and so on. On the wick of the five grasping sense consciousnesses the flame of the self-liberating non-grasping peformer of all burns bright. Ordinary understanding dissolves in the vastness free of decline. The non-duality of subject and object manifests as shining rays of light. In order to dispel the darkness of ignorance of all sentient beings we offer this to the guru, the three jewels, the three roots and all the deities. Please accept and bestow supreme and general accomplishments.

Wonderful!   In the pot of the view beyond the reach of thought swirls the oil of meditation free of preconceived objects. On the wick of immeasurable activity the flame of the result of mahamudra burns bright. The knot of object dissolves in the vastness of the subject as the depth of awareness unites releasing and immediacy. The creativity of the ground arises within the ground, manifesting as shining rays of light. Openness is not an object that can be described; immediacy eludes the words it reveals; spontaneity is everywhere. This is the naturally occurring lamp. In order to dispel the darkness of ignorance of all sentient beings we offer this to the pervading lord, our most kind guru Dorje Chang, and to the three jewels, the three roots, the three kayas and all the deities. Please accept and then bestow supreme and general accomplishments.

Wonderful! In the pot made with the five precious substances swirls the oil of butter coming from the concentrated essence of grasses and grains. On the wick wound with clean cotton wool the flame matching the light of the sun and moon burns bright. All darkness without exception dissolves in the vastness of light. The illumination of darkness everywhere manifests as shining rays of light. In order to dispel the darkness of ignorance of all beings we offer this to all the buddhas and bodhisattvas of the ten directions and to the guru, the three jewels, the three roots, and all the deities. Please accept and then bestow supreme and general accomplishments.

Wonderful! In the pot of glass free of outer and inner obscurations swirls the oil arising from the power of fire and water. On the wick made of glowing material the shining flame of radiant illumination burns bright. All demons, trouble-makers and obstructors dissolve in the vastness of the light which is free of fears, worries, terrors and fluctuating emotions. Unimpeded clarity without and within manifests as shining rays of light. In order to dispel the darkness of ignorance of all sentient beings we offer this to sentient beings, all of whom have the cause of buddhahood, and to the guru, the three jewels, the three roots and all the deities. Please accept and then bestow supreme and general accomplishments.

DEDICATION AND GURU YOGA

By the merit of offering these lamps all beings must be liberated from the ocean of samsara. Then, with the suffering of the darkness of ignorance completely removed, all must quickly gain omniscient perfect buddhahood and become identical with the noble Buddha Dipamkara.

****

[the sutra on Buddha Dipamkara may be read here or go to page 11]

THE SUTRA OF THE STORY OF THE LAMP OF KING GOLDEN HAND AND HIS ASPIRATION

Sanskrit: *rajakancanabahudipasyaprakriyapranidhana sutra*

Tibetan: *rGyal-Po gSer-Gyi Lag-Pa'i Mar-Me'i Lo-rGyus Dang sMon-Lam-Gyi mDo*

Salutation to the Three Jewels.

When Dipamkara, the Buddha of the earlier period[1], was teaching, King Golden Hand asked him, "Venerable One, what was the basis of the virtue that you created in former times resulting in you now displaying the major and minor signs of a Buddha and radiating infinite light from your body?"

Buddha Dipamkara replied, "Listen, great king! When I was an ordinary being, in front of all the Buddhas of the ten directions I developed bodhicitta[2]. Then I dipped one thousand cotton wicks in clarified butter and placed them on my body. Without hope or expectation I lit them as an offering to all the Buddhas of the ten directions and the three times. That is why I am now known as Buddha Dipamkara, 'the one who made the butterlamp.'"

The great king rejoiced at this. He wrapped his own right hand in cotton wool, dipped it in clarified butter and lit it. He raised his left hand to the sky and said, "Buddhas of the ten directions and Buddha Dipamkara, my teacher, please think of me."

With a mind free of regret he clearly visualised all the buddhas of the ten directions. He dedicated the merit of this offering given without expectation, and made this prayer of aspiration:

[Recite the sutra with your hands raised, palms facing the sky.]

May the pot of this lamp become as vast as the infinity of all the countless worlds. May the wick become as big as Mount Meru[3]. May the rays of its light reach from the top of this world down to the beings in the lowest Avici hell.

May the rays of its light reach beyond the iron mountains ringing our world system to reach the people who are living in the enveloping gloom of the darkness created by their own bad actions and who cannot even see the movements of their own hands. May this light spread illumination there.

May this light remain for the duration of all the periods of all the Buddhas of the past, present and future. May this light shine before the eyes of all the numberless Buddhas in the countless worlds which pervade the ten directions[4].

May the light from this lamp illuminate the formless realms. With that illumination, as soon as the gods of these realms are aroused, may they gain the major and minor signs of enlightenment and be freed from the mental absorptions of the four levels of subtle sensory support[5]. May entry to the various meditative states of the Tathagatha[6] be available to these fortunate ones.

May the light from this lamp illuminate the realm of the gods with form. May these gods enter meditative absorption and experience unwavering happiness and gain the stage of non-return[7].

May the light from this lamp illuminate the environment of the gods of the realm of desire. May these gods be free of attachment to the riches of their realm. May they look at their own minds and enter each of the four meditative absorptions[8] in turn. May they have the opportunity to experience that.

May the light from this lamp illuminate the realm of the demi-gods. May they be freed from their pride, fury, and crudity, and develop love, compassion, joyfulness and equanimity. May they develop minds that are calm.

May the light from this lamp illuminate the beings who inhabit the four continents. May they be freed from the eight sufferings[9]. May they gain transcendental diligence[10].

May the light from this lamp illuminate all who live in the animal realm. May they stop eating each other and be freed from the suffering of fighting, killing, being enslaved, and being dull and stupid. May they gain the wisdom of hearing, thinking about and meditating on the dharma.

May the light from this lamp illuminate the realm of the lord of death[11]. May these cruel ones cease from killing, cutting and beating. May they be taught the six transcendental qualities[12] by the Tathagathas and by this may they develop generous attitudes towards all beings.

May the light from this lamp illuminate the realms of the hungry ghosts. May they be freed from the misery of thirst and hunger. By the blessings of the great compassion of Akashagarbha Bodhisattva may they have an inexhaustible supply of easily available food and drink. May they gain the power of transcendental generosity.

May the light from this lamp illuminate the hell realms. Beings suffer there according to the ripening of their previous bad actions, experiencing intolerable heat and cold. By the blessings of the compassion of the Bodhisattva Arya Avalokitesvara may they be freed from the limitless sufferings of hell. May they realise the transcendent quality of patience.

May the light of this lamp illuminate the realms beyond this world system where, in the darkness, benighted people cannot even see their right hand held up in front of them. Due to the ripening of their previous bad actions they crave food and drink but scratch themselves with their iron claws as they reach out to the sky and so are unsatisfied. They are exhausted and cut their own flesh and eat it. By the blessing of the compassion of Buddha Amitabha may they be freed from the force of that great darkness and be reborn in the pure realm of Great Happiness [13].

May the light of this lamp illuminate the realm of the nagas [14]. May they be freed from the snares of stupidity and envy. May they practise generosity and be freed from the fear of predatory birds [15], heat, dry sand and the rest of the eight great fears [16]. May they take refuge in Buddha, Dharma and Sangha so that the life sustaining waterdrop of calm abiding rests in their hearts and all the nagas gain everything they desire.

May the light of this lamp illuminate the realm of the giant reptiles. May their sufferings be removed. May they gain the magical power to abide in oceans of happiness.

May the light from this lamp illuminate the areas beyond the continent of Jambudvipa [17] occupied by land gods, local gods, nagas, Pitali the king of the land gods, the great queen of the land, and the gods and denizens of oceans, seas, ponds and wells, big rivers, small rivers, springs, seasonal ponds and those who stay at the high glacial streams, black mountains, slate hills, water meadows, hill fields, big forests, solitary trees, temples, stupas, cities and villages – may all those who stay in these places be illuminated. May each of these beings have their own particular confusions removed. May they have unchanging faith in the Three Jewels. May they gain an altruistic intention towards enlightenment and establish the cause of liberation.

This concludes the aspiration of King Golden Hand.

By the sponsoring of these lamps and the offering of this transient display may I and all the infinite sentient beings be reborn at the feet of Buddha Dipamkara. May we gain perfect buddhahood and become benefactors of all beings.

****

Salutation! I bow to the gurus, deities and dakinis. Pervading lord, glorious guru Vajradhara, embodiment of the four modes and the five original knowings, from this time on in all my lives may I never separate from you, held by your compassion. May I serve and please you with my body, speech and mind!

Regarding this jewel-like human body possessing the freedoms and opportunities that are so difficult to gain, we do not know how long it will remain. Therefore, always keeping aware of the non-deceptive nature of karma, may we all be freed from this foul swamp of samsara.

Even at the cost of our lives we will never abandon the unsurpassed three jewels who protect from fear. Training our minds with the seven-part practice of cause and effect, may we never be separated from relative and absolute altruistic openness.

The outer container of the world with Mt. Meru and the four continents, the inner contents of all beings with their constituent aspects and all desirable phenomena, the secret unborn bodhicitta, my own awareness, the joyful secret mandala of awareness and hospitable space, all this, sole father of the buddhas, may we have the power to offer it to you!

Distinguishing clearly between object and subject, and then recognising that there is no actual basis for this, all outer and inner phenomena are seen to be illusory. Clearly experiencing that all possible appearances are the play of the mind, may we practise the profound offering assembly with our illusory bodies and thus make each of the four classes of guest happy.

Meditating on the guru as Vajrasattva on the crown of our heads may we confess with the four strong antidotes and keep our vows well. Glorious guru, you who are not different from Kunzang Heruka and Chomden Dema Chog, the source of all blessings — may we gain the blessing of the excellent yoga of the secret inconceivable vajras of your body, speech and mind.

Regarding this text, the great tantrica having Hinayana, Mahayana and Vajrayana vows who gained the excellent result, the incarnation of Vimalami-tra, Tsultrim Zangpo Yeshe Rolpa Tsal (Tshul Khrims bZang Po Ye Shes Rol Pa rTsal) ordered me to stay at the great pilgrimage place of mTsho Padma in the kingdom of Zahor. While living there without work in a loose retreat for a period of three years and six months the King of Zahor, Joginder Sen, was my sponsor providing all necessities. He generously gave offerings and butter lamps and food, as much as I wished. At that time for the general benefit and happiness of all sentient beings and in particular for the supreme precious incarnation Tsultrim Zangpo, or as he is also known, Terchen Yeshe Rolpa Tsal (gTer Chhen Ye Shes Rol Pa rTsal), whose most ordinary disciple I am, in order to remove the difficulties of his sixty-first year (that being a danger-ous year to be), so that he would stay for an ocean of kalpas, I wrote a prayer of aspiration for lamps to be joined with the Zab Thig Dechen Rang Shar Lae, Zilnon Yeshe Kyi Khandroma Senge Dongpa Chan Gyi Choekor (Zab Thig dDe Chhen Rang Shar Las, Zil gNon Ye Shes Kyi mKha' 'Gro Ma Seng Ge gDong Pa Chan Gyi Chhos sKor). With that as a basis, later on when I was fifty-seven years of age, before the great pilgrimage place of Bodhanath Stupa (Bya Rung Kha Shor) in Nepal, at the feet of the great representative of Padmasambhava, Dudjom Jigtral Yeshe Dorje (bDud 'Joms 'Jig Bral Ye Shes rDo rJe), from whom I was receiving initiations of Kama (bKa' Ma) and Terma (gTer Ma), during the intervening period when doing the tenth (Tsechu) and twenty-fifth day (Nyernga) practices I, Zilnon Lingpa (Zil gNon gLing Pa), (C.R. Lama), changed it slightly so as to make it suitable to join with any puja of the four schools.

Translated by C.R. Lama and James Low

Notes

1. That is the period before the appearance of Buddha Shakyamuni.

2. A profound and unwavering intention to benefit all beings.

3. Mount Meru, in traditional Buddhist cosmology, is the mountain at the centre of our world system. It is so high that night appears when the sun disappears behind it in the evening.

4. i.e. everywhere.

5. The four formless realms of increasingly rarefied experience

6. Another title indicating buddhahood.

7. Anagami, one who does not return to this world again.

8. bSam-gTan bZhi, the four concentrations: 1. with concepts and investigation, 2. with investigation but no concepts, 3. with mentation free of concepts and investigation, 4. with mentation linked with delight.

9. The eight sufferings are birth; aging; illness; death; separation from loved ones; being with the despised; not getting what one wants; the flourishing of the five skandhas.

10. Diligence is one of the six paramitas or transcendental qualities of a bodhisattva.

11. Yama - the one who judges us at death and whose minions punish the guilty.

12. The six paramitas are: generosity; moral discipline; patience; diligence; concentration and discriminative awareness.

13. This is the realm of Sukhavati or Dewachen where Amitabha resides.

14. The nagas are snake gods who protect the treasures of the earth and guard its resources.

15. In particular, garudas.

16. The eight great fears are: fears of fire, water, earth, air, elephants, snakes, thieves and kings.

17. This is one of the four large continents, and is the one on which we reside.

Part 2

མར་མེ་སྨོན་ལམ།།

The Offering Practice
of the
Butterlamp Prayer
by Chimed Rigdzin, Zilnon Lingpa

Recitation Format

 སྐྱབས་གསོལ།

INITIAL REQUEST

སྐྱབས་གནས་བསླུ་མེད་དཀོན་མཆོག་རིན་པོ་ཆེ།

KYAB NAE	LU ME	KON CHOG	RIN PO CHE
refuge place,	*unfailing,*	*jewel*	*precious*
protector	*never cheating*		

To the precious jewel who is our unfailing refuge,

ཐུགས་རྗེ་མངའ་བའི་ཨུ་རྒྱན་པདྨ་ལ།

THUG JE	NGA WAI	UR GYEN PAE MA	LA
compassion	*possessor*	*Padmasambhava*	*to*

Compassionate Padma from Urgyen,

བདག་གི་ཇི་ལྟར་གསོལ་བ་བཏབ་པ་བཞིན།

DAG GI	JI TAR	SOL WA	TAB PA	ZHIN
my	*like what,*	*prayer,*	*made*	*like that,*
	how it is	*request*		*accordingly*

We pray for your blessing – may whatever we request

མྱུར་དུ་འགྲུབ་པར་བྱིན་གྱིས་བརླབས་དུ་གསོལ།

NYUR DU	DRUB PAR	JIN GYI LAB	DU	SOL
quickly	*accomplish, fulfil*	*bless*	*as*	*pray*

Be quickly accomplished.

To the precious jewel who is our unfailing refuge, compassionate Padma from Urgyen, we pray for your blessing – may whatever we request be quickly accomplished.

ཚིག་བདུན་གསོལ་འདེབས།

SEVEN LINE PRAYER

ཧཱུྃ༔   ཨོ་རྒྱན་ཡུལ་གྱི་ནུབ་བྱང་མཚམས༔

HUNG	UR GYAN YUL	GYI	NUB	JANG	TSAM
bija, seed letter	*land of Urgyen in the*	*of*	*west*	*north*	*border,*
of Padmasambhava	*Sind Doab in Pakistan*				*corner*

Hung. In the north-west corner of the land of Urgyen,

པདྨ་གེ་སར་སྡོང་པོ་ལ༔

PAE MA GE SAR	DONG PO	LA
lotus, stamen	*stem*	*on*

Upon the stem and stamen of a lotus,

ཡ་མཚན་མཆོག་གི་དངོས་གྲུབ་བརྙེས༔

YAM TSAN	CHOG	GI	NGOE DRUB	NYE
marvellous,	*supreme*	*of*	*siddhis, accomplishments*	*got, has*
wonderful				

Are you who have the marvellous and supreme accomplishment,

པདྨ་འབྱུང་གནས་ཞེས་སུ་གྲགས༔

PAE MA JUNG NAE	ZHE SU	DRAG
Padmasambhava,	*famous*	*as*
Guru Rinpoche		

Padmasambhava of great renown

འཁོར་དུ་མཁའ་འགྲོ་མང་པོས་བསྐོར༔

KHOR DU	KHAN DRO	MANG POE	KOR
as retinue	*dakinis **	*many by*	*surrounded*

sky-goddesses (here means all deities inseparable from space)

With a retinue of many dakinis around you.

ཁྱེད་ཀྱི་རྗེས་སུ་བདག་བསྒྲུབ་ཀྱིས༔

KYE KYI	JE SU	DAG	DRUB	KYI
you	*following after*	*I*	*practice*	*by that*

Following and relying on you we do your practice, therefore,

བྱིན་གྱིས་བརླབ་ཕྱིར་གཤེགས་སུ་གསོལ༔

JIN GYI LAB	CHIR	SHEG SU SOL
blessing	*in order to*	*please come here.*

In order to grant your blessings, please come here.

 གུ་ར་པད་མེ་སི་ཏྟེ་ཧཱུྃ༔

GU RU   **PAE MA**   **SID DHI**   **HUNG**
master, guru   *Padmasambhava*   *accomplishment*   *give me*

Guru Padmasambhava grant us accomplishment!

HUNG. In the north-west corner of the land of Urgyen, upon the stem and stamen of a lotus, are you who have the marvellous and supreme accomplishment, Padmasambhava of great renown, with a retinue of many dakinis around you. Following and relying on you we do your practice, therefore, in order to grant your blessings, please come here. Guru Padmasambhava grant us accomplishment!

ལན་གསུམ་རྗེས༔ *(Recite this three times)*

སྐྱབས་འགྲོ་དང་སེམས་བསྐྱེད།

REFUGE AND BODHICITTA

སངས་རྒྱས་ཆོས་དང་ཚོགས་ཀྱི་མཆོག་རྣམས་ལ།

SANG GYE	CHO	DANG	TSOG	KYI	CHOG	NAM	LA
buddha	*dharma*	*and*	*sangha*	*of*	*supreme*	*(plural)*	*to*
	teaching		*(the assembly of committed practitioners)*				

To the Buddha, Dharma and Assembly of the Excellent Ones

བྱང་ཆུབ་བར་དུ་བདག་ནི་སྐྱབས་སུ་མཆི།

JANG CHUB	BAR DU	DAG NI	KYAB	SU	CHI
enlightenment	*until*	*I*	*refuge*	*for*	*go*

I go for refuge until enlightenment is gained.

བདག་གིས་སྦྱིན་སོགས་བགྱིས་པའི་བསོད་ནམས་ཀྱིས།

DAG GI	JIN	SOG	GYI PAI	SO NAM	KYI
I	*by*	*generosity*	*doing,*	*virtue*	*through*
		other	*practicing*		
		perfections *			

*discipline, patience, diligence, meditation, wisdom

Through the virtue of practicing generosity and the other perfections,

འགྲོ་ལ་ཕན་ཕྱིར་སངས་རྒྱས་འགྲུབ་པར་ཤོག།

DRO	LA	PHEN	CHIR	SANG GYE	DRUB PAR	SHO
all beings	*to*	*benefit*	*in order*	*buddha*	*accomplish*	*may it happen*

May I attain buddhahood for the benefit of all beings.

I go for refuge to the Buddha, Dharma and Assembly of the Excellent Ones until enlightenment is gained. Through the virtue of practicing generosity and the other perfections, may I attain buddhahood for the benefit of all beings.

ལན་གསུམ་རྗེས༔ *(Recite this three times)*

འཕགས་པ་བཟང་པོ་སྤྱོད་པའི་སྨོན་ལམ་གྱི་རྒྱལ་པོ་ལས་བྱུང་བའི་ཡན་ལག་བདུན་པ་
བཞུགས་སོ།།

THE SEVEN BRANCH PRACTICE

from

THE ASPIRATION OF GOOD DEEDS
BY BODHISATTVA SAMANTABHADRA

འཕགས་པ་འཇམ་དཔལ་གཞོན་ནུར་གྱུར་པ་ལ་ཕྱག་འཚལ་ལོ།

PHAG PA	JAM PAL	ZHO NUR GYUR PA	LA	CHAG TSHAL LO
noble	*Manjushri*	*who is young, never gets old*	*to*	*salutation*

Salutation to the noble Manjushri who is always young.

ཇི་སྙེད་སུ་དག་ཕྱོགས་བཅུའི་འཇིག་རྟེན་ན།

JI NYED	SU DAG	CHOG CHUI	JIG TEN	NA
as many as there are	*those, them*	*ten directions (i.e. everywhere)*	*world*	*in*

As many as there are in the ten directions of the world,

དུས་གསུམ་གཤེགས་པ་མི་ཡི་སེང་གེ་ཀུན།

DU	SUM	SHEG PA	MI	YI	SENG GE	KUN
time	*three (past,present,future) Buddha's title*	*going*	*men*	*of*	*lions*	*all*

(Just as the lion dominates all animals by its roar, so the Buddha's teaching on sunyata silences all expression of false views)

All those lions among men, the Buddhas of the three times,

བདག་གིས་མ་ལུས་དེ་དག་ཐམས་ཅད་ལ།

DAG	GI	MA LU	DE DAG	THAM CHE	LA
I	*by*	*without exception*	*them*	*all*	*to*

To all of them without exception,

ལུས་དང་ངག་ཡིད་དང་བས་ཕྱག་བགྱིའོ།

LU	DANG	NGAG	YID	DANG WAE	CHA GYI O
body	*and*	*speech*	*mind*	*faith, sincerity, by*	*make salutation, obeisance*

I sincerely make salutation with body, speech and mind.

Salutation to the noble Manjushri who is always young. As many as there are in the ten directions of the world, all those lions among men, the Buddhas of the three times, to all of them without exception, I sincerely make salutation with body, speech and mind.

བཟང་པོ་སྤྱོད་པའི་སྨོན་ལམ་སྟོབས་དག་གིས།

ZANG PO	CHO PAI	MON LAM	TOB DAG	GI
the Bodhisattva Samantabhadra*	conduct, practice	prayer of aspiration	strength	by

*The Bodhisattva Samantabhadra completed the two necessary accumulations of merit and wisdom and gained buddhahood by meditating that he had an infinite number of bodies, thus destroying body-centered egoism and so gaining wisdom. And with these bodies he made an unending stream of offerings to all the buddhas, thus destroying selfishness and gaining merit. By praying according to the same system we get his blessing and help.

By the power of aspiration following the practice of Samantabhadra,

རྒྱལ་བ་ཐམས་ཅད་ཡིད་ཀྱི་མངོན་སུམ་དུ།

GYAL WA	THAM CHE	YID	KYI	NGON SUM	DU
jinas, buddhas	all	mind	of	clarity (clearly imagining)	with

With all the buddhas clearly in mind,

ཞིང་གི་རྡུལ་སྙེད་ལུས་རབ་བཏུད་པ་ཡིས།

ZHING	GI	DUL	NYED	LU	RAB TUD PA	YI
realm, world, universe	of	dust particle	as many as there are	body	manifesting bodies which make obeisance	by

By manifesting as many bodies as there are dust particles in the universe,

རྒྱལ་བ་ཀུན་ལ་རབ་ཏུ་ཕྱག་འཚལ་ལོ།

GYAL WA	KUN	LA	RAB TU	CHA TSHAL LO
jinas	all	to	fully, deeply	make salutation

I make heartfelt salutation to all the buddhas.

By the power of aspiration following the practice of Samantabhadra, with all the buddhas clearly in mind, by manifesting as many bodies as there are dust particles in the universe, I offer sincere salutation to all the buddhas.

རྡུལ་གཅིག་སྟེང་ན་རྡུལ་སྙེད་སངས་རྒྱས་རྣམས།

DUL	CHIG	TENG NA	DUL	NYED	SANG GYE	NAM
particle of dust	one, each	on top of	dust, particles	as many as there are in the universe	buddha	all

On each particle of dust in the universe there are as many buddhas as there are particles of dust in the universe,

སངས་རྒྱས་སྲས་ཀྱི་དབུས་ན་བཞུགས་པ་དག།

SANG GYE SAE		KYI WU NA	ZHUG PA	DAG
Buddha's sons, bodhisattvas		*in the middle of*	*staying, sitting*	*them*

Each sitting in the midst of a host of bodhisattvas.

དེ་ལྟར་ཆོས་ཀྱི་དབྱིངས་རྣམས་མ་ལུས་པ།

DE TAR	CHO KYI YING	NAM	MA LU PA
like that	*dharmadhatu (everywhere)*	*(plural)*	*without exception*

Thus I believe that every possible space for appearance

ཐམས་ཅད་རྒྱལ་བ་དག་གིས་གང་བར་མོས།

THAM CHE	GYAL WA	DAG	GI	GANG WAR	MOE
all	*jinas*	*(plural)*	*by*	*filled, as*	*believe*

Is filled with buddhas.

On each particle of dust in the universe there are as many buddhas as there are particles of dust in the universe, each sitting in the midst of a host of bodhisattvas. Thus I believe that every possible space for appearance is filled with buddhas.

དེ་དག་བསྔགས་པ་མི་ཟད་རྒྱ་མཚོ་རྣམས།

DE DAG	NGAG PA	MI ZAD	GYAM TSHO	NAM
them	*praise*	*inexhaustible*	*ocean*	*all*

With inexhaustible oceans of praise,

དབྱངས་ཀྱི་ཡན་ལག་རྒྱ་མཚོ་སྒྲ་ཀུན་གྱིས།

YANG	KYI	YAN LAG	GYAM TSHO	DRA	KUN	GYI
melodies	*of*	*branches, variations*	*ocean*	*sounds*	*all*	*by*

Employing all the sounds of an ocean of different melodies,

རྒྱལ་བ་ཀུན་གྱི་ཡོན་ཏན་རབ་བརྗོད་ཅིང་།

GYAL WA	KUN	GYI	YON TAN	RAB	JOE CHING
jinas, victors buddhas	*all*	*of*	*good qualities*	*fully*	*expressing, saying*

By fully proclaiming the good qualities of all the jinas,

བདེ་བར་གཤེགས་པ་ཐམས་ཅད་བདག་གིས་བསྟོད།

DE WAR SHEG PA	THAM CHE	DAG	GI	TOE
sugatas, buddhas	*all*	*me*	*by*	*praised*

I praise all the sugatas.

With inexhaustible oceans of praise, employing all the sounds of an ocean of different melodies, by fully proclaiming the good qualities of all the Victors, I praise all those who are happily gone.

 མེ་ཏོག་དམ་པ་ཕྲེང་བ་དམ་པ་དང་།

ME TOG	DAM PA	TRENG WA	DAM PA	DANG
flowers	*excellent*	*garlands, necklaces*	*very best*	*and*

Splendid flowers and excellent garlands,

སིལ་སྙན་རྣམས་དང་བྱུག་པ་གདུགས་མཆོག་དང་།

SIL NYEN NAM	DANG	JUG PA	DUG	CHOG	DANG
music	*and*	*perfume*	*parasol*	*finest*	*and*

Music, perfumes, and the finest parasols,

མར་མེ་མཆོག་དང་བདུག་སྤོས་དམ་པ་ཡིས།

MAR ME	CHOG	DANG	DUG POE	DAM PA	YI
butter lamps	*best*	*and*	*incense*	*excellent*	*by*

Wonderful lamps and marvellous incense, with these

རྒྱལ་བ་དེ་དག་ལ་ནི་མཆོད་པར་བགྱི།

GYAL WA	DE DAG	LA NI	CHO PAR GYI
jinas	*these*	*to*	*offer, make offering*

I make offerings to the buddhas.

Splendid flowers and excellent garlands; music, perfumes and the finest parasols; wonderful lamps and marvellous incense, with these I make offerings to the buddhas.

ན་བཟའ་དམ་པ་རྣམས་དང་དྲི་མཆོག་དང་།

NAB ZA	DAM PA	NAM	DANG	DRI	CHOG	DANG
clothes, garments	*excellent*	*many*	*and*	*scent*	*excellent, finest*	*and*

Excellent garments and the finest scent, and

ཕྱེ་མ་ཕུར་མ་རི་རབ་མཉམ་པ་དང་།

CHE MA	PHUR MA	RI RAB	NYAM PA	DANG
pieces of cloth	*pleated, folded cloth*	*Mt. Meru (the vast mountain at the centre of the world)*	*equalling*	*and*

Pieces of cloth equalling Mt. Meru –

བཀོད་པ་ཁྱད་པར་འཕགས་པའི་མཆོག་ཀུན་གྱིས།

KOD PA	KHYE PAR	PHAG PAI	CHOG	KUN	GYI
display, set up	*special*	*noble, distinguished*	*excellent*	*all*	*by*

With all the best items most excellently arranged

རྒྱལ་བ་དེ་དག་ལ་ནི་མཆོད་པར་བགྱི།

GYAL WA	DE DAG	LA NI	CHO PAR	GYI
victors, buddhas	*those*	*to*	*offer*	*do*

I make offerings to these victors.

Excellent garments and the finest scent; and pieces of cloth and folded cloth equalling Mt. Meru – with all the best items most excellently arranged I make offerings to the buddhas.

མཆོད་པ་གང་རྣམས་བླ་མེད་རྒྱ་ཆེ་བ།

CHOD PA	GANG NAM	LA ME	GYA CHE WA
offerings	*whatever has been offered*	*unsurpassed (in quality)*	*very vast (in quantity)*

These offerings, unsurpassed in quality and vast in quantity,

དེ་དག་རྒྱལ་བ་ཐམས་ཅད་ལ་ཡང་མོས།

DE DAG	GYAL WA	THAM CHE	LA	YANG	MOE
these	*jinas*	*all*	*to*	*also*	*happy*

Make the victors happy.

བཟང་པོ་སྤྱོད་ལ་དད་པའི་སྟོབས་དག་གིས།

ZANG PO CHO	LA	DAE PAI	TOB DAG	GI
Samantabhadra's practice system	*to*	*faith's*	*strength*	*by*

By the power of faith in Samantabhadra's offering system,

རྒྱལ་བ་ཀུན་ལ་ཕྱག་འཚལ་མཆོད་པར་བགྱི།

GYAL WA	KUN	LA	CHAG TSHAL	CHOD PAR	GYI
Jinas, victors	*all*	*to*	*salutation*	*offer*	*do*

I make salutation and offerings to all the jinas.

These offerings unsurpassed in quality and vast in quantity, make the buddhas happy. By the power of faith in Samantabhadra's offering system, I make salutation and offerings to all the buddhas.

ददराक्षगाषानेस्रुदगहेसुग दवदगैषानी।

DOE CHAG	ZHE DANG	TI MUG	WONG	GI NI
desire	anger	stupidity *	power	by

*This stupidity arises from ignorance of our actual nature and it affects all beings in sam-
sara, no matter how intelligent they may seem.

Due to the power of desire, anger and stupidity,

लुषादरादगादरादेखबेषायैदगुबागुदा

LU	DANG	NGAG	DANG	DE ZHIN	YID	KYI	KYANG
body	and	speech	and	similarly	mind	by	also

By body, speech, mind

ष्टिगायाबदगागेषाबगुयषायाउेबाउेषाया

DIG PA		DAG	GI	GYI PA	CHI CHI PA
error,contaminating behaviour		me	by	done	whatever I did

I have acted in a poisonous way. Whatever poisonous acts I have done,

देदगाधयषाउदाबदगागेषासेसेराबगुगषा

DE DAG	THAM CHE	DAG	GI	SO SOR	SHAG
these	all	I, me	by	each	confess and repent

(I don't want to suffer the painful results of this bad karma)

Each and all of them I now confess and beg to be excused.

*Whatever poisonous acts of body, speech and mind I have done due to the
power of desire, anger and stupidity, each and all of them I now confess
and repent.*

धेगषाबाउुदेगुयाबागुनादरासदषागुषासुषा।

CHOG CHUI	GYAL WA	KUN	DANG	SANG GYE SAE
ten directions (everywhere)	jinas, buddhas	all	and	Buddha's sons, bodhisattvas

All the buddhas and bodhisattvas of the ten directions,

रदगुयाद्रमषादरस्रेबादरसिस्रेबादरा

RANG GYAL NAM	DANG	LOB	DANG	MI LOB	DANG
pratyekabuddhas	and	saiksa	and	asaiksa	and

(self-victorious' buddhas who practice in order to free themselves from suffering, and who on gaining that goal, just enjoy it by themselves without helping others.	('students', those practising the dharma up till the 4th way (marga) and 9th stage (bhumi). They still require a teacher.	('graduates' or 'non-students' are those who have reached the 5th way, 10th stage. They will now progress easily without danger of confusion of falling back, and so do not require a teacher.

The self-victorious, the students, the graduates, and

འགྲོ་བ་ཀུན་གྱི་བསོད་ནམས་གང་ལ་ཡང་།

DRO WA	KUN	GYI	SO NAM		GANG LA YANG
beings, those who move in samsara	*all*	*of*	*merit, virtues, the positive results of good deeds*		*whatever they have*

All beings in samsara – seeing all the merit they have gathered

དེ་དག་ཀུན་གྱི་རྗེས་སུ་བདག་ཡི་རང་།

DE DAG	KUN	GYI	JE SU	DAG	YI RANG
these	*all*	*of*	*after*	*I*	*feel, have*

(I am not jealous of their virtue and happiness)

I feel happy and joyful.

All the buddhas and the bodhisattvas in the ten directions, the self-victorious, the students and the graduates, and all beings in samsara – seeing all the merit they have gathered I feel happy and joyful.

གང་རྣམས་ཕྱོགས་བཅུའི་འཇིག་རྟེན་སྒྲོན་མ་རྣམས།

GANG NAM		CHOG CHUI	JIG TEN	DRON MA NAM
however many there are		*ten directions (everywhere)*	*world*	*lamps (buddhas)*

Lamps of the world, however many there are in the ten directions, and

བྱང་ཆུབ་རིམ་པར་སངས་རྒྱས་མ་ཆགས་བརྙེས།

CHANG CHUB	RIM PAR	SANG GYE	MA CHAG	NYE
enlightenment	*stages*	*buddhahood*	*free of desire*	*getting*

Those on the stages leading to enlightenment, those gaining buddhahood free of desire –

མགོན་པོ་དེ་དག་བདག་གིས་ཐམས་ཅད་ལ།

GON PO		DE DAG	DAG	GI	THAM CHE	LA
protectors, benefactors		*these*	*me*	*by*	*all*	*to*

I beseech all you protectors

འཁོར་ལོ་བླ་ན་མེད་པ་བསྐོར་བར་བསྐུལ།

KHOR LO	LA NA ME PA	KOR WAR	KUL
dharmachakra, wheel of dharma	*unsurpassed (i.e. teach the mahayana doctrine)*	*turn*	*request, beseech, encourage*

To turn the unsurpassed dharmachakra.

Lamps of the world, however many there are in the ten directions, and those on the stages leading to enlightenment, those gaining buddhahood free of desire – I beseech all you protectors to turn the unsurpassed wheel of dharma.

ཉ་ངན་འདའ་སྟོན་གང་བཞེད་དེ་དག་ལ།

NYA NGAN DA	TON	GANG	ZHE	DE DAG	LA
pass from sorrow, die, enter nirvana	showing	whoever	like to	them	to

All you (buddhas) who wish to show the passing away of your form,

འགྲོ་བ་ཀུན་ལ་ཕན་ཞིང་བདེ་བའི་ཕྱིར།

DRO WA	KUN	LA	PHEN ZHING	DE WAI	CHIR
beings	all	to	benefiting	happiness	in order to

In order to benefit all beings and make them happy,

བསྐལ་པ་ཞིང་གི་རྡུལ་སྙེད་བཞུགས་པར་ཡང་།

KAL PA	ZHING GI	DUL	NYED	ZHUG PAR	YANG
aeons, kalpas	realms, worlds	dust	as many as	stay	thus

Please stay for as many kalpas as there are particles of dust in the universe.

བདག་གིས་ཐལ་མོ་རབ་སྦྱར་གསོལ་བར་བགྱི།

DAG GI	THAL MO RAB JAR	SOL WAR	GYI
I by	with hands held in prayer (i.e. very sincerely)	pray	do

With hands held in prayer I request this of you.

In order to benefit all beings and make them happy, may all you who wish to show the passing away of your form, please stay for as many kalpas as there are particles of dust in the universe. With hands held in prayer I request this of you.

ཕྱག་འཚལ་བ་དང་མཆོད་ཅིང་བཤགས་པ་དང་།

CHAG TSAL WA	DANG	CHOD CHING	SHAG PA	DANG
salutation	and	offerings	confession	and

By salutations, offerings, and confession, and

རྗེས་སུ་ཡི་རང་བསྐུལ་ཞིང་གསོལ་བ་ཡི།

JE SU YI RANG	KUL ZHING	SOL WA YI
rejoicing at the merit of others	requesting dharma teaching	praying, requesting the buddhas to stay

By rejoicing at the merit of others, beseeching dharma teaching, and requesting the buddhas not to leave –

དགེ་བ་ཅུང་ཟད་བདག་གིས་ཅི་བསགས་པ།

GE WA	CHUNG ZAD	DAG	GI	CHI	SAG PA
virtue	small amount	me	by	whatever	collected

Whatever small amount of virtue I have collected

ཐམས་ཅད་བདག་གིས་བྱང་ཆུབ་ཕྱིར་བསྔོ།། ‖

THAM CHE	DAG	GI	JANG CHUB		CHIR	NGO WO
all	*me*	*by*	*enlightenment, bodhi*		*for the sake of (for all beings)*	*dedicate*

I dedicate it all for the enlightenment of all beings.

By salutations, offerings and confession, and by rejoicing at the merit of others, beseeching dharma teaching and requesting the buddhas not to leave – whatever small amount of virtue I have collected by doing this, I dedicate it all for the enlightenment of all beings.

འཇམ་དཔལ་དཔའ་བོས་ཇི་ལྟར་མཁྱེན་པ་དང་།

JAM PAL	PA WOE	JI TAR	KHYEN PA	DANG
Manjushri	*hero, by*	*like what*	*I know*	*and*

As much as is known by Manjushri the hero, and

ཀུན་ཏུ་བཟང་པོ་དེ་ཡང་དེ་བཞིན་ཏེ།

KUN TU ZANG PO	DE YANG	DE ZHIN	TE
Samantabhadra	*he also*	*like that*	*thus*

Is known by Samantabhadra,

དེ་དག་ཀུན་གྱི་རྗེས་སུ་བདག་སློབ་ཕྱིར།

DE DAG	KUN	GYI	JE SU	DAG	LOB	CHIR
that	*all*	*of*	*after*	*I*	*study and practice (present and future)*	*therefore*

All that I will follow in study and practice and

དགེ་བ་འདི་དག་ཐམས་ཅད་རབ་ཏུ་བསྔོ།། ‖

GE WA	DI DAG	THAM CHE	RAB TU	NGO
virtue	*this*	*all*	*fully*	*dedicate (give all of it to others)*

Dedicate the virtue arising from this to all beings.

As much as is known by Manjushri the hero, and as is known by Samantabhadra, I will follow the same in study and practice and dedicate the virtue arising from this to all beings.

མར་མེ་སྨོན་ལམ།།

THE BUTTERLAMP PRAYER

རང་རིག་ཏ་ཀྲི་དམར་མོ་གྲི་ཐོད་འཛིན༔

RANG	RIG	DAK KI	MAR MO	DRI	THOD	DZIN
my	*open awareness*	*dakini*	*red*	*curved knife*	*skull cup*	*holding*

My awareness is the red dakini holding a curved knife and a skull cup.

དེའི་ཐུགས་ལས་སྤྲུལ་པའི་མཁའ་འགྲོ་མ༔

DE EI	THUG	LAE	TRUL PAI	KHAN DRO MA
my	*heart, mind*	*from*	*emanated*	*dakini*

From my heart emanates a radiant white dakini

དཀར་གསལ་བཞིན་མཛེས་སྤྱན་གསུམ་ནམ་མཁར་གཟིགས༔

KAR	SAL	ZHIN	DZE	CHAN	SUM	NAM KHAR	ZIG
white	*shining*	*face*	*beautiful*	*eye*	*three*	*sky*	*looking*

Who has the most beautiful face with three eyes looking at the sky.

ཕྱག་གཉིས་ཐུགས་ཀར་ཐལ་མོ་སྦྱར་བའི་ནང༔

CHAG	NYI	THUG	KAR	THAL MO	CHAR WAI	NANG
hands	*two*	*heart*	*at*	*palms*	*joined*	*inside*

The palms of her two hands are joined together at her heart and

ཡིད་བཞིན་ནོར་བུ་དགོས་འདོད་ཀུན་འབྱུང་ལས༔

YID ZHIN	NOR BU	GOE	DOD	KUN	JUNG	LAE
wish fulfilling	*jewel, gem*	*need*	*desire*	*all*	*arising, source*	*from*
		(		*name of the jewel*		)

Hold the wish-fulfilling jewel, Source of all Satisfaction, from which

བགྲང་ཡས་འོད་ཟེར་དཔག་མེད་རབ་འཕྲོས་ཆེར༔

DRANG YAE	OD	ZER	PAG MED	RAB	TROE	TSER
numberless	*light*	*rays*	*countless, immeasurable*	*fully, really*	*come out, radiate*	*on top of*

Numberless rays of light radiate out endlessly spreading

མཆོད་པའི་ལྷ་མོ་གྲངས་མེད་བགྲང་ལས་འདས༔

CHOD PAI	LHA MO	DRANG MED	DRANG	LAE	DAE
offering	*goddess*	*numberless*	*counting,*	*from*	*passed*

Countless offering goddesses.

My awareness is the red dakini holding a curved knife and a skull cup. From my heart emanates a radiant white dakini who has the most wonderful face with three eyes looking at the sky. The palms of her two hands are joined together at her heart and hold the wish-fulfilling jewel, Source of all Satisfaction, from which numberless rays of light radiate out endlessly spreading countless offering goddesses.

རབ་མཛེས་རྒྱན་ལྡན་ལྷ་མོ་རེ་རེ་ཡིཿ

RAB	DZE	GYAN	DAN	LHA MO	RE RE	YI
very, most	beautiful	ornaments	having	goddess	each one	of
					(i.e. they each hold a pot)	

The goddesses have the most beautiful ornaments and each

ཕྱག་ཏུ་ཕྱི་ནང་གསང་བའི་སྒྲོན་མེ་འཛིནཿ

CHAG	TU	CHI	NANG	SANG WAI	DRON ME	DZIN
hands	in	outer	inner	secret	lamp	holding

Holds one of the outer, inner and secret lamps in her hands.

ཀོང་བུའི་ཚད་ནི་མཐའ་ཡི་ལྕགས་རི་དངཿ

KONG BUI		TSAD NI	THA	YI	CHAG	RI	DANG
pot	of	size, dimension	boundary	of	iron	mountain	and

The lamp pots are the size of the ring of iron mountains that contains the world.

མར་ཁུའི་ཚད་ནི་རྒྱ་མཚོ་ཆེན་པོ་མཉམཿ

MAR KUI		TSAD NI	GYAM TSO	CHEN PO	NYAM
oil	of	size, quantity	ocean	great	equally

Their quantity of oil equals a great ocean.

These goddesses have the most beautiful ornaments and each holds one of the outer, inner and secret lamps in her hands. The lamp pots are the size of the ring of iron mountains that contains the world. Their quantity of oil equals a great ocean.

སྡོང་བུའི་ཚད་ནི་རི་རྒྱལ་ལྷུན་པོ་དངཿ

DONG BUI		TSAD NI	RI GYAL LHUN PO		DANG
wick	of	size, dimension	Mt. Meru, the central axis of the world		and

Their wicks are the size of Mt. Meru and

མེ་ལྕེའི་ཚད་ནི་སྲིད་རྩེའི་བར་དུ་ཁྱབཿ

ME CHEI	TSAD NI	SID	TSEI	BAR DU	KHYAB
fire, flame	dimension	world	peak, top	until	fill, pervade

Their flames reach the top of the world.

འོད་ནི་ཉི་མ་དུང་ཕྱུར་འབུམ་ལས་ལྷག༔

OD NI	**NYI MA**	**DUNG CHUR**	**BUM**	**LAE**	**LHAG**
light	*sun*	*a hundred million*	*one hundred thousand*	*than*	*better*

Their light is brighter than a million million suns.

ནུས་པས་ཕྱི་ནང་མུན་པ་ཀུན་བསལ་ནས༔

NUE PAE	**CHI**	**NANG**	**MUN PA**	**KUN**	**SAL**	**NAE**
power, by	*outer*	*inner*	*darkness*	*all*	*clear, remove*	*then*

By their power all outer and inner darkness is cleared away and thus

འགྲོ་ཀུན་འཁོར་བའི་ཚང་ཚིང་རབ་བསྲེག་གྱུར༔

DRO	**KUN**	**KHOR WAI**	**TSANG TSING**	**RAB**	**SEG GYUR**
beings	*all*	*samsara*	*fuel, the small sticks used to light a fire**	*fully, well*	*burn*

**i.e. all the wrong views, etc. that keep beings revolving in samsara*

The fuel of samsara belonging to all beings is completely burned up.

Their wicks are the size of Mt. Meru and their flames reach the top of the world. Their light is brighter than a million million suns. By their power all outer and inner darkness is cleared away and thus the fuel of samsara belonging to all beings is completely burned up.

ན་མོ་རཏྣ་ཏྲ་ཡཱ་ཡ༔ ན་མོ་བྷ་ག་ཝ་ཏེ༔

NA MO	**RAT NA**	**TRA YA YA**	**NA MO**	**BHA GA WA TE**
salutation	*jewels*	*three**	*salutation*	*Bhagawan, Buddhas, Perfect Ones*

**Buddha, Dharma, Sangha; Guru, Deva, Dakini; Dharmakaya, Sambhogakaya, Nirmanakaya*

Salutation to the Three Jewels. Salutation to the Perfect Ones.

བཛྲ་སཱ་ར་པྲ་མ་རྡ་ནི༔ ཏ་ཐཱ་ག་ཏཱ་ཡ༔

BEN DZA	**SA RA**	**PRA MA DHA NI**	**TA THA GA TA YA**
vajra, indestructible	*essence*	*great gift (sunyata)*	*all Tathagatas, Thus Gone*

Vajra essence! Great gift! All Tathagatas,

ཨརྷ་ཏེ༔ སམྱཀ་སཾ་བུདྡྷཱ་ཡ༔ ཏདྱ་ཐཱ༔

AR HA TE	**SAM YAK SAM BUD DHA YA**	**TA DYA THA**
Arhat, vanquishers	*completely enlightened Buddhas*	*it is like that*

Arhats, Samyak Sambuddhas are like that.

Salutation to the Three Jewels. Salutation to the Perfect Ones. Vajra essence. Great gift. All Tathagatas, Arhats, Samyak Sambuddhas are like that.

ཨོཾ་བཛྲ་བཛྲ་མ་ཧཱུ་བཛྲ་མ་ཧཱུ་ཏེ་ཛ་བཛྲ

OM	BEN DZE	BEN DZE	MA HA	BEN DZE	MA HA	TE DZA	BEN DZE
five wisdoms	*vajra*	*vajra*	*great*	*vajra*	*great*	*shining*	*vajra*

Om. Vajra, vajra, great vajra, great shining vajra.

མ་ཧཱ་བི་དྱ་བཛྲ་མ་ཧཱ་བོ་དྷི་ཙིཏྟ་བཛྲ

MA HA	BI DYA	BEN DZE	MA HA	BO DHI CHIT TA	BEN DZE
great	*vidya, awareness*	*vajra*	*great*	*bodhicitta, expansive awareness*	*vajra*

Great vidya vajra. Great bodhicitta vajra.

མ་ཧཱ་བོ་དྷི་མ་ནོ་ཏཿ

MA HA	BO DHI	MA NO TA
great	*bodhi, enlightenment*	*meaning*

Great enlightenment's meaning.

Om. Vajra, vajra, great vajra, great shining vajra. Great vidya vajra. Great bodhicitta vajra. Great enlightenment's meaning.

ཨུད་བྷ་སོ་ཀྲ་མ་ན་བཛྲ་སརྦ་ཀརྨ༔

UD BHA	SAM KRA MA NA	BEN DZE	SAR WA	KAR MA
come out	*by stages*	*vajra, very strong*	*all*	*deeds*

Coming out by stages, all deeds like vajras.

ཨ་ཝ་རཎི་བི་ཤུ་དྷ་ནི་བཛྲ་ཡེ་སྭ་ཧཱུ༔

A WA RA NI	BI SHU DHA NI	BEN DZE	YE SWA HA
experience	*very pure*	*strong*	*come*

Experience becomes very pure and strong.

Coming out by stages, all deeds like vajras. Experience becomes very pure and strong.

ཨོཾ་བཛྲ་དྷརྨ་རཎི་ཏ༔   པྲ་རཎི་ཏ༔

OM	BEN DZA	DHAR MA	RA NI TA	PRA RA NI TA
five jnana, bija	*vajra*	*dharma*	*jewel, wisdom*	*life (not quickly ending)*

Om. Vajradharma jewel. Long life.

སོ་པྲ་རཎི་ཏ༔   སརྦ་བུ་དྡྷེ་ཏྲ༔

SAM	PRA RA NI TA	SAR WA	BUD DHA	KSHE TRA
good	*life*	*all*	*buddha*	*realms*

Excellent life. All buddha realms.

ཕུ་ཙ་ལི་ཏི༔   ཕུ་ཙྪུ་ར་མི་ཏ༔

PRA TSA LI TI   **PRA DZNYA**   **PA RA MI TA**
knowing (the pure realms   *prajna, wisdom,*   *paramita, transcendental*
and wisdom itself)   *(knowledge of sunyata)*

Knowledge. Transcendent wisdom.

ནཱ་དྷ་སྭ་བྷཱ་ཝེ་བཛྲ་དྷརྨ་ཧྲྀ་ད་ཡ༔

NA DA   SWA BHA VE   BEN DZA   DHAR MA   HRI DA YA
sound   natural   vajra   dharma   heart, essence
(it has sunyata's nature)

Sound naturally has vajra dharma essence.

སནྟོ་ཥ་ནི་ཧཱུྃ་ཧཱུྃ་ཧཱུྃ་ཧོ་ཧོ་ཧོ་ཨ་ཁཾ་སྭ་ཧཱུྃ༔

SAN TO SHA NI   HUNG HUNG HUNG HO HO HO   A KHAM SWA HA
satisfy (all beings)   all come out (ceaseless flow)   filling the sky

Satisfying all, they rise out endlessly filling the sky.

Om Vajradharma jewel. Long life. Excellent life. All buddha realms. Knowledge. Transcendent wisdom. Sound naturally has vajra dharma essence. Satisfying all, they rise out endlessly filling the sky.

ཧོཿ ཆོས་དབྱིངས་ཀུན་ལ་ཁྱབ་པའི་ཀོང་བུ་རུཿ

HO	CHOE YING	KUN	LA	KHYAB PAI	KONG BU	RU
wonderful!	*dharmadhatu*	*all*	*to*	*pervading, filling*	*pot*	*in*
	(unborn space,					
	the source and site of everything)					

Wonderful! In the pot of all-pervading hospitable space

དོན་དམ་བྱང་ཆུབ་སེམས་ཀྱི་མར་ཁུ་འཁྱིལཿ

DON DAM	JANG CHUB SEM	KYI	MAR KHU	KHYIL
absolute,	*bodhicitta,*	*of*	*clarified butter, oil*	*swirling*
non-dual	*enlightened mind*			

Swirls the oil of non-dual awareness.

མི་རྟོག་ཏིང་ངེ་འཛིན་གྱི་སྡོང་བུ་ལཿ

MI TOG	TING NGE DZIN	GYI	DONG BU	LA
free of dualistic	*samadhi, absorbed*	*of*	*wick, stick*	*on*
thoughts	*contemplation*			

On the wick of absorbed contemplation free of dualistic thought,

རིག་པ་རང་བྱུང་གསལ་བའི་མེ་ལྕེ་འབརཿ

RIG PA	RANG JUNG	SAL WAI	ME CHE	BAR
vidya, natural	*self-existing,*	*shining,*	*flame*	*burning*
awareness	*self-occurring*	*illuminating*	*(of dharmadhatu jnana)*	

The flame of the self-existing clarity of awareness burns bright.

ཉོན་མོངས་གཏི་མུག་རྟོག་པ་རང་སར་གྲོལཿ

NYON MONG	TI MUG	TOG PA	RANG	SAR	DROL
affliction, kleshas	*stupidity,*	*thoughts*	*own place*	*in*	*liberate, go free*
(of all beings)	*assumption*				

Thoughts arising from the affliction of stupidity are liberated in their own place.

མ་སྤང་ཆོས་ཉིད་དེ་བཞིན་ཀློང་དུ་ཐིམཿ

MA PANG	CHOE NYID	DE ZHIN	LONG	DU	THIM
*without rejecting**	*dharmata#*	*natural, tathata,*	*vast*	*in*	*melt, go°*
		givenness			

*neither inhibiting nor stopping   # original condition, actuality free of projections
° the stupidity is self-liberated in this way

Without being rejected they dissolve in the vastness of the actuality of what is.

Wonderful! In the pot of all-pervading hospitable space swirls the oil of non-dual awareness. On the wick of absorbed contemplation free of dualistic thought, the flame of the self-existing clarity of awareness burns bright. Thoughts arising from the affliction of stupidity are liberated in their own place. Without being rejected they dissolve in the vastness of the actuality of what is.

ཆོས་དབྱིངས་ཡེ་ཤེས་རང་བཞིན་འོད་ཟེར་འཚེར༔

CHOE YING	YE SHE	RANG ZHIN	OD	ZER	TSER
dharmadhatu, all encompassing space	jnana, original knowing	nature, show	light	rays	shining

Original knowing as hospitable space manifests as shining rays of light.

འགྲོ་བའི་མ་རིག་མུན་པ་སེལ་ཕྱིར་དུ༔

DRO WAI	MA RIG	MUN PA	SEL	CHIR DU
being	avidya, ignorance	darkness	clear away	in order to

In order to dispel the darkness of ignorance of all sentient beings

བླ་མ་སངས་རྒྱས་རིགས་ཀྱི་ལྷ་ཚོགས་ལ༔

LA MA	SANG GYAE	RIG	KYI	LHA TSHOG	LA
guru*	buddha	kula, family #	of	gods	to

*the guru is not different from these gods   # i.e. Vairocana and his circle

We offer this to the guru and the gods of the Buddha clan.

འབུལ་ལོ་བཞེས་ནས་མཆོག་ཐུན་དངོས་གྲུབ་སྩོལ༔

BUL LO	ZHE	NE	CHOG	THUN	NGOE DRUB	TSOL
offer	accept	then	supreme	general	siddhis, accomplishments	grant

Please accept and then bestow supreme and general accomplishments.

Original knowing as hospitable space manifests as shining rays of light. In order to dispel the darkness of ignorance of all sentient beings we offer this to the guru and the gods of the Buddha clan. Please accept and then bestow supreme and general accomplishments.

ཧོ༔   ཕྱོགས་མེད་མཐའ་དབུས་བྲལ་བའི་ཀོང་བུ་རུ༔

HO	CHOG MED	THA	WUE	DRAL WAI	KONG BU	RU
wonderful	not going to one side*	edge, end	centre	free of ≠	pot	in

*going everywhere without bias or preference or limitation   ≠ no sense of duality

Wonderful! In the pot free of bias, without centre or circumference

ཞེན་པ་གཞི་ལ་བྲལ་བའི་མར་ཁུ་འཁྱིལ༔

ZHEN PA	ZHI	LA	DRAL WAI	MAR KHU	KHYIL
hopes, habits, attachments	ground*	on	free of	oil	swirling

*on knowledge of the truth all false notions go free

Swirls the oil of liberating attachment on the natural ground.

བདེ་གསལ་རང་རོ་ཤེས་པའི་སྡོང་བུ་ལ༔

DE	SAL	RANG NGO	SHE PAI	DONG BU	LA
happy	*clear*	*own nature*	*know*	*stick, wick*	*on*

On the wick of knowing one's own nature of happiness and clarity

རིག་པ་རང་གསལ་ཤར་བའི་མེ་ལྕེ་འབར༔

RIG PA	RANG SAL		SHAR WAI	ME CHE	BAR
awareness	*naturally clear, shining*		*rising*	*flame*	*burning*
					(of adarsha jnana)

The flame of the arising of the natural clarity of awareness burns bright.

ཉོན་མོངས་ཞེ་སྡང་རྟོག་པ་རང་སར་གྲོལ༔

NYON MONG	ZHE DANG	TOG PA	RANG SAR	DROL
affliction	*anger*	*thoughts*	*in own place*	*liberate*

Thoughts arising from the affliction of anger are liberated in their own place.

མ་སྤང་གསལ་སྟོང་གཉིས་མེད་ཀློང་དུ་ཐིམ༔

MA PANG	SAL	TONG	NYI MED	LONG	DU	THIM
not rejecting, not stopping	*clear, shining*	*empty*	*not different*	*vast*	*in*	*dissolve, melt*

Without being rejected they dissolve in the vastness of the non-duality of clarity and emptiness.

Wonderful! In the pot free of bias, without centre or circumference, swirls the oil of liberating attachment on the natural ground. On the wick of knowing one's own nature of happiness and clarity the flame of the arising of the natural clarity of awareness burns bright. Thoughts arising from the affliction of anger are liberated in their own place. Without being rejected they dissolve in the vastness of the non-duality of clarity and emptiness.

མེ་ལོང་ཡེ་ཤེས་རང་བཞིན་འོད་ཟེར་འཚེར༔

ME LONG	YE SHE	RANG ZHIN	OD ZER	TSER
adarsha, mirror	*jnana, original knowing*	*nature, show*	*light rays*	*shining*

Original knowing as mirroring manifests as shining rays of light.

འགྲོ་བའི་མ་རིག་མུན་པ་སེལ་ཕྱིར་དུ༔

DRO WAI	MA RIG	MUN PA	SEL	CHIR DU

In order to dispel the darkness of ignorance of all sentient beings

བླ་མ་རྡོ་རྗེ་རིགས་ཀྱི་ལྷ་ཚོགས་ལ༔

LA MA	DOR JE	RIG	KYI	LHA TSOG	LA
guru	vajra, indestructible	kula, family*	of	gods	to

* Akshobya and his circle

We offer this to the guru and the gods of the Vajra clan.

འབུལ་ལོ་བཞེས་ནས་མཆོག་ཐུན་དངོས་གྲུབ་སྩོལ༔

BUL LO	ZHE	NE	CHOG	THUN	NGOE DRUB	TSOL

Please accept and then bestow supreme and general accomplishments.

Original knowing as mirroring manifests as shining rays of light. In order to dispel the darkness of ignorance of all sentient beings we offer this to the guru and the gods of the Vajra clan. Please accept and then bestow supreme and general accomplishments.

ཧོཿ   ཆོས་དབྱིངས་མཉམ་པར་བརྡལ་བའི་ཀོང་བུ་རུཿ

HO	CHOE YING	NYAM PAR	DAL WAI	KONG BU	RU
wonderful	dharmadhatu, space of everything	equal*	spread, pervade	pot	in

*It goes everywhere equally and everything is equal within it

Wonderful! In the pot of hospitable space that is the same everywhere

ཀུན་རྫོབ་བྱང་ཆུབ་སེམས་ཀྱི་མར་ཁུ་འཁྱིལ༔

KUN DZOB	JANG CHUB SEM	KYI	MAR KHU	KHYIL
relative*	bodhicitta#	of	oil	swirling

*working in terms of subject and object   # altruistic aspiration for enlightenment

Swirls the oil of dualistic altruism.

སྣང་སྟོང་ཟུང་དུ་འཇུག་པའི་སྡོང་བུ་ལ༔

NANG	TONG	ZUNG DU JUG PAI	DONG BU	LA
appearances, ideas	empty	joined in union, fully merged	wick	on

On the wick of the union of appearance and emptiness

རིག་པ་རྗེན་པར་རྟོགས་པའི་མེ་ལྕེ་འབར༔

RIG PA	JEN PAR	TOG PAI	ME CHE	BAR
awareness	raw, naked, unobscured	actualise directly	flame (of samanta jnana)	burning

The flame of actualising naked awareness burns bright.

ཉོན་མོངས་ང་རྒྱལ་རྟོག་པ་རང་སར་གྲོལ༔

NYON MONG	NGA GYAL	TOG PA	RANG SAR	DROL
affliction	pride	thoughts	own place	liberated

Thoughts arising from the affliction of pride are liberated in their own place.

མ་སྤང་མཉམ་པ་ཉིད་ཀྱི་ཀློང་དུ་ཐིམ༔

MA PANG	NYAM PA NYID	KYI	LONG	DU	THIM
without abandoning, without stopping	equality (sunyata)	of	vastness	in	melt, merge

Without being rejected they dissolve in the vastness of perfect equality.

Wonderful! In the pot of hospitable space that is the same everywhere swirls the oil of dualistic altruism. On the wick of the union of appearance and emptiness the flame of actualising naked awareness burns bright. Thoughts arising from the affliction of pride are liberated in their own place. Without being rejected they dissolve in the vastness of perfect equality.

མཉམ་ཉིད་ཡེ་ཤེས་རང་བཞིན་འོད་ཟེར་འཚེར༔

NYAM NYID	YE SHE	RANG ZHIN	OD	ZER	TSER
samanta, equality*	jnana, original knowing	nature, show	light	rays	shining

*all phenomena have the same nature whatever their different aspects; they share identity

Original knowing as identity manifests as shining rays of light

འགྲོ་བའི་མ་རིག་མུན་པ་སེལ་ཕྱིར་དུ༔

DRO WAI	MA RIG	MUN PA	SEL	CHIR DU

In order to dispel the darkness of ignorance of all sentient beings

བླ་མ་རིན་ཆེན་རིགས་ཀྱི་ལྷ་ཚོགས་ལ༔

LA MA	RIN CHEN	RIG	KYI	LHA TSOG	LA
guru	ratna, jewel	kula, family*	of	gods	to

* Ratnasambhava and his circle

We offer this to the guru and the gods of the Ratna clan.

འབུལ་ལོ་བཞེས་ནས་མཆོག་ཐུན་དངོས་གྲུབ་སྩོལ༔

BUL LO	ZHE	NE	CHOG	THUN	NGOE DRUB	TSOL

Please accept and then bestow supreme and general accomplishments.

Original knowing as identity manifests as shining rays of light. In order to dispel the darkness of ignorance of all sentient beings we offer this to the guru and the gods of the Ratna clan. Please accept and then bestow supreme and general accomplishments.

ཧོཿ ཆོས་ཀུན་རྣམ་པར་འབྱེད་པའི་ཀོང་བུ་རུཿ

HO	CHOE KUN	NAM PAR	JED PAI	KONG BU	RU
wonderful	*all dharmas, phenomena**	*fully, clearly*	*distinguish, separate and identify*	*pot*	*in*

*all that is experienced in samsara and nirvana

Wonderful! In the pot of attention to the distinct features of all phenomena

ཟག་མེད་བདེ་བ་ཆེན་པོའི་མར་ཁུ་འཁྱིལཿ

ZAG MED	DE WA	CHEN POI	MAR KHU	KHYIL
no leaks, no distractions	*happy*	*great*	*oil*	*swirling*

Swirls the oil of undeclining great happiness.

བདེ་སྟོང་ཟུང་དུ་འཇུག་པའི་སྡོང་བུ་ལཿ

DE	TONG	ZUNG DU JUG PAI	DONG BU	LA
happiness	*emptiness*	*union*	*wick, stick*	*on*

On the wick of the union of happiness and emptiness,

རིག་རྩལ་སོ་སོར་རྟོགས་པའི་མེ་ལྕེ་འབརཿ

RIG	TSAL	SO SOR	TOG PAI	ME CHE	BAR
awareness	*energy flow, radiance*	*each one, as*	*know, see*	*flame (of pratika jnana)*	*blazing*

The flame of the energy of awareness revealing each appearance as it is burns bright.

ཉོན་མོངས་འདོད་ཆགས་རྟོག་པ་རང་སར་གྲོལཿ

NYON MONG	DOD CHAG	TOG PA	RANG SAR	DROL
affliction	*desire*	*thoughts*	*in own place*	*liberate*

Thoughts arising from the affliction of desire are liberated in their own place.

མ་སྤང་གཉིས་མེད་བདེ་ཆེན་ཀློང་དུ་ཐིམཿ

MA PANG	NYI MED	DE	CHEN	LONG	DU	THIM
without rejection	*non-dual*	*happiness*	*great*	*depth*	*in*	*dissolve*

Without being rejected they dissolve in the vastness of non-dual great happiness.

Wonderful! In the pot of attention to the distinct features of all phenomena swirls the oil of undeclining great happiness. On the wick of the union of happiness and emptiness, the flame of the energy of awareness revealing each appearance as it is burns bright. Thoughts arising from the affliction of desire are liberated in their own place. Without being rejected they dissolve in the vastness of non-dual great happiness.

སོར་རྟོགས་ཡེ་ཤེས་རང་བཞིན་འོད་ཟེར་འཚེར༔

SOR TOG	YE SHE	RANG ZHIN	OD	ZER	TSER
pratika*	jnana, wisdom	natural, show	light	rays	shining

*clear distinction, knowing each thing just as it is, discerning

Original knowing as precise discernment manifests as shining rays of light.

འགྲོ་བའི་མ་རིག་མུན་པ་སེལ་ཕྱིར་དུ༔

DRO WAI	MA RIG	MUN PA	SEL	CHIR DU

In order to dispel the darkness of ignorance of all sentient beings

བླ་མ་པདྨ་རིགས་ཀྱི་ལྷ་ཚོགས་ལ༔

LA MA	PAD MA	RIG	KYI	LHA TSOG	LA
guru	padma, lotus	kula, family*	of	gods	to

*Amitabha and his circle

We offer this to the guru and the gods of the Padma clan.

འབུལ་ལོ་བཞེས་ནས་མཆོག་ཐུན་དངོས་གྲུབ་སྩོལ༔

BUL LO	ZHE	NE	CHOG	THUN	NGOE DRUB	TSOL

Please accept and then bestow supreme and general accomplishments.

Original knowing as precise discernment manifests as shining rays of light. In order to dispel the darkness of ignorance of all sentient beings we offer this to the guru and the gods of Padma clan. Please accept and bestow supreme and general accomplishments.

ཧོ༔   བྱ་བ་ལས་ཀྱི་འཁོར་ལོའི་ཀོང་བུ་རུ༔

HO	JA WA LAE	KYI	KHOR LOI	KONG BU	RU
wonderful	deeds, actions	of	chakra, wheel	pot	in

Wonderful! In the pot of the wheel of continuous activity

རྩོལ་མེད་ལྷུན་གྱིས་གྲུབ་པའི་མར་ཁུ་འཁྱིལ༔

TSOL MED	LHUN GYI DRUB PAI	MAR KHU	KHYIL
free of striving and trying	effortlessly arising	oil	swirling

Swirls the oil of effortless accomplishment free of striving.

གསལ་སྟོང་ཟུང་དུ་འཇུག་པའི་སྡོང་བུ་ལ༔

SAL	TONG	ZUNG DU JUG PAI	DONG BU	LA
clarity	emptiness	union	wick, stick	on

On the wick of the union of clarity and emptiness

རིག་པ་ཐོག་མཐའ་བྲལ་བའི་མེ་ལྕེ་འབར༔

RIG PA	THOG	THA	DRAL WAI	ME CHE	BAR
awareness	*beginning*	*end*	*free of*	*flame*	*blaze, burn*
					(of Amogasiddhi jnana)

The flame of awareness free of beginning and end burns bright.

ཉོན་མོངས་ཕྲག་དོག་རྟོག་པ་རང་སར་གྲོལ༔

NYON MONG	THRAG DOG	TOG PA	RANG SAR	DROL
affliction	*jealousy*	*thoughts*	*in their own place*	*liberate*

Thoughts arising from the affliction of jealousy are liberated in their own place.

མ་སྤང་བྱ་རྩོལ་བྲལ་བའི་ཀློང་དུ་ཐིམ༔

MA PANG	JA	TSOL	DRAL WAI	LONG	DU	THIM
without rejection	*work*	*effort*	*free of*	*vast*	*in*	*dissolve*
or stopping			*(i.e. non-duality)*			

Without being rejected they dissolve in the vastness of freedom from work and effort.

Wonderful! In the pot of the wheel of continuous activity swirls the oil of effortless accomplishment free of striving. On the wick of the union of clarity and emptiness the flame of awareness free of beginning and end burns bright. Thoughts arising from the affliction of jealousy are liberated in their own place. Without being rejected they dissolve in the vastness of freedom from work and effort.

བྱ་གྲུབ་ཡེ་ཤེས་རང་བཞིན་འོད་ཟེར་འཚེར༔

JA DRUB	YE SHE	RANG ZHIN	OD ZER	TSER
effective action	*jnana, wisdom*	*nature, show*	*light rays*	*shining*

Original knowing as effective action manifests as shining rays of light.

འགྲོ་བའི་མ་རིག་མུན་པ་སེལ་ཕྱིར་དུ༔

DRO WAI	MA RIG	MUN PA SEL	CHIR DU

In order to dispel the darkness of ignorance of all sentient beings

བླ་མ་ལས་ཀྱི་རིགས་ཀྱི་ལྷ་ཚོགས་ལ༔

LA MA	LAE KYI	RIG	KYI	LHA TSOG	LA
guru	*activity, karma*	*kula, family**	*of*	*gods*	*to*

* Amogasiddhi and his circle

We offer this to the guru and the gods of the Karma clan.

འབུལ་ལོ་བཞེས་ནས་མཆོག་ཐུན་དངོས་གྲུབ་རྩོལ༔

BUL LO   ZHE   NE   CHOG   THUN   NGOE DRUB   TSOL

Please accept and then bestow supreme and general accomplishments.

Original knowing as effective action manifests as shining rays of light. In order to dispel the darkness of ignorance of all sentient beings we offer this to the guru and the gods of the Karma clan. Please accept and then bestow supreme and general accomplishments.

ཧོ༔   ཀུན་གཞི་འཁྲུལ་པས་བཅིང་པའི་ཀོང་བུ་རུ༔

HO	KUN ZHI	TRUL PAE	CHING PAI	KONG BU	RU
Wonderful	*alaya, ground of all*	*confusion, by*	*bound***	*pot*	*in*

* the natural freedom is not experienced due to a focus on limitations

Wonderful! In the pot of the ground of all bound by delusion

ཉེ་ཉོན་རྟོག་པའི་ཚོགས་ཀྱི་མར་ཁུ་འཁྱིལ༔

NYE NYON	TOG PAI	TSOG	KYI	MAR KHU	KHYIL
minor afflictions*	*thoughts*	*hosts*	*of*	*oil*	*swirling*

*the main five afflictions are listed in the five preceding verses: ignorance, anger, jealousy, desire, pride

Swirls the oil of the many thoughts arising from the minor afflictions.

མ་རིག་བདག་ཏུ་འཛིན་པའི་སྡོང་བུ་ལ༔

MA RIG	DAG	TU	DZIN PAI	DONG BU	LA
avidya, ignorance	*self- essence*	*to*	*grasping, believing*	*wick, stick*	*on*

On the wick of belief in self-existing entities that arises from ignoring,

བདག་མེད་ཡེ་ཤེས་ཆེན་པོའི་མེ་ལྕེ་འབར༔

DAG MED	YE SHE	CHEN POI	ME CHE	BAR
anatma, without essence	*original knowing*	*great*	*flame*	*blazing, burning*

The flame of the great original knowing free of reification burns bright.

ཉོན་སྒྲིབ་ཆ་དང་བཅས་པ་རང་སར་གྲོལ༔

NYON DRIB CHA	DANG CHAE PA	RANG SAR	DROL
kleshavarana, obscuration of the afflictions	*together*	*in own place*	*liberate*

The obscuration arising from the afflictions is liberated in its own place.

 མ་སྤང་ཆོས་ཀྱི་བདག་མེད་ཀློང་དུ་ཐིམ༔

MA PANG	CHOE KYI DAG MED	LONG	DU	THIM
without rejecting	*dharmanatma**	*vast*	*in*	*dissolve*

**absence of inherent self-nature in phenomena*

Without being rejected it dissolves in the vastness of the absence of inherent self-nature in all phenomena.

Wonderful! In the pot of the ground of all bound by delusion swirls the oil of the many thoughts arising from the minor afflictions. On the wick of belief in self-existing entities that arises from ignoring, the flame of the great original knowing free of reification burns bright. The obscuration arising from the afflictions is liberated in its own place. Without being rejected it dissolves in the vastness of the absence of inherent self-nature in all phenomena.

ཕྱོགས་མེད་ཡེ་ཤེས་ཆེན་པོའི་རང་འོད་འཚེར༔

CHOG	ME	YE SHE	CHEN POI	RANG	OD	TSER
direction, side, limitation, (i.e. impartially pervasive)	*without*	*jnana*	*great*	*own*	*light*	*shining*

The great impartial original knowing manifests its own shining light.

འགྲོ་བའི་མ་རིག་མུན་པ་སེལ་ཕྱིར་དུ༔

DRO WAI	MA RIG	MUN PA SEL	CHIR DU

In order to dispel the darkness of ignorance of all sentient beings

བླ་མ་མཆོག་གསུམ་རྩ་གསུམ་ལྷ་ཚོགས་ལ༔

LA MA	CHOG	SUM	TSA	SUM	LHA TSOG	LA
guru	*excellent**	*three*	*root#*	*three*	*gods*	*to*

**buddha, dharma, sangha   # guru, deva, dakini*

We offer this to the guru, the three jewels, the three roots, and all the deities.

འབུལ་ལོ་བཞེས་ནས་མཆོག་ཐུན་དངོས་གྲུབ་སྩོལ༔

BUL LO	ZHE	NE	CHOG	THUN	NGOE DRUB TSOL

Please accept and then bestow supreme and general accomplishments.

The great impartial original knowing manifests its own shining light. In order to dispel the darkness of ignorance of all sentient beings we offer this to the guru, the three jewels, the three roots and all the deities. Please accept and then bestow supreme and general accomplishments.

ཧོྃ ཆོས་དབྱིངས་བདལ་ཁྱབ་ཆེན་པོའི་ཀོང་བུ་རུ༔

HO	CHOE YING	DAL KHYAB	CHEN POI	KONG BU	RU
wonderful	dharmadhatu, all-encompassing space	vast, pervasive, infinite	great	pot	in

Wonderful! In the pot of infinite hospitable space

ཕྲ་བའི་རྟོག་ཚོགས་ལྷུན་འགྲུབས་མར་ཁུ་འཁྱིལ༔

TRA WAI	TOG	TSOG	LHUN	JAM	MAR KHU	KHYIL
small	thought	many	quickly, always	moving	oil	swirling

Swirls the oil of the many small thoughts that appear ceaselessly.

ཤེས་པ་རང་འོད་གསལ་བའི་སྡོང་བུ་ལ༔

SHE PA	RANG	OD	SAL WAI	DONG BU	LA
mind, awareness	own	light	shining	wick, stick	on

On the wick of the radiant natural light of knowing,

དུག་ལྔ་ལྷག་མེད་འཇོམས་པའི་མེ་ལྕེ་འབར༔

DUG NGA	LHAG	MED	JOM PAI	ME CHE	BAR
five poisons*	left-over, residue remainder	without	destroying	flame	burning

*stupidity, anger, desire, pride, jealousy

The flame of the traceless destruction of the five poisons burns bright.

ཤེས་བྱའི་སྒྲིབ་པ་ལྷག་མེད་རང་སར་གྲོལ༔

SHE JAI DRIB PA	LHAG MED	RANG SAR	DROL
obscurations by and to knowledge	without residue	in its own place	liberate

Obscuration by and to knowledge is liberated in its own place without residue.

མ་སྤང་གང་ཟག་བདག་མེད་ཀློང་དུ་ཐིམ༔

MA PANG	GANG ZAG DAG MED	LONG	DU	THIM
without rejecting	pudgalanatma*	vast	in	dissolve

*absence of inherent self-nature in beings

Without being rejected it dissolves in the vastness of the absence of inherent self-nature in all beings.

Wonderful! In the pot of infinite hospitable space swirls the oil of the many small thoughts that appear ceaselessly. On the wick of the radiant natural light of knowing, the flame of the traceless destruction of the five poisons burns bright. Obscuration by and to knowledge is liberated in its own place without residue. Without being rejected it dissolves in the vastness of the absence of inherent self-nature in all beings.

ཀུན་ཁྱབ་རང་གསལ་དག་པའི་རང་འོད་འཚེར༔

KUN KHYAB   RANG   SAL   DAG PAI   RANG   OD   TSER
all-pervading   own, natural   clarity   pure   own   light   shining

The all-pervading natural clarity manifests as the purity of its own shining light.

འགྲོ་བའི་མ་རིག་མུན་པ་སེལ་ཕྱིར་དུ༔

DRO WAI   MA RIG   MUN PA   SEL   CHIR DU

In order to dispel the darkness of ignorance of all sentient beings

བླ་མ་མཆོག་གསུམ་རྩ་གསུམ་ལྷ་ཚོགས་ལ༔

LA MA   CHOG   SUM   TSA   SUM   LHA TSOG   LA

We offer this to the guru, the three jewels, the three roots, and all the deities.

འབུལ་ལོ་བཞེས་ནས་མཆོག་ཐུན་དངོས་གྲུབ་སྩོལ༔

BUL LO   ZHE   NE   CHOG   THUN   NGOE DRUB   TSOL

Please accept and then bestow supreme and general accomplishments.

The all-pervading natural clarity manifests as the purity of its own shining light. In order to dispel the darkness of ignorance of all sentient beings we offer this to the guru, the three jewels, the three roots and all the deities. Please accept and then bestow supreme and general accomplishments.

ཧོ༔   འཁོར་བ་ཤེས་བྱ་ཡུལ་གྱི་ཀོང་བུ་རུ༔

HO   KHOR WA   SHE JA   YUL   KYI   KONG BU   RU
wonderful   samsara   knowable,   objects   of   pot   in
                        knowledge*

*all that constitutes samsara, seemingly separate entities

Wonderful! In the pot of samsaric objects of knowledge

ལས་ཉོན་གཟུང་འཛིན་འཁྲུལ་པའི་མར་ཁུ་འཁྱིལ༔

LAE   NYON   ZUNG   DZIN   THRUL PAI   MAR KHU   KHYIL
karma,   afflictions   graspable   grasping   confusion   oil   swirling
actions   object   subject

Swirls the oil of dualistic confusion which generates karma and the afflictions.

བདེ་སྡུག་གཉིས་སུ་མེད་པའི་སྡོང་བུ་ལ༔

DE   DUG   NYI SU MED PAI   DONG BU   LA
happy   sorrow   not different, same nature   wick   on

On the wick of the non-duality of happiness and sorrow

ཡེ་ཤེས་རང་ལས་བྱུང་བའི་མེ་ལྕེ་འབར༔

YE SHE	RANG	LAE	JUNG WAI	ME CHE	BAR
original knowing	*self*	*from*	*arise*	*flame*	*burning*

The flame that arises from original knowing burns bright.

འཁྲུལ་པའི་སེམས་ཅན་ཚོགས་རྣམས་རང་སར་གྲོལ༔

THRUL PAI	SEM CHEN	TSOG NAM	RANG	SAR	DROL
confused, bewildered	*sentient beings*	*hosts, all*	*in its own*	*place*	*liberate*

All confused sentient beings are liberated in their own place.

མ་སྤང་གཟུང་འཛིན་གཉིས་མེད་ཀློང་དུ་ཐིམ༔

MA PANG	ZUNG	DZIN	NYI MED	LONG	DU	THIM
without abandoning	*graspable objects*	*grasping mind*	*not different*	*vast*	*in*	*dissolves*

Without being rejected they dissolve in the vastness of the non-duality of graspable object and grasping mind.

Wonderful! In the pot of samsaric objects of knowledge swirls the oil of dualistic confusion which generates karma and the afflictions. On the wick of the non-duality of happiness and sorrow the flame that arises from original knowing burns bright. All confused sentient beings are liberated in their own place. Without being rejected they dissolve in the vastness of the non-duality of graspable object and grasping mind.

འཛིན་མེད་ཡེ་ཤེས་ཆེན་པོའི་རང་འོད་འཆོར༔

DZIN MED	YE SHE	CHEN POI	RANG	OD	TSER
without grasping	*original knowing*	*great*	*own*	*light*	*shines*

The great original knowing free of grasping manifests its own shining light.

འགྲོ་བའི་མ་རིག་མུན་པ་སེལ་ཕྱིར་དུ༔

DRO WAI	MA RIG	MUN PA	SEL	CHIR DU

In order to dispel the darkness of ignorance of all sentient beings

བླ་མ་མཆོག་གསུམ་རྩ་གསུམ་ལྷ་ཚོགས་ལ༔

LA MA	CHOG	SUM	TSA	SUM	LHA TSOG	LA

We offer this to the guru, the three jewels, the three roots, and all the deities.

འབུལ་ལོ་བཞེས་ནས་མཆོག་ཐུན་དངོས་གྲུབ་སྩོལ༔

BUL LO	ZHE	NE	CHOG	THUN	NGOE DRUB	TSOL

Please accept and then bestow supreme and general accomplishments.

The great original knowing free of grasping manifests its own shining light. In order to dispel the darkness of ignorance of all sentient beings we offer this to the guru, the three jewels, the three roots and all the deities. Please accept and then bestow supreme and general accomplishments.

ཧོཿ བྱམས་པ་ཚད་མེད་བློ་འདས་ཀོང་བུ་རུཿ

HO	JAM PA	TSAD MED	LO DAE	KONG BU	RU
wonderful	*love*	*immeasurable*	*beyond thought*	*pot*	*in*
	(wanting beings to be happy)		*(i.e. very large)*		

Wonderful! In the pot of inconceivable measureless love

སྙིང་རྗེ་ཚད་གཟུང་མེད་པའི་མར་ཁུ་འཁྱིལཿ

NYING JE	TSAD ZUNG	MED PAI	MAR KHU	KHYIL
compassion	*measurable*	*without*	*oil*	*swirling*
(acting to free beings from samsara)				

Swirls the oil of immeasurable compassion.

བཏང་སྙོམས་ཚད་མེད་རྣམ་དག་སྡོང་བུ་ལཿ

TANG NYOM	TSAD MED	NAM DAG	DONG BU	LA
*equanimity**	*immeasurable*	*very pure*	*wick*	*on*

not discriminating between friend and foe

On the wick of very pure immeasurable equanimity

དགའ་བ་ཚད་མེད་རྒྱས་པའི་མེ་ལྕེ་འབརཿ

GA WA	TSAD MED	GYAE PAI	ME CHE	BAR
*joy**	*immeasurable*	*spreading*	*flame*	*blazing*

wishing unlimited joy for others

The flame of spreading immeasurable joy burns bright.

ཉོན་མོངས་དུག་ལྔའི་རྟོག་པ་རང་སར་གྲོལཿ

NYON MONG	DUG	NGAI	TOG PA	RANG SAR	DROL
afflictions	*poisons*	*five**	*thoughts*	*in own place*	*liberate*

stupidity, desire, anger, jealousy, pride

Thoughts arising from the five afflicting poisons are liberated in their own place.

ཚད་མེད་ཁྱབ་གདལ་ཆེན་པོའི་ཀློང་དུ་ཐིམཿ

TSAD MED	KHYAB DAL	CHEN POI	LONG	DU	THIM
immeasurable	*infinitude, pervasion*	*great*	*vast*	*in*	*dissolve*

They dissolve in the vastness of the great infinitude of the immeasurable.

Wonderful! In the pot of inconceivable measureless love swirls the oil of immeasurable compassion. On the wick of very pure immeasurable equanimity the flame of spreading immeasurable joy burns bright. Thoughts arising from the five afflicting poisons are liberated in their own place. They dissolve in the vastness of the great infinitude of the immeasurable.

གཉིས་མེད་བློ་ལས་འདས་པའི་རང་འོད་འཚེར༔

NYI ME	LO LAE DAE PAI	RANG	OD	TSER
non-dual	*inconceivable, beyond mentation*	*own*	*light*	*shining*

Inconceivable non-duality manifests its own shining light.

འགྲོ་བའི་མ་རིག་མུན་པ་སེལ་ཕྱིར་དུ༔

DRO WAI	MA RIG	MUN PA	SEL	CHIR DU

In order to dispel the darkness of ignorance of all sentient beings

བླ་མ་མཆོག་གསུམ་རྩ་གསུམ་ལྷ་ཚོགས་ལ༔

LA MA	CHOG	SUM	TSA	SUM	LHA TSOG	LA

We offer this to the guru, the three jewels, the three roots, and all the deities.

འབུལ་ལོ་བཞེས་ནས་མཆོག་ཐུན་དངོས་གྲུབ་སྩོལ༔

BUL LO	ZHE	NE	CHOG	THUN	NGOE DRUB TSOL

Please accept and then bestow supreme and general accomplishments.

Inconceivable non-duality manifests its own shining light. In order to dispel the darkness of ignorance of all sentient beings we offer this to the guru, the three jewels, the three roots and all the deities. Please accept and then bestow supreme and general accomplishments.

ཧོ༔   འགྲོ་ཀུན་ཕ་མར་ཤེས་པའི་ཀོང་བུ་རུ༔

HO	DRO	KUN	PHA MAR	SHE PAI	KONG BU	RU
wonderful	*beings*	*all**	*as parents*	*knowing*	*pot*	*in*

*they have all been my parents in my countless past lives in samsara

Wonderful! In the pot of knowing all beings to be my parents

དྲིན་གྱིས་བཀྱང་བར་དྲན་པའི་མར་ཁུ་འཁྱིལ༔

DRIN	GYI	KYANG WAR	DRAN PAI	MAR KHU	KHYIL
kindness	*by*	*hold**	*remember*	*oil*	*swirling*

*take care of and keep one's affectionate thoughts

Swirls the oil of remembrance of the kindness with which they have held me.

ཏྲིན་ལན་གཐོ་བར་འདོད་པའི་སྡོང་བུ་ལ༔

DRIN	LAN ZO WAR	DOD PAI	DONG BU	LA
kindness	*repay*	*wish to, want to*	*wick, stick*	*on*

On the stick of the desire to repay their kindness

ཡིད་དུ་འོང་བའི་བྱམས་པའི་རས་བལ་ཀྱིས༔

YID DU ONG WAI	JAM PAI	RAE BAL	KYI
*attractive, fascinating**	*love*	*cotton*	*by, with*

pure and genuine love free of the taint of wanting some reward

The cotton of very beautiful love

བརྩེ་བའི་སྙིང་རྗེའི་དམ་དུ་རབ་དཀྲིས་པར༔

TSE WAI	NYING JEI	DAM	DU	RAB	TRI	PAR
loving compassion	*compassion*	*binding*	*as, with*	*fully, well*	*wind*	*as*

Is wound well with the power of tender compassion.

ལྷག་བསམ་རྣམ་པར་དག་པའི་མེ་ལྕེ་འབར༔

LHAG SAM	NAM PAR DAG PAI	ME CHE	BAR
very excellent	*very pure*	*flame*	*burning*

The flame of the most excellent purity burns bright.

བདག་གཞན་འབྲེལ་མེད་རྟོག་པ་རང་སར་གྲོལ༔

DAG	ZHAN	DREL	MED	TOG PA	RANG SAR	DROL
self, me	*other, you*	*connection*	*without*	*thoughts*	*in its own place*	*liberate*

Thoughts of the absence of connection between oneself and others are liberated in their own place and

དམིགས་བཅས་དམིགས་མེད་ཆེན་པོའི་ཀློང་དུ་ཐིམ༔

MIG CHAE	MIG MED	CHEN POI	LONG	DU	THIM
*with conceptualised objects **	*without conceptualised objects #*	*great*	*vast*	*in*	*dissolve*

the accumulation of merit   # the accumulation of insight

Dissolve in the vastness of great compassion with and without an object.

Wonderful. In the pot of knowing all beings to be my parents swirls the oil of remembrance of the kindness with which they have held me. On the stick of the desire to repay their kindness the cotton of very beautiful love is wound well with the power of tender compassion. The flame of the most excellent purity burns bright. Thoughts of the absence of connection between myself and others are liberated in their own place and dissolve in the vastness of great compassion with and without an object.

རང་འབྲས་བླ་མེད་རྫོགས་བྱང་འོད་དུ་འཚེར༔

RANG	DRAE	LA MED	DZOG	JANG	OD	DU	TSER
own	result	unsurpassed	complete	bodhi, enlightenment	light	as	burning

The light of our own result of unsurpassed complete enlightenment is shining.

འགྲོ་བའི་མ་རིག་མུན་པ་སེལ་ཕྱིར་དུ༔

DRO WAI	MA RIG	MUN PA	SEL CHIR DU

In order to dispel the darkness of ignorance of all sentient beings

བླ་མ་མཆོག་གསུམ་རྩ་གསུམ་ལྷ་ཚོགས་ལ༔

LA MA	CHOG	SUM	TSA	SUM	LHA	TSOG	LA

We offer this to the guru, the three jewels, the three roots, and all the deities.

འབུལ་ལོ་བཞེས་ནས་མཆོག་ཐུན་དངོས་གྲུབ་སྩོལ༔

BUL LO	ZHE	NE	CHOG	THUN	NGOE DRUB	TSOL

Please accept and then bestow supreme and general accomplishments.

The light of our own result of unsurpassed complete enlightenment is shining. In order to dispel the darkness of ignorance of all sentient beings we offer this to the guru, the three jewels, the three roots and all the deities. Please accept and then bestow supreme and general accomplishments.

ཧོ༔   ཚུལ་ཁྲིམས་རྣམ་པར་དག་པའི་ཀོང་བུ་རུ༔

HO	TSUL THRIM	NAM PAR DAG PAI	KONG BU	RU
wonderful	morality	very pure, perfect (performed in sunyata)	pot	in

Wonderful! In the pot of very pure morality

སྦྱིན་པ་རྣམ་དག་འཛད་མེད་མར་ཁུ་འཁྱིལ༔

JIN PA	NAM DAG	DZAD MED	MAR KHU	KHYIL
generosity	very pure	inexhaustible	oil	swirling

Swirls the inexhaustible oil of very pure generosity.

བསམ་གཏན་རྣམ་པར་དག་པའི་སྡོང་བུ་ལ༔

SAM TEN	NAM PAR DAG PAI	DONG BU	LA
samadhi, concentration mental stability	very pure	wick, stick	on

On the stick of very pure concentration,

བརྩོན་འགྲུས་རྣམ་པར་དག་པའི་སྒྲོས་བླང་ཏེ༔

TSON DRUE   **NAM PAR DAG PAI**   **LOE**   **LANG**   **TE**
diligence,   *very pure*   *intellect,*   *take up,*   *then*
endeavour   *mind*   *practice*

With the very pure attitude of diligence,

བཟོད་པ་རྣམ་པར་དག་པའི་རས་བལ་དཀྲིས༔

ZOD PA   **NAM PAR DAG PAI**   **RAE BAL**   **TRI**
endurance, patience   *very pure*   *cotton*   *tie, bind*

The cotton of very pure patience is tied.

ཤེས་རབ་རྣམ་པར་དག་པའི་མེ་ལྕེ་འབར༔

SHE RAB   **NAM PAR DAG PAI**   **ME CHE**   **BAR**
prajna, true knowing   *very pure*   *flame*   *burning*

The flame of very pure true knowing burns bright.

རང་དོན་གཙོར་འདོད་གཞན་དོན་ཀློང་དུ་ཐིམ༔

RANG DON   **TSOR**   **DOD**   **ZHEN**   **DON**   **LONG**   **DU**   **THIM**
own benefit   *as chief*   *desire*   *others*   *benefit,*   *vast*   *in*   *dissolves*
                            welfare

The desire to privilege one's own welfare dissolves in the vastness of benefiting others.

Wonderful! In the pot of very pure morality swirls the inexhaustible oil of very pure generosity. On the stick of very pure concentration, with the very pure attitude of diligence, the cotton of very pure patience is tied. The flame of very pure true knowing burns bright. The desire to privilege one's own welfare dissolves in the vastness of benefiting others.

ཐུགས་རྗེའི་ཐབས་དང་སྨོན་ལམ་སྟོབས་རྒྱས་ཏེ༔

THUG JEI   **THAB**   **DANG**   **MON LAM**   **THOB**   **GYAE**   **TE**
compassionate   *method*   *and*   *aspiration*   *strength*   *increase*   *then*

With the increase of power, compassionate method and aspiration,

ཡེ་ཤེས་ཕ་རོལ་ཕྱིན་པའི་རང་འོད་འཚེར༔

YE SHE   **PA ROL CHIN PAI**   **RANG**   **OD**   **TSER**
jnana, original knowing   *paramita, transcendent**   *own*   *light*   *shining*

*the essence of the paramitas listed above, generosity, concentration, diligence...

Transcendent original knowing manifests its own shining light.

འགྲོ་བའི་མ་རིག་མུན་པ་སེལ་ཕྱིར་དུ༔

DRO WAI   **MA RIG**   **MUN PA**   **SEL CHIR DU**

In order to dispel the darkness of ignorance of all sentient beings

 བླ་མ་མཆོག་གསུམ་རྩ་གསུམ་ལྷ་ཚོགས་ལ༔

LA MA   CHOG   SUM   TSA   SUM   LHA   TSOG   LA

We offer this to the guru, the three jewels, the three roots, and all the deities.

འབུལ་ལོ་བཞེས་ནས་མཆོག་ཐུན་དངོས་གྲུབ་སྩོལ༔

BUL LO   ZHE   NE   CHOG   THUN   NGOE DRUB   TSOL

Please accept and then bestow supreme and general accomplishments.

With the increase of power, compassionate method and aspiration, transcendent original knowing manifests its own shining light. In order to dispel the darkness of ignorance of all sentient beings we offer this to the guru, the three jewels, the three roots and all the deities. Please accept and then bestow supreme and general accomplishments.

ཧོ༔   ལྷག་པ་ཚུལ་ཁྲིམས་གཙང་མའི་ཀོང་བུ་རུ༔

HO	**LHAG PA**	**TSUL THRIM**	**TSANG MAI**	**KONG BU**	**RU**
wonderful	*excellent, finest*	*morality*	*pure*	*pot*	*in*

Wonderful! In the pot of the finest pure morality

འཕགས་ལམ་ཡན་ལག་བརྒྱད་ཀྱི་མར་ཁུ་འཁྱིལ༔

PHAG LAM YAN LAG GYAD	**GYI**	**MAR KHU**	**KHYIL**
aryastangigmarga, noble eightfold path*	*by*	*oil*	*swirling*

*right view, understanding, speech, action, living, exertion, recollection, meditation

Swirls the oil of the noble eightfold path.

གཡོ་མེད་ཏིང་འཛིན་བརྟན་པོའི་སྡོང་བུ་ལ༔

YO MED	**TING DZIN**	**TAN POI**	**DONG BU**	**LA**
unwavering	*samadhi, absorbed contemplation*	*steady*	*wick, stick*	*on*

On the wick stick of unwavering, steady absorbed contemplation

སེམས་གནས་དགུ་དང་ཡིད་བྱེད་བཞི་ཡིས་དཀྲིས༔

SEM	**NAE**	**GU**	**DANG**	**YID JED**	**ZHI**	**YI**	**TRI**
mind	*staying*	*nine**	*and*	*manaskara*	*four #*	*by*	*wind*

*nine methods of controlling the mind and making it peaceful: 1. interiorising, 2. duration fixation, 3. refixation, 4. close fixation, 5. disciplined, 6. pacified, 7. completely pacified, 8. one-pointed, 9. even fixation (full meditation)

 # these are technical terms of the sutra system: equality, antidote, purification, clarification

The nine methods of mind control and the four aspects of mental development are tied.

སྟོབས་དྲུག་རྣམ་པར་དག་པའི་གྲུབ་འབྲས་ལ༔

TOB	DRUG	NAM PAR DAG PAI		DRUB	DRAE	LA
powers	six*	very pure		attainment	result	with

*hearing, thinking, memory, knowledge, exertion, full understanding

With the result of the perfect attainment of the six powers,

ཐོས་བསམ་བསྒོམ་པའི་ཤེས་རབ་མེ་ལྕེ་འབར༔

THOE	SAM	GOM PAI	SHE RAB	ME CHE	BAR
hearing, reflection	meditation	true knowing	flame		burning
i.e. study					

The flame of true knowing arising from study, reflection and meditation burns bright.

རྟོག་དཔྱོད་རྣམ་པར་མི་རྟོག་ཀློང་དུ་ཐིམ༔

TOG	CHOD	NAM PAR MI TOG	LONG	DU	THIM
thought	judgement, discrimination	fully without dualistic thoughts	vast	in	dissolves

Judgemental thoughts dissolve in the vastness of complete freedom from thoughts.

Wonderful! In the pot of the finest pure morality, swirls the oil of the noble eightfold path. On the wick stick of unwavering, steady absorbed contemplation the nine methods of mind control and the four aspects of mental development are tied. With the result of the perfect attainment of the six powers, the flame of true knowing arising from study, reflection and meditation burns bright. Judgemental thoughts dissolve in the vastness of complete freedom from thoughts.

བསླབ་གསུམ་རྣམ་པར་དག་པའི་རང་འོད་འཚེར༔

LAB	SUM	NAM PAR DAG PAI		RANG	OD	TSER
trainings	three*	very pure		own	light	shining

*morality, absorbed contemplation, true knowing

The completely pure three trainings manifest their own shining light.

འགྲོ་བའི་མ་རིག་མུན་པ་སེལ་ཕྱིར་དུ༔

DRO WAI	MA RIG	MUN PA SEL	CHIR DU

In order to dispel the darkness of ignorance of all sentient beings

བླ་མ་མཆོག་གསུམ་རྩ་གསུམ་ལྷ་ཚོགས་ལ༔

LA MA	CHOG	SUM	TSA	SUM	LHA TSOG	LA

We offer this to the guru, the three jewels, the three roots, and all the deities.

འབུལ་ལོ་བཞེས་ནས་མཆོག་ཐུན་དངོས་གྲུབ་སྩོལ༔

BUL LO	ZHE	NE	CHOG	THUN	NGOE DRUB TSOL

Please accept and then bestow supreme and general accomplishments.

The completely pure three trainings manifest their own shining light. In order to dispel the darkness of ignorance of all sentient beings we offer this to the guru, the three jewels, the three roots and all the deities. Please accept and bestow supreme and general accomplishments.

ཧོཿ ཕྱི་སྣོད་ཞིང་ཆེན་གཡང་གཞིའི་ཀོང་བུ་རུཿ

HO	CHI	NOD	ZHING CHEN YANG ZHI	KONG BU	RU
wonderful	*outer*	*pot, container*	*full human hide*	*pot*	*in*

Wonderful! In the pot of the outer vessel of an entire human skin

ནང་བཅུད་ཤ་ཁྲག་རུས་པའི་མར་ཁུ་འཁྱིལཿ

NANG	CHUD	SHA	THRAG	RUE PAI	MAR KHU	KHYIL
inner	*contents*	*flesh*	*blood*	*bone*	*oil*	*swirling*

Swirls the oil of the inner contents of flesh, blood and bones.

གསལ་བྱེད་ཙིཏྟ་རྩ་ཡི་སྡོང་བུ་ལཿ

SAL JED	TSIT TA	TSA	YI	DONG BU	LA
shining	*heart*	*veins, nerves, channels*	*of*	*wick, stick*	*on*

On the wick stick of the shining heart and channels

དོན་སྣོད་འབྱུང་བ་ལྔ་ཡི་རས་བལ་དཀྲིས༔

DON NOD	JUNG WA	NGA	YI	RAE BAL	TRI
entrails*	*elements*	*five*	*of*	*cotton*	*tied, wound*

*stomach, liver, lungs, gall bladder, kidneys, heart, bladder, etc

Is wound the cotton of the organs and entrails made from the five elements.

ཕུང་ཁམས་བཀྲག་མདངས་འཚེར་བའི་མེ་ལྕེ་འབར༔

PHUNG	KHAM	TRAG DANG	TSER WAI ME	CHE	BAR
5 skandhas*	*18 dhatus #*	*radiant, bright*	*shining*	*flame*	*burning*

*form, feeling, perception, conception, consciousness

 # the six sense organs, the six consciousnesses, the six sense objects

The flame of all the radiant components of existence burns bright.

སྙིགས་མའི་སྒྱུ་ལུས་འོད་ཕུང་ཀློང་དུ་ཐིམས༔

NYIG MAI	GYU	LUE	OD	PUNG	LONG	DU	THIM
rough, defiled	*illusory*	*body*	*light*	*body, mass*	*vast*	*in*	*dissolve*

The debased illusory body dissolves in the vastness of a mass of light.

Wonderful! In the pot of the outer vessel of an entire human skin swirls the inner contents of flesh, blood and bones. On the wick stick of the shining heart and channels is wound the cotton of the organs and entrails made from the five elements. The flame of all the radiant components of existence burns bright. The debased illusory body dissolves in the vastness of a mass of light.

རིག་པའི་ཡེ་ཤེས་རང་རྩལ་འོད་ཟེར་འཚེར༔

RIG PAI	YE SHE		RANG	TSAL	OD	ZER	TSER
awareness	*original knowing*		*own*	*energy*	*light*	*rays*	*shining*

The diversifying energy of the original knowing of natural presence manifests as shining rays of light.

འགྲོ་བའི་མ་རིག་མུན་པ་སེལ་ཕྱིར་དུ༔

DRO WAI	MA RIG	MUN PA	SEL	CHIR DU

In order to dispel the darkness of ignorance of all sentient beings

བླ་མ་མཆོག་གསུམ་རྩ་གསུམ་ལྷ་ཚོགས་ལ༔

LA MA	CHOG	SUM	TSA	SUM	LHA	TSOG	LA

We offer this to the guru, the three jewels, the three roots, and all the deities.

འབུལ་ལོ་བཞེས་ནས་མཆོག་ཐུན་དངོས་གྲུབ་སྩོལ༔

BUL LO	ZHE	NE	CHOG	THUN	NGOE DRUB	TSOL

Please accept and then bestow supreme and general accomplishments.

The diversifying energy of the original knowing of natural presence manifests as shining rays of light. In order to dispel the darkness of ignorance of all sentient beings we offer this to the guru, the three jewels, the three roots and all the deities. Please accept and bestow supreme and general accomplishments.

ཧོ༔   ཀུན་གཞི་ཁྱབ་གདལ་ཡངས་པའི་ཀོང་བུ་རུ༔

HO	KUN ZHI	KHYAB DAL	YANG PA	KONG BU	RU
wonderful	*alaya, ground of all*	*pervasive*	*vast*	*pot*	*in*

Wonderful! In the vast pot of the pervasive ground of all

ལྷན་སྐྱེས་ཀུན་བཏགས་རྨོངས་པའི་མར་ཁུ་འཁྱིལ༔

LHAN KYE	KUN TAG		MONG PAI	MAR KHU	KHYIL
simultaneous	*discriminating and identifying karma**		*stupidity towards*	*oil*	*swirling*

* *these are the three modes of ignorance which give rise to samsara*

Swirls the oil of simultaneous, discriminating and complaisant ignorance.

བདག་འཛིན་མ་རིག་པ་ཡི་སྡོང་བུ་ལ༔

DAG DZIN		MA RIG PA	YI	DONG BU	LA
belief in inherent self-nature		*ignorance*	*of*	*wick, stick*	*on*

On the wick stick of the ignorant belief in inherent self-nature

ཉོན་ཤེས་སྒྲིབ་པ་གཉིས་ཀྱི་རས་བལ་དཀྲིས༔

NYON	SHE	DRIB PA	NYI	KYI	RAE BAL	TRI
afflictions	*cognisable, knowledge*	*obscuration*	*two**	*of*	*cotton*	*wind*

*obscurations of the afflictions and of knowledge

Is wound the cotton of the obscurations arising from afflictions and false knowledge.

ཀུན་ཁྱབ་རིག་པའི་རང་དང་མེ་ལྕེ་འབར༔

KUN KHYAB	RIG PAI	RANG DANG	ME CHE	BAR
all-pervading	*awareness*	*self expression, own quality or radiance*	*flame*	*burning*

The flame of the natural radiance of all-pervading awareness burns bright.

ལྷན་སྐྱེས་ཀུན་བཏགས་མ་རིག་དབྱིངས་སུ་ཐིམ༔

LHAN KHYE	KUN TAG	MA RIG	YING	SU	THIM
simultaneous	*distinguishing*	*ignorance*	*dharmadhatu*	*in*	*dissolve*

Simultaneous and discriminating ignorance dissolve in the vastness of hospitable space.

Wonderful! In the pot of the pervasive ground of all swirls the oil of simultaneous, discriminating and complaisant ignorance. On the wick stick of the ignorant belief in inherent self-nature is wound the cotton of the obscurations arising from afflictions and false knowledge. The flame of the natural radiance of all-pervading awareness burns bright. Simultaneous and discriminating ignorance dissolve in the vastness of hospitable space.

བདག་མེད་རིག་པའི་ཡེ་ཤེས་རང་འོད་འཚེར༔

DAG MED		RIG PAI	YE SHE	RANG	OD	TSER
without inherent self-nature self-nature		*awareness*	*original knowing*	*own*	*light*	*shining*

Original knowing of natural presence free of reification manifests as shining rays of light.

འགྲོ་བའི་མ་རིག་མུན་པ་སེལ་ཕྱིར་དུ༔

DRO WAI	MA RIG	MUN PA	SEL CHIR DU

In order to dispel the darkness of ignorance of all sentient beings

ས་མ་མཆོག་གསུམ་རྩ་གསུམ་ལྷ་ཚོགས་ལ༔

LA MA   CHOG   SUM   TSA   SUM   LHA TSOG   LA

We offer this to the guru, the three jewels, the three roots, and all the deities.

འབུལ་ལོ་བཞེས་ནས་མཆོག་ཐུན་དངོས་གྲུབ་སྩོལ༔

BUL LO   ZHE   NE   CHOG   THUN   NGOE DRUB   TSOL

Please accept and then bestow supreme and general accomplishments.

Original knowing of natural presence free of reification manifests as shining rays of light. In order to dispel the darkness of ignorance of all sentient beings we offer this to the guru, the three jewels, the three roots and all the deities. Please accept and then bestow supreme and general accomplishments.

ཧོ༔   མིག་སོགས་དབང་པོ་ལྔ་ཡི་ཀོང་བུ་རུ༔

HO		MIG	SOG		WANG PO	NGA	YI	KONG BU	RU
wonderful		*eye*	*and so forth*	*organs*		*five**	*of*	*pot*	*in*

*eyes, ears, tongue, nose, body

Wonderful! In the pot of the five sense organs, the eyes and so on,

གཟུགས་སོགས་འདོད་ཡོན་ལྔ་ཡི་མར་ཁུ་འཁྱིལ༔

ZUG	SOG		DOD YON		NGA	YI	MAR KHU	KHYIL
form*	*and so forth#*		*desirable qualities+*		*five*	*of*	*oil*	*swirling*

*symbolised by a mirror   # sounds, tastes, smells, sensations   +pleasing to the senses

Swirls the oil of the five desirable qualities of form and so on.

འཛིན་བྱེད་དབང་ཤེས་ལྔ་ཡི་སྡོང་བུ་ལ༔

DZIN JED	WANG SHE		NGA	YI	DONG BU	LA
grasping	*sense consciousness*		*five**	*of*	*wick*	*on*

*of the five senses

On the wick of the five grasping sense consciousnesses

ཀུན་བྱེད་འཛིན་མེད་རང་གྲོལ་མེ་ལྕེ་འབར༔

KUN JED	DZIN MED	RANG DROL	ME CHE	BAR
all-doing (natural mind)	*without grasping*	*self-liberating*	*flame*	*burning*

The flame of the self-liberating non-grasping performer of all burns bright.

ཐ་མལ་ཤེས་པ་ཟག་མེད་ཀློང་དུ་ཐིམ༔

THA MAL	SHE PA	ZAG MED	LONG	DU	THIM
ordinary	*mind, thoughts*	*without lack or decline*	*vast*	*in*	*dissolve*
(i.e. dualistic)		*(i.e. sunyata)*			

Ordinary understanding dissolves in the vastness free of decline.

Wonderful! In the pot of the five sense organs, the eyes and so on, swirls the oil of the five desirable qualities of form and so on. On the wick of the five grasping sense consciousnesses the flame of the self-liberating non-grasping performer of all burns bright. Ordinary understanding dissolves in the vastness free of decline.

གཟུང་འཛིན་གཉིས་སུ་མེད་པའི་འོད་ཟེར་འཚེར༔

ZUNG	DZIN	NYI SU MED PAI	OD	ZER	TSER
graspable	*grasping*	*non-dual*	*light*	*rays*	*radiate*
object	*mind*				

The non-duality of subject and object manifests as shining rays of light.

འགྲོ་བའི་མ་རིག་མུན་པ་སེལ་ཕྱིར་དུ༔

DRO WAI	MA RIG	MUN PA	SEL CHIR	DU

In order to dispel the darkness of ignorance of all sentient beings

བླ་མ་མཆོག་གསུམ་རྩ་གསུམ་ལྷ་ཚོགས་ལ༔

LA MA	CHOG	SUM	TSA	SUM	LHA TSOG	LA

We offer this to the guru, the three jewels, the three roots, and all the deities.

འབུལ་ལོ་བཞེས་ནས་མཆོག་ཐུན་དངོས་གྲུབ་སྩོལ༔

BUL LO	ZHE	NE	CHOG	THUN	NGOE DRUB	TSOL

Please accept and then bestow supreme and general accomplishments.

The non-duality of subject and object manifests as shining rays of light. In order to dispel the darkness of ignorance of all sentient beings we offer this to the guru, the three jewels, the three roots and all the deities. Please accept and bestow supreme and general accomplishments.

ཧོ༔   ལྟ་བ་བློ་ལས་འདས་པའི་ཀོང་བུ་རུ༔

HO	TA WA	LO LAE DAE PAI	KONG BU	RU
wonderful	*view*	*inconceivable,*	*pot*	*in*
		vast beyond thoughts		

Wonderful! In the pot of the view beyond the reach of thought

བསྒོམ་པ་དམིགས་གཏད་བྲལ་བའི་མར་ཁུ་འཁྱིལཿ

GOM PA	MIG TAD	DRAL WA	MAR KHU	KHYIL
meditation	*conceptualised object**	*without*	*wick, stick*	*swirling*

*i.e. its object is just whatever comes

Swirls the oil of meditation free of preconceived objects.

སྤྱོད་པ་ཚད་ལས་འདས་པའི་སྡོང་བུ་ལཿ

CHOD PA		TSAD LAE DAE PAI	DONG BU	LA
conduct, activities		*immeasurable**	*wick, stick*	*on*

*they cannot be limited or assessed as being this or that

On the wick of immeasurable activity

འབྲས་བུ་ཕྱག་རྒྱ་ཆེན་པོའི་མེ་ལྕེ་འབརཿ

DRAE BU	CHAG GYA CHEN POI	ME CHE	BAR
result	*mahamudra (enlightenment)*	*flame*	*burning*

The flame of the result of mahamudra burns bright.

ཡུལ་གྱི་མདུད་པ་ཡུལ་ཅན་ཀློང་དུ་ཐིམཿ

YUL	GYI	DUD PA	YUL CHEN	LONG	DU	THIM
object	*of*	*knot*	*subject*	*vast*	*in*	*dissolves*

The knot of object dissolves in the vastness of the subject

ཁྲེགས་ཆོད་ཐོད་རྒལ་ཟུང་འཇུག་སེམས་ཀྱི་ཀློངཿ

THREG CHOD	THOD GAL	ZUNG JUG	SEM	KYI	LONG
release*	*immediate#*	*union*	*mind*	*of*	*depth, space*

*release mental activity into the primordial purity of its ground
 # immediate presence in and as the emergent field of experience

As the depth of awareness unites releasing and immediacy.

Wonderful! In the pot of the view beyond the reach of thought swirls the oil of meditation free of preconceived objects. On the wick of immeasurable activity the flame of the result of mahamudra burns bright. The knot of object dissolves in the vastness of the subject as the depth of awareness unites releasing and immediacy.

གཞི་སྣང་གཞི་ལ་ཤར་བའི་རང་འོད་འཚེརཿ

ZHI	NANG	ZHI	LA	SHAR WAI	RANG	OD	TSER
ground	*idea*	*ground*	*on*	*rising**	*own*	*light*	*shining*
	(of object into subject)						

*just as the rays of the sun falling back on the sun cause it to shine much brighter

The creativity of the ground arises within the ground, manifesting as shining rays of light.

བརྗོད་བྱའི་ཡུལ་ལས་འདས་པའི་ངོ་བོ་ལ༔

JOD JAI	YUL	LAE DAE PAI		NGO WO	LA
expressible	*object*	*transcending, going beyond*		*true nature*	*to, with*

Openness is not an object that can be described;

བརྗོད་བྱེད་ཚིག་ལས་འདས་པའི་རང་བཞིན་གྱི༔

JOD JE	TSIG	LAE DAE PAI	RANG ZHIN	GYI
expressing	*words*	*transcending*	*natural quality*	*of*

Immediacy eludes the words it reveals;

ཐུགས་རྗེ་ཀུན་ཁྱབ་རང་བྱུང་སྒྲོན་མེ་འདི༔

THUG JE	KUN KHYAB	RANG JUNG	DRON ME	DI
compassion	*all-pervading*	*naturally occurring*	*lamp*	*this*

Spontaneity is everywhere. This is the naturally occurring lamp.

འགྲོ་བའི་མ་རིག་མུན་པ་སེལ་ཕྱིར་དུ༔

DRO WAI	MA RIG	MUN PA	SEL CHIR DU

In order to dispel the darkness of ignorance of all sentient beings

ཁྱབ་བདག་དྲིན་ཆེན་བླ་མ་རྡོ་རྗེ་འཆང༔

KHYAB DAG	DRIN CHEN	LA MA	DOR JE CHANG
pervading lord	*most kind*	*guru*	*Vajradhara, supreme buddha*

We offer this to the pervading lord, our most kind guru Dorje Chang, and

མཆོག་གསུམ་རྩ་གསུམ་སྐུ་གསུམ་ལྷ་ཚོགས་ལ༔

CHOG	SUM	TSA	SUM	KU	SUM	LHA	TSOG	LA
excellent	*three*	*roots*	*three*	*kayas*	*three*	*deities*	*host*	*to*

To the three jewels, the three roots, the three kayas and all the deities.

འབུལ་ལོ་བཞེས་ནས་མཆོག་ཐུན་དངོས་གྲུབ་སྩོལ༔

BUL LO	ZHE	NE	CHOG	THUN	NGOE DRUB	TSOL

Please accept and then bestow supreme and general accomplishments.

The creativity of the ground arises within the ground, manifesting as shining rays of light. Openness is not an object that can be described; immediacy eludes the words it reveals; spontaneity is everywhere. This is the naturally occurring lamp. In order to dispel the darkness of ignorance of all sentient beings we offer this to the pervading lord, our most kind guru Dorje Chang, and to the three jewels, the three roots, the three kayas and all the deities. Please accept and then bestow supreme and general accomplishments.

ཧོཿ རིན་ཆེན་སྣ་ལྔའི་རྒྱུ་ཡི་ཀོང་བུ་རུཿ

HO	RIN CHEN	NA	NGAI	GYU	YI	KONG BU	RU
wonderful	jewels	kinds	five	materials	of	pot	on
	(gold, silver, turquoise, coral, pearl)						

Wonderful! In the pot made with the five precious substances

ཙི་བཅུད་འབྲུ་མར་འབྱུང་བའི་མར་ཁུ་འཁྱིལཿ

TSI	CHUD	DRU	MAR	JUNG WAI	MAR KHU	KHYIL
juice	natural vitamins	grains	butter	arising	oil	swirling

Swirls the oil of butter coming from the concentrated essence of grasses and grains.

གཙང་མའི་རས་བལ་དཀྱིས་པའི་སྡོང་བུ་ལཿ

TSANG MAI	RAE BAL	TRI PAI	DONG BU	LA
clean	ordinary cotton	winding	wick, stick	on

On the wick wound with clean cotton wool

ཉི་ཟླའི་འོད་ལ་འགྲན་པའི་མེ་ལྕེ་འབརཿ

NYI	DAI	OD	LA DRAN PAI	ME CHE	BAR
sun	moon	light	similar to, equalling	flame	burning

The flame matching the light of the sun and moon burns bright.

མུན་པ་མ་ལུས་སྣང་བའི་ཀློང་དུ་ཐིམཿ

MUN PA	MA LUE	NANG WAI	LONG	DU	THIM
darkness	without exception	light	vast	in	dissolves

All darkness without exception dissolves in the vastness of light.

Wonderful! In the pot made with the five precious substances swirls the oil of butter coming from the concentrated essence of grasses and grains. On the wick wound with clean cotton wool the flame matching the light of the sun and moon burns bright. All darkness without exception dissolves in the vastness of light.

ཀུན་ཁྱབ་མུན་པ་སེལ་བའི་རང་འོད་འཚེརཿ

KUN KHYAB	MUN PA	SEL WAI	RANG	OD	TSER
all-pervading	darkness	clearing	own	light	shining

The illumination of darkness everywhere manifests as shining rays of light.

འགྲོ་བའི་མ་རིག་མུན་པ་སེལ་ཕྱིར་དུཿ

DRO WAI	MA RIG	MUN PA	SEL CHIR DU

In order to dispel the darkness of ignorance of all sentient beings

ཕྱོགས་བཅུའི་རྒྱལ་བ་སྲས་བཅས་ཐམས་ཅད་དང་ཿ

CHOG	CHUI	GYAL WA	SAE CHAE	THAM CHAE	DANG
directions	*ten*	*jina*	*bodhisattvas*	*all*	*and*

We offer this to all the buddhas and bodhisattvas of the ten directions, and

བླ་མ་མཆོག་གསུམ་རྩ་གསུམ་ལྷ་ཚོགས་ལ་ཿ

LA MA	CHOG	SUM	TSA	SUM	LHA TSOG	LA

To the guru, the three jewels, the three roots, and all the deities.

འབུལ་ལོ་བཞེས་ནས་མཆོག་ཐུན་དངོས་གྲུབ་སྩོལ་ཿ

BUL LO	ZHE	NE	CHOG	THUN	NGOE DRUB	TSOL

Please accept and then bestow supreme and general accomplishments.

The illumination of darkness everywhere manifests as shining rays of light. In order to dispel the darkness of ignorance of all beings we offer this to all the buddhas and bodhisattvas of the ten directions and to the guru, the three jewels, the three roots, and all the deities. Please accept and then bestow supreme and general accomplishments.

ཧོཿ ཕྱི་ནང་སྒྲིབ་མེད་ཤེལ་གྱི་ཀོང་བུ་རུཿ

HO	CHI	NANG	DRIB	MED	SHEL	GYI	KONG BU	RU
wonderful	*outer*	*inner*	*obscuration*	*without*	*crystal*	*of*	*pot*	*in*
			(i.e. transparent)		*(i.e. glass)*			

Wonderful! In the pot of glass free of outer and inner obscurations

མེ་ཆུའི་རྡུལ་ཤུགས་ལས་བྱུང་མར་ཁུ་འཁྱིལ་ཿ

ME	CHUI	DUL	SHUG	LAE	JUNG	MAR KHU	KHYIL
fire	*water*	*atoms*	*power, energy wave i.e. electricity*	*from*	*arising*	*oil*	*swirling*

Swirls the oil arising from the power of fire and water.

དངས་མའི་རྫས་ལས་གྲུབ་པའི་སྡོང་བུ་ལ་ཿ

DANG MAI	DZAE	LAE	JAE PAI	DONG BU	LA
shining, glowing	*material*	*from*	*arising*	*wick (the filament of the bulb)*	*on*

On the wick made of glowing material

གསལ་བྱེད་བཀྲག་མདངས་འཚེར་བའི་མེ་ལྕེ་འབར་ཿ

SAL	JED	TRAG DANG	TSER WAI	ME CHE	BAR
shining, illuminating		*very brightly*	*shining*	*flame (the electric lamp)*	*burning*

The shining flame of radiant illumination burns bright.

འདྲེ་གདོན་བགེགས་རིགས་འོད་ཀྱི་ཀློང་དུ་ཐིམ༔

DRE	DON	GEG	RIG	OD	KYI	LONG	DU	THIM
demons	*trouble-makers*	*obstructors*	*groups*	*light*	*of*	*vast*	*in*	*dissolve*

(no demons come where there is bright light)

All demons, trouble-makers and obstructors dissolve in the vastness of the light

ཡ་ང་བག་ཚ་འཇིགས་སྐྲག་རེ་དོག་བྲལ༔

YA NGA	BAG TSA	JIG	TRAG	RE	DOG	DRAL
small fear	*fear from seeing the suffering of others*	*fear*	*terror*	*hopes*	*doubts*	*free of*

Which is free of fears, worries, terrors and fluctuating emotions.

Wonderful! In the pot of glass free of outer and inner obscurations swirls the oil arising from the power of fire and water. On the wick made of glowing material the shining flame of radiant illumination burns bright. All demons, trouble-makers and obstructors dissolve in the vastness of the light which is free of fears, worries, terrors and fluctuating emotions.

ཕྱི་ནང་ཟང་ཐལ་གསལ་བའི་འོད་ཟེར་འཚེར

CHI	NANG	ZANG THAL	SAL WAI	OD	ZER	TSER
outer	*inner*	*direct*	*shining*	*light*	*rays*	*burning*

Unimpeded clarity without and within manifests as shining rays of light.

འགྲོ་བའི་མ་རིག་མུན་པ་སེལ་ཕྱིར་དུ༔

DRO WAI	MA RIG	MUN PA	SEL	CHIR DU

In order to dispel the darkness of ignorance of all sentient beings

སངས་རྒྱས་རྒྱུ་ཅན་སྐྱེ་དགུ་ཐམས་ཅད་དང༔

SANG GYAE	GYU	CHEN	KYE GU	THAM CHAE	DANG
buddha	*cause*	*having*	*sentient beings*	*all*	*and*

We offer this to sentient beings all of whom have the cause of buddhahood, and

བླ་མ་མཆོག་གསུམ་རྩ་གསུམ་ལྷ་ཚོགས་ལ༔

LA MA	CHOG	SUM	TSA	SUM	LHA	TSOG LA

To the guru, the three jewels, the three roots, and all the deities.

འབུལ་ལོ་བཞེས་ནས་མཆོག་ཐུན་དངོས་གྲུབ་སྩོལ༔

BUL LO	ZHE	NE	CHOG	THUN	NGOE DRUB	TSOL

Please accept and then bestow supreme and general accomplishments.

Unimpeded clarity without and within manifests as shining rays of light. In order to dispel the darkness of ignorance of all sentient beings we offer this to sentient beings, all of whom have the cause of buddhahood, and to the guru, the three jewels, the three roots and all the deities. Please accept and then bestow supreme and general accomplishments.

དེ་ལྟར་མར་མེ་ཕུལ་བའི་བསོད་ནམས་ཀྱིས༔

DE TAR	MAR ME	PUL WAI	SO NAM	KYI
like that	*lamp*	*offering*	*merit*	*by*

By the merit of offering these lamps

འགྲོ་ཀུན་སྲིད་པའི་རྒྱ་མཚོ་ལས་བསྒྲལ་ནས༔

DRO	KUN	SID PAI	GYAM TSO	LAE	DRAL	NAE
beings	*all*	*world (samsara)*	*ocean*	*from*	*liberate*	*then*

All beings must be liberated from the ocean of samsara.

མ་རིག་མུན་པའི་གདུང་བ་རབ་བསལ་ཞིང༔

MA RIG	MUN PAI	DUNG WA	RAB	SAL ZHING
ignorance	*darkness*	*suffering*	*fully*	*clearing*

Then, with the suffering of the darkness of ignorance completely removed,

རྣམ་མཁྱེན་རྫོགས་པའི་སངས་རྒྱས་མྱུར་ཐོབ་ནས༔

NAM KHYEN	DZOG PAI	SANG GYE	NYUR	THOB	NAE
omniscient	*complete*	*buddhahood*	*quickly*	*obtain*	*then*

All must quickly gain omniscient perfect buddhahood and

འཕགས་པ་མར་མེ་མཛད་དང་དབྱེར་མེད་ཤོག༔

PHAG PA	MAR ME DZAD	DANG	YER MED	SHOG
Arya	*Buddha Dipamkara*	*and*	*not different*	*must become*

Become identical with the noble Buddha Dipamkara.

By the merit of offering these lamps all beings must be liberated from the ocean of samsara. Then, with the suffering of the darkness of ignorance completely removed, all must quickly gain omniscient perfect buddhahood and become identical with the noble Buddha Dipamkara.

[At this point the sutra concerning Buddha Dipamkara may be read as follows. If not go to page 84]

རྒྱལ་པོ་གསེར་གྱི་ལག་པའི་མར་མེའི་ལོ་རྒྱུས་དང་སྨོན་ལམ་གྱི་མདོ་བཞུགས་སོ།།

THE SUTRA OF THE STORY OF THE LAMP OF KING GOLDEN HAND AND HIS ASPIRATION

༄༅། རྒྱ་གར་སྐད་དུ། རྦཛྫ་ཀཱུ་ཙུ་བྲ་ཏུ་དཱི་པ་སུ་པ་ཀྲི་ཡཱ་པ་ཙི་ཊྚ་སུ་ཏྲ། བོད་སྐད་དུ། རྒྱལ་པོ་གསེར་གྱི་ལག་པའི་མར་མེའི་ལོ་རྒྱུས་དང་སྨོན་ལམ་གྱི་མདོ། དཀོན་མཆོག་གསུམ་ལ་ཕྱག་འཚལ་ལོ། སྟོན་པ་སངས་རྒྱས་མར་མེ་མཛད་ཀྱིས་ སྟོན་པ་མཛད་པའི་དུས་ན། རྒྱལ་པོ་གསེར་གྱི་ལག་པ་ཞེས་བྱ་བས། ཚོམ་ལྟུན་ འདས་མར་མེ་མཛད་ལ་འདི་སྐད་ཅེས་གསོལ་ཏོ། བཙུན་པ་བྱོན་སྟོན་གྱི་དུས་ན་ དགེ་བའི་རྩ་བ་ཅི་ཞིག་སྤྱད་ན། དཔལ་འབྱོར་མཚན་དང་དཔེ་བྱད་དུ་ལྡན་ཏེ། སྐུ་ལས་ འོད་ཟེར་མཐའ་ཡས་པ་འབྱུང་བའི་རྒྱ་གང་ལགས། ཆེན་གང་ལགས། བཅོམ་ ལྡན་འདས་ཀྱིས་བཀའ་སྩལ་པ། རྒྱལ་པོ་ཆེན་པོ་ཉོན་ཅིག། ངས་སྔོན་སྦྱིན་ པོའི་དུས་ན། ཕྱོགས་བཅུའི་སངས་རྒྱས་ཐམས་ཅད་ལ་བྱང་ཆུབ་ཏུ་སེམས་བསྐྱེད་ ནས། ལུས་ལ་རས་བལ་གྱི་ཡེ་ཏུ་ཊིལ་མར་གྱི་ནང་དུ་བཙོས་པ་སྟོང་བཙུགས་ ཏེ། ཕྱོགས་བཅུ་དུས་གསུམ་གྱི་སངས་རྒྱས་ཐམས་ཅད་ལ། གཏན་པ་མེད་ པའི་མཆོད་པར་ཕུལ་བས། དཔར་དངེད་སངས་རྒྱས་མར་མེ་མཛད་ཅེས་བྱ་བར་ གྱུར་པ་ཡིན་ནོ་ཞེས་གསུངས་པ་དང་། དེ་ལ་རྒྱལ་པོ་ཆེན་པོ་ཞིན་ཏུ་ཡི་རངས་ཏེ། དེ་ནས་རྒྱལ་པོ་དེས་རང་གི་ལག་པ་གཡས་ན་རས་བལ་མར་གྱིས་བཙོས་པས་ དཀྲིས་ཏེ་མེ་བཏང་ནས། ལག་པ་གཡོན་པ་བར་སྤྲངས་ལ་བཀྲང་སྟེ། ཕྱོགས་ བཅུའི་སངས་རྒྱས་ཐམས་ཅད་དང་། བདག་གི་སྟོན་པ་བཙོམ་ལྡན་འདས་མར་མེ་ མཛད་དགོངས་སུ་གསོལ་ལོ། འགྱོད་པ་མེད་པའི་སེམས་ཀྱིས། ཕྱོགས་བཅུའི་ སངས་རྒྱས་ཐམས་ཅད་ཡིད་ཀྱིས་མཆོམ་སུམ་དུ་དམིགས་ཏེ། གཏན་པ་མེད་པའི་ མཆོད་པར་བསྒོས་ནས་སྨོན་ལམ་འདེབས་ཏེ། འདི་སྐད་དོ།

Sanskrit: *rajakancanabahudipasyaprakriyapranidhana sutra*

Tibetan: *rGyal-Po gSer-Gyi Lag-Pa'i Mar-Me'i Lo-rGyus*
Dang sMon-Lam-Gyi mDo

Salutation to the Three Jewels.

When Dipamkara, the Buddha of the earlier period before the time of Buddha Shakyamuni, was teaching, King Golden Hand asked him, "Venerable One, what was the basis of the virtue that you created in former times resulting in you now displaying the major and minor signs of a Buddha and radiating infinite light from your body?"

Buddha Dipamkara replied, "Listen, great king! When I was an ordinary being, in front of all the Buddhas of the ten directions I developed altruistic bodhicitta. Then I dipped one thousand cotton wicks in clarified butter and placed them on my body. Without hope or expectation I lit them as an offering to all the Buddhas of the ten directions and the three times. That is why I am now known as Buddha Dipamkara, 'the one who made the butter lamp'."

The great king rejoiced at this. He wrapped his own right hand in cotton wool, dipped it in clarified butter and lit it. He raised his left hand to the sky and said, "Buddhas of the ten directions and Buddha Dipamkara, my teacher, please think of me."

With a mind free of regret he clearly visualised all the buddhas of the ten directions. He dedicated the merit of this offering given without expectation, and made this prayer of aspiration:

[Recite the sutra with your hands raised, palms facing the sky.]

མར་མེའི་སྣོད་ནི་སྟོང་གསུམ་གྱི་སྟོང་ཆེན་པོའི

MAR MEI	NOE	NI	TONG	SUM	GYI	TONG	CHEN POI
butter lamp	*pot*	*this*	*thousand*	*three (infinite)*	*of*	*thousand*	*great*

May the pot of this lamp become as vast as the infinity

འཇིག་རྟེན་གྱི་ཁམས་ཚམ་དུ་གྱུར་ཅིག

JIG TEN	GYI	KHAMS	TSAM DU	GYUR CHIG
worlds	*of*	*realms*	*as much as*	*become*

Of all the countless worlds.

སྙིང་པོ་ནི་རིའི་རྒྱལ་པོ་རི་རབ་ཚམ་དུ་གྱུར་ཅིག

NYING PO	NI	RI	GYAL PO	RI RAB	TSAM DU	GYUR CHIG
wick	*this*	*mountains*	*king*	*Mt. Meru**	*like*	*become*

*Mount Meru, in traditional Buddhist cosmology, is the mountain at the centre of our world system. It is so high that night appears when the sun disappears behind it in the evening.

May the wick become as big as Mount Meru, the king of mountains.

འོད་ཀྱིས་ནི་སྲིད་པའི་རྩེ་མོ་མན་ཆད་ནས

WOE	KYI	NI	SI PAI	TSE MO	MEN CHAE	NAE
light	*by*	*this*	*world*	*top*	*down*	*from*

May the rays of its light reach from the top of this world

མནར་མེད་པའི་སེམས་ཅན་དམྱལ་བ་ཡན་ཆད་ནས

NAR ME PAI	SEM CHEN	NYAL WA	YAN CHAE	NAE
name of the lowest hell	*sentient beings*	*hell*	*above*	*also*

Down to the beings in the lowest Avici hell.

May the pot of this lamp become as vast as the infinity of all the countless worlds. May the wick become as big as Mount Meru, the king of mountains. May the rays of its light reach from the top of this world down to the beings in the lowest Avici hell.

གཞན་ཡང་ལྕགས་རི་ཆེན་པོའི་ཕྱི་རྒྱབ་ན

ZHAN YANG	CHAG	RI	CHEN POI	CHI GYAB	NA
moreover	*iron*	*mountain*	*great*	*behind, beyond*	*at*

May the rays of light reach beyond the iron mountains ringing our world system

སེམས་ཅན་རང་གི་ལས་ཀྱིས་སྒྲིབ་པས་

SEM CHEN	RANG	GI	LAE	KYI	DRIB PAE
sentient beings	*own*		*actions*	*by*	*obscuring*

To reach the people who are living in the enveloping gloom of

བསྒྲིབས་པའི་མུན་ནག་ཆེན་པོའི་ནང་ན།

DRIB PAI	MU	NAG	CHEN POI	NANG NA
covering	*darkness*	*black*	*great*	*in*

The darkness created by their own bad actions and

རང་གི་ལག་པ་བརྐྱང་བསྐུམ་ཡང་མི་མཐོང་བའི་གནས་

RANG GI	LAG PA	KYANG KUM	YANG	MI	THONG PAI	NAE
own	*hand*	*moving, waving*	*also*	*not*	*see*	*place*

Who cannot even see the movements of their own hands.

ཚུན་ཆད་སྣང་ཞིང་གསལ་བར་གྱུར་ཅིག

TSHUN CHAE	NANG ZHING	SAL WAR	CHIG
as far as	*light*	*illuminate*	*become*

May this light spread illumination there.

May the rays of its light reach beyond the iron mountains ringing our world system to reach the people who are living in the enveloping gloom of the darkness created by their own bad actions and who cannot even see the movements of their own hands. May this light spread illumination there.

ཡུན་ནི་དུས་གསུམ་གྱི་སངས་རྒྱས་ཇི་སྲིད་བཞུགས་པ་

YUN NI	DUE SUM	GYI	SANG GYE	JI SRI	ZHUG PA
duration	*times three*	*of*	*buddhas*	*as long as that*	*staying*

May this light remain for the duration of all the periods of all the Buddhas

དེ་སྲིད་དུ་གནས་པར་གྱུར་ཅིག

DE SRI	DU	NAE PAR	GYUR CHIG
as much	*for*	*stay*	*make, may*

Of the past, present and future.

གྲངས་ནི་ཕྱོགས་བཅུ་འཇིག་རྟེན་གྱི་ཁམས་མཐའ་ཡས་པ་ན་བཞུགས་པའི་

DRANG NI	CHOG	CHU	JIG TEN	GYI	KHAM	THA YAE PA...
enumeration	*directions*	*ten**	*world*	*of*	*realms*	*limitless*

...NA	ZHUG PAI
in	*staying*

**ten direction, i.e. everywhere*

May this light shine before the eyes of all the numberless Buddhas

སངས་རྒྱས་གྲངས་མེད་པར་རེ་རེའི་སྤྱན་ལམ་དུ་གསལ་བར་གྱུར་ཅིག།

SANG GYE	DRANG ME PAR	RE REI	CHEN	LAM DU	SAL WAR...
buddhas	*countless*	*each*	*eye*	*in front of*	*shine*

...GYUR CHIG
make

In the countless worlds which pervade the ten directions.

May this light remain for the duration of all the periods of all the Buddhas of the past, present and future. May this light shine before the eyes of all the numberless Buddhas in the countless worlds which pervade the ten directions.

མར་མེ་འདི་གཟུགས་མེད་པའི་གནས་སུ་སྣང་ཞིང་

MAR ME	DI	ZUG ME PAI	NAE	SU	NANG ZHING
butterlamp	*this*	*formless*	*place*	*in*	*appearing*

May the light from this lamp illuminate

གསལ་བར་གྱུར་ཅིག།   དེ་ལྟར་གསལ་བའི་མོད་ལ།

SAL WAR	GYUR CHIG		DE TAR	SAL WAI	MOE LA
illuminating	*make, may*		*in that way*	*shining*	*immediately*

The formless realms.   With that illumination,

གཟུགས་མེད་པའི་ལྷ་རྣམས་མར་མེའི་འོད་ཀྱིས་བསྐུལ་མ་ཐག་ཏུ།

ZUG ME PAI	LHA	NAM	MAR MEI	WOE	KYI	KUL	MA TAG TU
formless	*gods*	*all*	*butterlamp*	*light*	*by*	*arouse*	*as soon as*

As soon as the gods of these realms are aroused

མཚན་དང་དཔེ་བྱད་དུ་ལྡན་ནས་

TSHAN	DANG	PE JE	DU DEN	NE
major signs	*and*	*minor signs*	*gain*	*then*
(of a buddha's body)				

May they gain the major and minor signs of enlightenment and

སྙོམས་པར་འཇུག་པའི་སྐྱེ་མཆེད་བཞི་ལས་གྲོལ་ཏེ།

NYOM PAR JUG PAI	KYEM CHE	ZHI	LAE	DROL	TE
mental absorption	*sensory supports*	*four*	*from*	*freed*	*then*
	(these are the four formless levels)				

Be freed from the mental absorptions of the four levels of subtle sensory support.

དེ་བཞིན་གཤེགས་པའི་བསམ་གཏན་ལ་སོགས་པར་

DE ZHIN SHEG PAI   SAM TAN   LA   SOG PAR
Buddha, tathagata,   stable forms of   different

May entry to the various meditative states of the Tathagata

སྙོམས་པར་འཇུག་པའི་སྐལ་པ་དང་ལྡན་པར་གྱུར་ཅིག །

NYOM PAR JUG PAI   KAL PA   DANG DEN PAR   GYUR   CHIG
contemplation   fortunate   have   make, may

Be available to these fortunate ones.

*May the light from this lamp illuminate the formless realms. With that il-
lumination, as soon as the gods of these realms are aroused, may they gain
the major and minor signs of enlightenment and be freed from the mental
absorptions of the four levels of subtle sensory support. May entry to the
various meditative states of the Tathagata be available to these fortunate
ones.*

མར་མེ་འདི་གཟུགས་ན་སྤྱོད་པའི་ལྷ་རྣམས་ཀྱི་

MAR ME   DI   ZUG   NA   CHOE PAI   LHA NAM   KYI
butterlamp   this   form   with   acting   gods   of

May the light from this lamp illuminate

གནས་སུ་གསལ་བར་གྱུར་ཅིག །

NAE   SU   SAL WAR   GYUR CHIG
place   to   illuminate   make, may

The realm of the gods with form.

གཟུགས་ན་སྤྱོད་པའི་ལྷ་རྣམས་ཏིང་ངེ་འཛིན་གྱི་

ZUG   NA   CHOE PAI   LHA NAM   TING NGE DZIN   GYI
form   in, with   acting   gods   undisturbed contemplation of

May these gods enter meditative absorption and

དགའ་བདེ་རྩེ་གཅིག་ལ་ཉམས་སུ་མྱོང་ནས །

GA   DE   TSE   CHIG   LA   NYAM SU NYONG   NAE
happy   joy   pointed   one   in   experience   then

Experience unwavering happiness and

ཕྱིར་མི་ལྡོག་པའི་ས་ཐོབ་པར་གྱུར་ཅིག །

CHIR MI DOG PAI   SA   THOB PAR   GYUR   CHIG
irreversible   stage   get   make, may*

*state of non return, Anagami,one who does not return to this world again

Gain the state of non-return.

May the light from this lamp illuminate the realm of the gods with form. May these gods enter meditative absorption and experience unwavering happiness and gain the stage of non-return.

མར་མེ་འདི་འདོད་ཁམས་ཀྱི་ལྷ་རྣམས་ཀྱི་གནས་སུ་

MAR ME	DI	DOE	KHAM	KYI	LHA NAM	KYI	NAE	SU
butterlamp	*this*	*desire*	*realm*	*of*	*gods*	*of*	*place*	*to*

May the light from this lamp illuminate the environment

སྣང་ཞིང་གསལ་བར་གྱུར་ཅིག

NANG ZHING	SAL WAR	GYUR CHIG
showing	*illuminating*	*make, may*

Of the gods of the realm of desire.

འདོད་ཁམས་ཀྱི་ལྷ་རྣམས་ཀྱང་

DOE	KHAM	KYI	LHA NAM	KYANG
desire	*realm*	*of*	*gods*	*also*

May these gods

ལྷའི་འདོད་པའི་ལོངས་སྤྱོད་ལ་སེམས་མ་ཆགས་ཤིང་

LHAI	DOE PAI	LONG CHO	LA	SEM	MA	CHAG SHING
god's	*desirable*	*wealth*	*to*	*mind*	*not*	*attaching*

Be free of attachment to the riches of their realm.

རང་གི་སེམས་ལ་ལྟ་ཞིང་

RANG GI	SEM	LA	TA ZHING
own	*mind*	*to*	*look, see*

May they look at their own minds and

བསམ་གཏན་བཞི་ལ་རིམ་གྱིས་སྙོམས་པར་འཇུག་པའི་

SAM TEN ZHI	LA	RIM	GYI	NYOM PAR JUG PAI
mental	*on*	*in sequence*	*by*	*enter that state,*
four*				*settle into stability*

*four concentrations: 1. with concepts and investigation, 2.with investigation but no concepts, 3.with mentation free of concepts and investigation, 4. with mentation linked with delight.

Enter each of the four meditative absorptions in turn.

སྐལ་པ་དང་ལྡན་པར་གྱུར་ཅིག

KAL PA	DANG DAN PAR	GYUR	CHIG
fortunate	*have*	*make, may*	
opportunity			

May they have the opportunity to experience that.

*May the light from this lamp illuminate the environment of the gods of
the realm of desire. May these gods be free of attachment to the riches of
their realm. May they look at their own minds and enter each of the four
meditative absorptions in turn. May they have the opportunity to experience that.*

མར་མེ་འདི་ལྷ་མ་ཡིན་རྣམས་ཀྱི་གནས་སུ་

MAR ME	DI	LHA MA YIN NAM	KYI	NAE	SU
butterlamp	this	demi-gods, asuras	of	place	to

May the light from this lamp illuminate

སྣང་ཞིང་གསལ་བར་གྱུར་ཅིག

NANG ZHING	SAL WAR	GYUR	CHIG
showing	illuminate	make, may	

The realm of the demi-gods.

ལྷ་མ་ཡིན་གྱི་ང་རྒྱལ་དང་།   ཁྲོ་གཏུམ་དང་།

LHA MA YIN	GYI	NGA GYAL	DANG	TRO TUM	DANG
asuras, jealous demi-gods	of	pride	and	fury, rage	and

May they be freed from their pride, fury, rage and crudity,

སེམས་ཀྱི་གདུག་པ་ཞི་ནས་ཚད་མེད་པ་བཞི་དང་ལྡན་ནས།

SEM KYI DUG PA	ZHI	NE	TSAE ME PA	ZHI	DANG DEN	NE
crudity, roughness of attitude	pacify	then	immeasurable (love, compassion, joy, equanimity)	four	gain	then

And develop love, compassion, joyfulness and equanimity.

ཞི་གནས་ཀྱི་སེམས་ཡིད་ལ་བྱེད་པ་དང་ལྡན་པར་གྱུར་ཅིག

ZHI NE	KYI	SEM	YID LA JE PA	DANG DEN PAR	GYU CHIG
calm, peaceful	of	mind	practice	gain, have	make, may

May they develop minds that are calm.

*May the light from this lamp illuminate the realm of the demi-gods. May
they be freed from their pride, fury, and crudity, and develop love, compassion, joyfulness and equanimity. May they develop minds that are calm.*

མར་མེ་འདི་གླིང་བཞིའི་མི་རྣམས་ཀྱི་གནས་སུ་

MAR ME	DI	LING	ZHI	MI NAM	KYI	NAE	SU
butterlamp	this	continent	four (the four islands around Mt. Meru)	inhabitants	of	place	to

May the light from this lamp illuminate

སྣང་ཞིང་གསལ་བར་གྱུར་ཅིག།

NANG ZHING   SAL WAR   GYUR   CHIG
showing   illuminate   make,may

All who live in the four continents.

གླིང་བཞིའི་མི་རྣམས་ཀྱང་སྡུག་བསྔལ་བརྒྱད་ལས་ཐར་ནས།

LING   ZHI   MI NAM   KYANG   DUG NGAL   GYAE   LAE   THAR   NE
continents   four   inhabitants   also   suffering   eight   from   free   then*

*birth, aging, illness, death, separation from loved ones, being with the despised, not get-
ting what one wants, the flourishing of the five skandhas.*

May they be freed from the eight sufferings.

བརྩོན་འགྲུས་ཀྱི་ཕ་རོལ་ཏུ་ཕྱིན་པ་དང་ལྡན་པར་གྱུར་ཅིག།

TSON DRUE   KYI   PA ROL TU JIN PA   DANG DAN PAR   GYUR   CHIG
diligence   of   transcendental quality   gain   make, must*

*transcendental diligence: one of the six paramitas or transcendental qualities of a bod-
hisattva*

May they gain transcendental diligence.

*May the light from this lamp illuminate the beings who inhabit the four
continents. May they be freed from the eight sufferings. May they gain
transcendental diligence.*

མར་མེ་འདི་བྱོལ་སོང་རྣམས་ཀྱི་གནས་སུ་

MAR ME   DI   JOL SONG NAM   KYI   NAE   SU
butterlamp   this   animals   of   place   to

May the light from this lamp illuminate

སྣང་ཞིང་གསལ་བར་གྱུར་ཅིག།

NANG ZHING   SAL WAR   GYUR   CHIG
showing, light up   illuminate   make, may

All who live in the animal realm.

བྱོལ་སོང་དེ་དག་གཅིག་ལ་གཅིག་ཟ་བ་དང་།

JOL SONG   DE DAG   CHIG LA CHIG   ZA WA   DANG
animals   these   one   to   one   eat   and
                                (i.e. each other)

May they stop eating each other, and

བརྡེག་བཏུང་དང་།   གསད་པ་དང་།

DEG DUNG   DANG   SAD PA   DANG
fighting   and   killing   and

Be freed from the suffering of fighting, killing,

བཀོལ་བའི་སྡུག་བསྔལ་དང་།   གླེན་ལྐུགས་ལས་ཐར་ནས།

KOL WAI	DUG NGAL	DANG	LUN MONG	LAE	THAR	NE
enslaved, captured, domesticated	suffering	and	stupidity, mental dullness	from	freed	then

Being enslaved, and being dull and stupid.

ཤེས་རབ་རྣམ་པ་གསུམ་དང་ལྡན་པར་གྱུར་ཅིག

SHE RAB	NAM PA	SUM	DANG DAN PAR	GYUR	CHIG
wisdom (hearing, reflecting on, meditating on dharma teachings)	kinds	three	gain		make, may

May they gain the wisdom of hearing, thinking about and meditating on the dharma.

May the light from this lamp illuminate all who live in the animal realm. May they stop eating each other and be freed from the suffering of fighting, killing, being enslaved, and being dull and stupid. May they gain the wisdom of hearing, thinking about and meditating on the dharma.

མར་མེ་འདི་གཤིན་རྗེའི་འཇིག་རྟེན་དུ་སྣང་ཞིང་

MAR ME	DI	SHIN JEI	JIG TEN	DU	NANG ZHING
butterlamp	this	lord of death*	realm, world	to	show

 Yama, the one who judges us at death and whose minions punish the guilty.

May the light from this lamp illuminate

གསལ་བར་གྱུར་ཅིག

SAL WAR	GYUR	CHIG
illuminate	make, may	

The realm of the lord of death.

གཤིན་རྗེ་རྣམས་གསོད་གཅོད་བྱེད་པ་དང་བརྡེག་བརྡུང་གི་ལས་ཐར་ནས།

SHIN JE NAM	SOE CHOE	JE PA	DANG	DEG DUNG	GI	LE...
Yama gods	killing	cutting	and	beating	of	activity

...THAR	NE
freed	then

May these cruel ones cease from killing, cutting and beating.

དེ་བཞིན་གཤེགས་པ་ཐམས་ཅད་ཀྱིས་ཕ་རོལ་ཏུ་ཕྱིན་པ་བསྟགས་པས།

DE ZHIN SHEG PA	THAM CHE	KYI	PHA ROL TU CHIN PA	DRAG PAE
tathagata, buddha	all	by	paramitas*, transcendent	teach, hear

generosity; morality; patience; diligence; concentration and wisdom

May they be taught the six transcendental qualities by the Tathagathas, and

 སེམས་ཅན་ཐམས་ཅད་གཏོང་བའི་སེམས་འབྱུང་བར་གྱུར་ཅིག།

SEM CHEN	THAM CHE	TONG WAI	SEM	JUNG WAR	GYUR CHIG
sentient beings	*all*	*generous, giving*	*mind attitude*	*arise gain*	*make, may*

By this may they develop generous attitudes towards all beings.

May the light from this lamp illuminate the realm of the lord of death. May these cruel ones cease from killing, cutting and beating. May they be taught the six transcendental qualities by the Tathagathas and by this may they develop generous attitudes towards all beings.

མར་མེ་འདི་ཡི་ཡི་དྭགས་གནས་སུ་གསལ་བར་གྱུར་ཅིག །

MAR ME	DI	PRE TAI	NAE	SU	SAL WAR	GYUR	CHIG
butterlamp	*this*	*hungry ghost*	*place*	*to*	*illuminate*	*make, may*	

May the light from this lamp illuminate the realms of the hungry ghosts.

ཡི་ཏུ་རྣམས་ཀྱང་བཀྲེས་སྐོམ་གྱི་སྡུག་བསྔལ་ལས་ཐར་ནས།

PRE TA NAM	KYANG	TRE	KOM	GYI	DUG NGAL	LE...
hungry ghosts	*also*	*hunger*	*thirst*	*of*	*suffering*	*from*

...THAR	NE
free	*then*

May they be freed from the misery of thirst and hunger.

བྱང་ཆུབ་སེམས་དཔའ་ནམ་མཁའ་མཛོད་ཀྱི་

JANG CHUB SEM PA	NAM KHA DZOE	KYI
bodhisattva	*sky treasure akashagarbha*	*of*

By the blessings of the great compassion

ཐུགས་རྗེ་ཆེན་པོའི་བྱིན་གྱི་རླབས་ཀྱིས།

THUG JE	CHEN POI	JIN GYI LAB	KYI
compassion	*great*	*blessing*	*by*

Of Bodhisattva Akashagarbha

ཟས་དང་སྐོམ་གྱིས་མི་འཕོངས་པའི་ལོངས་སྤྱོད

ZAE	DANG	KOM	GYI	MI PHONG PAI	LONG CHO
food	*and*	*drink*	*by*	*luxurious, rich*	*supplies, resources*

May they have an inexhaustible supply

ཟད་མི་ཤེས་པ་དང་ལྡན་ཞིང་།

ZAE PA MI SHE PA	DANG DEN ZHING
inexhaustible	*have*

Of easily available food and drink.

སྦྱིན་པའི་ཕ་རོལ་ཏུ་ཕྱིན་པའི་དབང་དང་ལྡན་པར་གྱུར་ཅིག །

JIN PAI	PHA ROL TU CHIN PAI	WANG	DANG DEN PAR	GYUR CHIG
generosity	paramitas, transcendent quality	power	have, gain	must, make

May they gain the power of transcendental generosity.

May the light from this lamp illuminate the realms of the hungry ghosts. May they be freed from the misery of thirst and hunger. By the blessings of the great compassion of Bodhisattva Akashagarbha may they have an inexhaustible supply of easily available food and drink. May they gain the power of transcendental generosity.

མར་མེ་འདི་ན་རག་རྣམས་ཀྱི་གནས་སུ་གསལ་བར་གྱུར་ཅིག །

MAR ME	DI	NA RAG NAM	KYI	NAE	SU	SAL WAR	GYUR CHIG
butterlamp	this	hells	of	places	to	illuminate	make, may

May the light from this lamp illuminate the hell realms.

ན་རག་ནི་སྔོན་གྱི་ལས་ངན་པའི་རྣམ་པར་སྨིན་པས་

NA RAG NI	NYON GYI	LAE	NGAN	PAI	NAM PAR MIN PAE
hells	former	actions	bad	by	ripening

Beings suffer there according to the ripening of their previous bad actions,

ཚ་གྲང་གི་སྡུག་བསྔལ་བཟོད་པར་དཀའ་བ་ཉམས་སུ་མྱོང་པ་ལས།

TSHA	DRANG	GI	DUG NGAL	ZOE PAR	KA WA ...
heat	cold	of	suffering	bear, endure	difficult

...NYAM SU NYONG PA	LE
experience	then

Experiencing intolerable heat and cold.

འཕགས་པ་སྤྱན་རས་གཟིགས་དབང་ཕྱུག་གི་ཐུགས་རྗེའི་བྱིན་གྱི་རླབས་ཀྱིས།

PHAG PA	CHEN RE ZIG WANG CHUG	GI	THUG JEI...
arya, noble	Avalokitesvara	of	compassion

...JIN GYI LAB	KYI
blessing	by

By the blessings of the compassion of the Bodhisattva Arya Avalokitesvara

དམྱལ་བའི་སྡུག་བསྔལ་ཚད་མེད་པ་ལས་ཐར་ནས།

NYAL WAI	DUG NGAL	TSHE ME PE	LE	THAR	NE
hell's	suffering	limitless	from	freed	then

May they be freed from the limitless sufferings of hell.

བཟོད་པའི་ཕ་རོལ་ཏུ་ཕྱིན་པ་དང་ལྡན་པར་གྱུར་ཅིག།

ZOE PAI	PHA ROL TU CHIN PA	DANG DEN PAR	GYUR CHIG
patience	*paramita*	*gain*	*make, may*

May they realise the transcendent quality of patience.

May the light from this lamp illuminate the hell realms. Beings suffer there according to the ripening of their previous bad actions, experiencing intolerable heat and cold. By the blessings of the compassion of the Bodhisattva Arya Avalokitesvara may they be freed from the limitless sufferings of hell. May they realise the transcendent quality of patience.

མར་མེ་འདིས་འཛམ་བུ་གླིང་གི་ཕྱི་རོལ་ན་མུན་ནག་གི་

MAR ME	DI	DZAM BU LING	GI	CHI ROL NA	MUN NAG	GI
butterlamp	*this*	*jambhudvipa, our world*	*of*	*outside, beyond*	*profound darkness*	*of*

May the light of this lamp illuminate the realms beyond this world system where,

ནང་ན་འཐོམས་པའི་

NANG	NA	THOM PAI
in	*there*	*benighted, dulled*

In the darkness, benighted people cannot

སེམས་ཅན་རང་གི་ལག་པ་གཡས་པ་བཀྱང་བ་ཡང་

SEM CHEN	RANG GI	LAG PA	YAE PA	KYANG WA	YANG
beings	*own*	*hand*	*right*	*held up in front of them*	*yet*

Even see their own right hand

མི་མཐོང་བའི་གནས་སུ་གསལ་བར་གྱུར་ཅིག།

MI THONG WAI	NAE	SU	SAL WAR	GYUR CHIG
not see	*place*	*to*	*illuminate*	*make, may*

Held up in front of them.

དེ་དག་སྔོན་གྱི་ལས་ངན་པའི་རྣམ་པར་སྨིན་པས་

DE DAG	NGON GYI	LAE	NGAN PAI	NAM PAR MIN PAE
they	*former*	*actions* *bad*	*by*	*ripening*

Due to the ripening of their previous bad actions

ཟས་དང་སྐོམ་འདོད་པ་ལས།

ZAE	DANG	KOM	DOE PA	LAE
food	*and*	*drink*	*desire*	*yet*

They crave food and drink

ནམ་མཁའ་ལ་རང་གི་ལྕགས་ཀྱི་སེན་མོ་ཡོད་པས་

NAM KHA	LA	RANG GI	CHAG	KYI	SEN MO	YOE PAE
sky	*to*	*own*	*iron*	*of*	*claws*	*that they have*

But scratch themselves with their iron claws

བསྐོགས་པས་ཟས་དང་སྐོམ་མ་རྙེད་ནས།

NYOG WAE	ZAE	DANG	KOM	MA	NYE	NE
scratch, tear	*food*	*and*	*drink*	*not*	*get*	*then*

As they reach out to the sky and so are unsatisfied.

རང་གི་ལུས་ཟིན་པ་དང་ཤ་བཅད་ཅིང་བཟའ་པ་

RANG GI	LU	ZIN PA	DANG	SHA	CHED CHING	ZAE PA
own	*body*	*exhausted*	*and*	*flesh*	*cutting*	*eat*

They are exhausted and cut their own flesh and eat it.

དེ་དག་དེ་བཞིན་གཤེགས་པ་འོད་དཔག་མེད་ཀྱི་

DE DAG	DE ZHIN SHEG PA	WOE PAG ME	KYI
these beings	*tathagata, buddha*	*Amitabha*	*of*

By the blessing of the compassion of Buddha Amitabha

ཐུགས་རྗེའི་བྱིན་གྱི་རླབས་ཀྱིས། མུན་ནག་ཆེན་པོའི་ཐོམས་པ་ལས་ཐར་ནས།

THUG JEI	JIN GYI LAB	KYI	MUN NAG	CHEN POI	THOM PA...
compassion	*blessing*	*by*	*profound darkness*	*great*	*dazed, stunned*

...LAE	THAR	NE
from	*freed*	*then*

May they be freed from the force of that great darkness and

བདེ་བ་ཅན་གྱི་ཞིང་ཁམས་སུ་སྐྱེ་བར་གྱུར་ཅིག།

DE WA CHEN	GYI	ZHING KHAM	SU	KYE WA	GYUR CHIG
*sukhavati**	*of*	*realm*	*in*	*born*	*make, may*

*or Dewachen, the buddha realm where Amitabha resides

Be reborn in the pure realm of Great Happiness.

May the light of this lamp illuminate the realms beyond this world system where, in the darkness, benighted people cannot even see their own right hand held up in front of them. Due to the ripening of their previous bad actions they crave food and drink but scratch themselves with their iron claws as they reach out to the sky and so are unsatisfied. They are exhausted and cut their own flesh and eat it. By the blessing of the compassion of Buddha Amitabha may they be freed from the force of that great darkness and be reborn in the pure realm of Great Happiness.

གཞན་ཡང་མར་མེ་འདི་ཀླུའི་གནས་སུ་སྣང་ཞིང་

ZHAN YANG	MAR ME	DI	LUI	NAE	SU	NANG ZHING
moreover, furthermore	butterlamp	this	nagas*	place	to	showing

*snake gods who protect the treasures of the earth and guard its resource

May the light of this lamp illuminate

གསལ་བར་གྱུར་ཅིག

SAL WAR	GYUR CHIG
illuminating	make, may

The realm of the nagas.

དེ་རྣམས་གཏི་མུག་དང་སེར་སྣའི་མདུད་པ་ལས་བཀྲོལ་ཏེ་

DE NAM	TI MUG	DANG	SER NAI	DUD PA	LAE	TROL	TE
they	stupidity	and	envy	snare, knot	from	freed, untied	then

May they be freed from the snares of stupidity and envy.

གཏོང་བའི་བློ་དང་ལྡན་ཞིང་

TONG WAI	LO	DANG DEN	ZHING
generosity	attitude	have, gain	and

May they practise generosity and

ནམ་མཁའ་ལྡིང་གི་འཇིགས་པ་དང་

NAM KHA DING	GI	JIG PA	DANG
predatory birds, garudas, eagles etc.	of	fear	and

Be freed from the fear of predatory birds,

མེ་ཚན་ཕྱི་ཚན་ལ་སོགས་ཏེ།

ME TSHAN	CHE TSHAN	LA SOG TE
hot air	dry sand	and so on

Heat, dry sand, and

འཇིགས་པ་ཆེན་པོ་བརྒྱད་ལས་ཐར་ནས།

JIG PA	CHEN PO	GYE	LAE	THAR	NE
fears	great	eight	from	freed	then

(eight great fears: fear of fire, water, earth, air, elephants, snakes, thieves and kings)

The rest of the eight great fears.

སངས་རྒྱས་དང་།   ཆོས་དང་།   དགེ་འདུན་ལ་སྐྱབས་སུ་འགྲོ་ཞིང་

SANG GYE	DANG	CHO	DANG	GEN DUN	LA...
buddha	and	dharma	and	sangha	to

...KYAB SU DRO ZHING
take refuge in

May they take refuge in Buddha, Dharma and Sangha

སྲོག་འཚོ་བའི་ཞི་གནས་ཀྱི་ཆུའི་ཐིག་ལེ་སྙིང་ལ་གནས་ནས་

SOG	TSHO WAI	ZHI NAE	KYI	CHUI	THIG LE	NYING
life	*sustaining* *nourishing* *replenishing*	*calm* *abiding*	*of*	*water* *(cooling and purifying the heart/mind)*	*drop*	*heart*

...LA   NAE   NE
in   stay   then

So that the life sustaining waterdrop of calm abiding rests in their hearts and

ཀླུ་རྣམས་འདོད་པའི་ཡོན་ཏན་དང་ལྡན་པར་གྱུར་ཅིག

LU NAM	DOE PAI	YON TAN	DANG DEN PAR	GYUR CHIG
nagas	*desirable qualities*	*good*	*gain*	*make, may*

All the nagas gain everything they desire.

May the light of this lamp illuminate the realm of the nagas. May they be freed from the snares of stupidity and envy. May they practise generosity and be freed from the fear of predatory birds, heat, dry sand and the rest of the eight great fears. May they take refuge in Buddha, Dharma and Sangha so that the life sustaining waterdrop of calm abiding rests in their hearts and all the nagas gain everything they desire.

མར་མེ་འདི་སྦྲོ་འཕྱེ་ཆེན་པོའི་གནས་སུ་སྣང་ཞིང་

MAR ME	DI	TO CHE	CHEN POI	NAE	SU	NANG ZHING
butterlamp	*this*	*reptiles*	*great*	*place*	*to*	*showing*

May the light of this lamp illuminate

གསལ་བར་གྱུར་ཅིག

SAL WAR	GYUR CHIG
illuminate	*make, may*

The realm of the giant reptiles.

དེས་སྦྲོ་འཕྱེ་ཆེན་པོའི་སྡུག་བསྔལ་ཞི་ནས་

DE	TO CHE	CHEN POI	DUG NGAL	ZHI	NE
by this	*reptiles*	*great, big*	*suffering*	*pacify*	*then*

May their sufferings be removed.

དགའ་བ་རྒྱ་མཚོ་རྣམ་པར་འཕྲུལ་པའི་ཤུགས་

GA WA	GYAM TSO	NAM PAR	TRUL PAI	SHUG
happiness	*ocean*	*form*	*magical*	*power*

May they gain the magical power to abide

དང་ལྡན་པར་གྱུར་ཅིག།

DANG DEN PAR	GYUR CHIG
possess	*make, may*

In oceans of happiness.

May the light of this lamp illuminate the realm of the giant reptiles. May their sufferings be removed. May they gain the magical power to abide in oceans of happiness.

མར་མེ་འདི་འཛམ་བུ་གླིང་གི་ཕྱིར་གནས་པའི་

MAR ME	DI	DZAM BU LING	GI	CHIR	NAE PAI
butterlamp	*this*	*this world*	*of*	*outwith, beyond*	*places*

May the light from this lamp illuminate the areas beyond the continent of Jambudvipa occupied

ས་བདག་དང་།   ལྷ་དང་།   ཀླུ་དང་།

SA DAG	DANG	LHA	DANG	LU	DANG
land gods, protectors of place	*and*	*local*	*and*	*nagas*	*and*

By land gods, local gods, nagas,

ས་བདག་གི་རྒྱལ་པོ་པ་ཏི་ལི་དང་།

SA DAG	GI	GYAL PO	PA TI LI	DANG
land gods	*of*	*king*	*his name*	*and*

Pitali the king of the land gods,

སའི་རྒྱལ་མོ་ཆེན་པོ་དང་།   རྒྱ་མཚོ་ཆེན་པོ་དང་།

SAI GYAL MO	CHEN PO	DANG	GYAM TSHO	CHEN PO	DANG
land queen	*great*	*and*	*(the gods of) oceans*	*great*	*and*

The great queen of the land, and the gods of oceans,

མཚོ་བུན་དང་།   རྫིང་དང་།   ཁྲོན་པ་ལ་གནས་པ་དང་།

TSHO TRAN	DANG	DZING	DANG	TRON PA	LA	NAE PA	DANG
seas	*and*	*ponds*	*and*	*wells*	*at*	*staying*	*and*

Seas, ponds and wells,

ཀླུང་ཆེན་པོ་དང་།   ཀླུང་ཕྲ་མོ་དང་།

LU   CHEN PO   DANG   LU   TRA MO   DANG
rivers *big*   *and*   *rivers* *small*   *and*

Big rivers, small rivers,

ཆུ་མིག་དང་།   ལུ་མ་ལ་གནས་པ་དང་།

CHU MIG   DANG   LU MA   LA   NAE PA   DANG
springs   *and*   *seasonal* *at*   *staying*   *and*
                                  ponds

Springs, seasonal ponds and

གངས་རི་མཐོན་མོའི་རྒྱུད་ལ་གནས་པ་དང་།

GANG RI   THÖN MOI   GYUD   LA   NAE PA   DANG
snow   mountain *high*   *flow*   *at*   *stay*   *and*
(glacial stream)

Those who stay at the high glacial streams.

རི་ནག་པོ་དང་།   གཡའ་དང་།   ཤ་སྲང་དང་།

RI   NAG PO   DANG   YA   DANG   SHA SANG   DANG
mountain *black*   *and*   *slate* *and*   *water meadows* *and*

Black mountains, slate hills, water meadows,

སྤང་རི་དང་།   ནགས་ཆེན་པོ་དང་།   ཤིང་གཅིག་པ་དང་།

PANG RI   DANG   NAG   CHEN PO   DANG   SHING   CHIG PA   DANG
hill fields *and*   *forest* *big*   *and*   *tree*   *solitary*   *and*

Hill fields, big forests and solitary trees,

གཙུག་ལག་ཁང་དང་།   མཆོད་རྟེན་དང་།   གྲོང་ཁྱེར་དང་།

TSUG LAG KHANG   DANG   CHO TEN   DANG   DRONG KHYER   DAN
temples   *and*   *stupas*   *and*   *cities*   *and*

Temples, stupas, cities and

གྲོང་ན་གནས་པའི་གནས་སུ་སྣང་ཞིང་གསལ་བར་གྱུར་ཅིག།

JONG   NA   NAE PAI   NAE   SU   NANG ZHING   SAL WAR...
villages *in*   *staying*   *places* *in*   *showing*   *illuminating*
...GYUR   CHIG
   make, may

villages – may all those who stay in these places be illuminated.

དེ་དག་སོ་སོའི་འཁྲུལ་པའི་རྟོག་པ་ཐམས་ཅད་བྱང་ནས།   ཐམས་ཅད་བྱང་ནས།

DE DAG	SO SOI	TRUL PAI	TOG PA	THAM CHE	JANG	NE
they	*each, individual*	*confusion, delusion*	*thoughts*	*all*	*clear, remove*	*then*

May each of these beings have their own particular confusions removed.

དཀོན་མཆོག་གསུམ་ལ་མི་ཕྱེད་པའི་དད་པ་དང་ལྡན་ཏེ།

KON CHOG	SUM	LA	MI CHED PAI	DAE PA	DANG DEN	TE
jewels	*three*	*to*	*unchanging*	*faith*	*gain*	*then, thus*

May they have unchanging faith in the Three Jewels.

བྱང་ཆུབ་ཀྱི་སེམས་དང་ལྡན་ནས་ཐར་པ་

JANG CHUB KYI SEM	DANG DEN	NE	THAR PA
bodhisattva's altruistic intention	*gain, have*	*then*	*liberation*

May they gain an altruistic intention towards enlightenment and

ཐོབ་པའི་རྒྱུ་རུ་གྱུར་ཅིག།

THOB PAI	GYU	RU	GYUR CHIG
gain	*cause*	*as*	*develop, establish*

Establish the cause of liberation.

May the light from this lamp illuminate the areas beyond the continent of Jambudvipa occupied by land gods, local gods, nagas, Pitali the king of the land gods, the great queen of the land, and the gods and denizens of oceans, seas, ponds and wells, big rivers, small rivers, springs, seasonal ponds and those who stay at the high glacial streams, black mountains, slate hills, water meadows, hill fields, big forests, solitary trees, temples, stupas, cities and villages – may all those who stay in these places be illuminated. May each of these beings have their own particular confusions removed. May they have unchanging faith in the Three Jewels. May they gain an altruistic intention towards enlightenment and establish the cause of liberation.

རྒྱལ་པོ་གསེར་གྱི་ལག་པའི་སྨར་མེའི་སྨོན་ལམ་གྱི་མཛད་རྫོགས་སོ།

This concludes the aspiration of King Golden Hand.

དེ་ལྟར་དེང་མར་མེ་འདིའི་ཡོན་བདག་ཀྱིས་ཀྱང་།   གཏན་པ་མེད་པའི་མཆོད་
པའི་དེ་ཕུལ་བས།   བདག་དང་མཐའ་ཡས་པའི་སེམས་ཅན་རྣམས་དེ་བཞིན་ག
གཤེགས་པ་མར་མེ་མཛད་ཀྱི་ཞབས་དྲུང་དུ་སྐྱེས་ཏེ།   མཚན་པར་རྫོགས་པར་
སངས་རྒྱས་ནས།   སེམས་ཅན་ཐམས་ཅད་ཀྱི་དཔལ་མགོན་དུ་གྱུར་ཅིག།།

*By the sponsoring of these lamps and the offering of this transient display
may I and all the infinite sentient beings be reborn at the feet of Buddha
Dipamkara. May we gain perfect Buddhahood and become benefactors of
all beings.*

****

...Continued from page 64.

ན་མོ་གུ་རུ་དེ་ཝ་ཌཱ་ཀི་ནི་ཡེ༔

NA MO	GU RU	DE VA	DA KI NI YE
salutation	*guru*	*deva, gods*	*dakini*

Salutation! I bow to the gurus, deities and dakinis.

དེང་ནས་བཟུང་སྟེ་ཚེ་རབས་ཐམས་ཅད་དུ༔

DENG	NAE	ZUNG TE	TSE RAB	THAM CHAD	DU
this time, today	*from*	*onwards*	*lives*	*all*	*in*

From this time on in all my lives,

ཁྱབ་བདག་དཔལ་ལྡན་བླ་མ་རྡོ་རྗེ་འཆང་༔

KHYAB DAG	PAL DEN	LA MA	DOR JE CHANG
pervading lord	*glorious*	*guru*	*Vajradhara (i.e. one's root guru)*

Pervading lord, glorious Guru Vajradhara,

སྐུ་བཞི་ཡེ་ཤེས་ལྔ་ཡི་བདག་ཉིད་ཅན༔

KU	ZHI	YE SHE	NGA	YI	DAG NYID	CHEN
mode, kaya*	*four*	*original knowing*	*five #*	*of*	*nature*	*having*

**dharmakaya/natural mode, sambhogakaya/revelatory mode, nirmanakaya/manifest mode,
svabhavikakaya/inseperable mode   # see the first five offering verses*

With the nature of the four modes and the five original knowings,

ཁྱོད་དང་འབྲལ་མེད་བརྩེ་བའི་རྗེས་བཟུང་ནས༔

KHYOD	DANG	DRAL MED	TSE WAI	JE ZUNG	NAE
you	*and*	*never separate*	*compassion*	*hold me*	*then*

May I never separate from you, held by your compassion.

མཉེས་པ་གསུམ་གྱི་སྒོ་ནས་ཁྱོད་བསྟེན་ཤོག༔

NYE PA	SUM	GYI	GO	NAE	KHYON	TEN	SHOG
happiness	*three**	*of*	*door*	*from*	*you*	*serve #*	*must, may I*

* body, speech and mind # With your body doing whatever tasks the guru gives you. With your speech being in agreement with whatever he tells you. With your mind doing whatever meditation and practice he tells you. By doing these three things the guru will be pleased.

May I serve and please you with my body, speech and mind!

Salutation! I bow to the gurus, deities and dakinis. Pervading lord, glorious guru Vajradhara, embodiment of the four modes and the five original knowings, from this time on in all my lives may I never separate from you, held by your compassion. May I serve and please you with my body, speech and mind!

ཐོབ་དཀའི་དལ་འབྱོར་མི་ལུས་རིན་ཆེན་འདི༔

THOB	KAI	DAL	JOR	MI LUE	RIN CHEN	DI
get	*difficult*	*freedoms*	*opportunities*	*human body*	*precious, jewel-like*	*this*

Regarding this jewel-like human body possessing the freedoms and opportunities that are so difficult to gain,

ཇི་ཙམ་འདུག་དབང་ཡོད་པར་མི་ཤེས་པས༔

CHI TSAM	DUG	WANG	YOD PAR	MI SHE PAE
how much, how long	*stay*	*power*	*have*	*not know, therefore*

We do not know how long it will remain.

བསླུ་མེད་ལས་འབྲས་ཁྱད་དུ་མི་གསོད་ཅིང༔

LU MED	LAE DRAE	KHYAD DU	MI SOD CHING
undeceiving	*karma*	*distinctions*	*not destroyed**

*i.e. do not believe that good actions bring bad results or vice versa

Therefore, always keeping aware of the non-deceptive nature of karma,

འཁོར་བའི་འདམ་རྫབ་འདི་ལས་བསྒྲལ་དུ་གསོལ༔

KHOR WAI	DAM DZAB	DI	LAE	DRAL	DU SOL
samsara	*filthy swamp, cess-pit*	*this*	*from*	*free (I and all beings)*	*pray*

May we all be freed from this foul swamp of samsara.

Regarding this jewel-like human body possessing the freedoms and opportunities that are so difficult to gain, we do not know how long it will remain. Therefore, always keeping aware of the non-deceptive nature of karma, may we all be freed from this foul swamp of samsara.

འཇིགས་ལས་སྐྱོབས་བྱེད་བླ་མེད་དཀོན་མཆོག་གསུམ༔

JIG	LAE	KYOB JED	LA MED	KON CHOG	SUM
fear	*from*	*protecting*	*unsurpassed*	*jewel*	*three**

*buddha, dharma, sangha

The unsurpassed three jewels who protect from fear

སྲོག་ལ་བབ་ཀྱང་ཡལ་བར་མི་འདོར་ཞིང༔

SOG	LA	BAB	KYANG	YAL WAR	MI DOR ZHING
life	*to*	*fall*	*although*	*diminish*	*not sending, not allowing to go*

We will never abandon even at the cost of our lives.

རྒྱུ་འབྲས་མན་ངག་བདུན་ལ་བློ་སྦྱངས་ཏེ༔

GYU	DRAE	MEN NGAG	DUN	LA	LO CHANG	TE
cause	*result*	*doctrine, advice*	*seven**	*with*	*mental training*	*then*

*the seven part practice: 1. all sentient beings have been our mother, 2. they were very kind to us, 3. we must replay that kindness, 4. we must love all our mothers, 5. we must have true compassion for our mothers, 6. we must develop the two bodhicittas: a) all beings must get enlightenment, b) for their benefit I must develop bodhicitta, 7. our own result will be enlightenment

Training our minds with the seven-part practice of cause and effect

རྣམ་གཉིས་བྱང་ཆུབ་སེམས་དང་མི་འབྲལ་ཤོག༔

NAM	NYI	JANG CHUB SEM	DANG	MI DRAL	SHOG
kinds	*two*	*bodhicitta (absolute and relative)*	*and*	*not separate*	*may we*

May we never be separated from relative and absolute altruistic openness.

Even at the cost of our lives we will never abandon the unsurpassed three jewels who protect from fear. Training our minds with the seven-part practice of cause and effect, may we never be separated from relative and absolute altruistic openness.

ཕྱི་སྣོད་འཇིག་རྟེན་རི་རབ་གླིང་བཞི་དང༔

CHI	NOD	JIG TEN	RI RAB	LING	ZHI	DANG
outer	*container**	*world*	*Mt. Meru*	*islands, continents*	*four*	*and*

* the outside world, trees, mountains, rivers...

The outer container of the world with Mt. Meru and the four continents,

ནང་བཅུད་ཕུང་ཁམས་སྐྱེ་མཆེད་འདོད་ཡོན་ཚོགས༔

NANG	CHUD	PUNG	KHAM	KYEM CHED	DOE YON	TSOG
inner	contents*	skandhas #	dhatus+	ayatanas~	desirable qualities	lots

(i.e. things pleasing to them)

*all sentient beings   # form, feeling, perception, conception, consciousness +six sense organs, six sense consciousnesses, six sense objects   ~ six sense consciousnesses and their objects

The inner contents of all beings with their constituent aspects and all desirable phenomena,

གསང་བ་རང་རིག་སྐྱེ་མེད་བྱང་ཆུབ་སེམས༔

SANG WA	RANG RIG	KYE MED	JANG CHUB SEM
secret, innermost	own awareness	unborn	bodhicitta

The secret unborn bodhicitta, my own awareness,

ཡང་གསང་དབྱིངས་རིག་བདེ་ཆེན་མཎྜལ་འདི༔

YANG SANG	YING	RIG	DE CHEN	MAN DAL	DI
most secret	dhatu, all encompassing space	vidya, awareness	great happiness	mandala	this

The most secret joyful mandala of awareness and hospitable space, all this,

རྒྱལ་བའི་ཡབ་གཅིག་ཁྱོད་ལ་འབུལ་ནུས་ཤོག༔

GYAL WAI	YAB CHIG	KHYO	LA	BUL	NUE	SHOG
jinas	sole father (i.e. my guru)	you	to	offer	power	must have

Sole father of the buddhas, may we have the power to offer it to you!

The outer container of the world with Mt. Meru and the four continents, the inner contents of all beings with their constituent aspects and all desirable phenomena, the secret unborn bodhicitta, my own awareness, the joyful secret mandala of awareness and hospitable space, all this, sole father of the buddhas, may we have the power to offer it to you!

ཆོས་དང་ཆོས་ཅན་རྣམ་པར་དབྱེ་བྱས་ནས༔

CHOE	DANG	CHOE CHEN	NAM PAR JE	JAE	NAE
object	and	subject	clearly distinguish	do	then

Distinguishing clearly between object and subject, and then

བདེན་པར་མ་གྲུབ་ཕྱི་ནང་སྒྱུ་མའི་ཆོས༔

DEN PAR MA DRUB	CHI	NANG	GYU MAI	CHOE
without actual reality	outer	inner	illusory, magical	dharmas, phenomena*

*everything in samsara and nirvana

Recognising that there is no actual basis for this, all outer and inner phenomena are seen to be illusory.

སྣང་སྲིད་སེམས་སུ་ཡིན་པར་ཐག་ཆོད་ཅིངཿ

NANG SID	SEM	SU	YIN PAR	THAG CHOD CHING
all possible appearances	mind	as, in	to be	deciding, eliminating doubt

Clearly experiencing that all possible appearances are the play of the mind,

སྒྱུ་ལུས་ཟབ་མོའི་ཚོགས་འཁོར་བསྐོར་བྱས་ནསཿ

GYU	LUE	ZAB MOI	TSOG KHOR	KOR	JAE	NAE
illusory	body	deep	ganachakra, assembly circle	turn*	do	then

*i.e. do the practice of chod

May we practise the profound offering assembly with our illusory bodies and thus

རྣམ་བཞིའི་མགྲོན་རྣམས་སོ་སོར་མཉེས་བྱེད་ཤོགཿ

NAM	ZHI	DRON NAM	SO SOR	NYE	JED	SHOG
kinds	four*	guests	each to	happy	make	may I

*1. the higher guests, Buddha, dharma, sangha 2. bodhisattvas, devas, dakinis 3. all sentient beings 4. people to whom I owe something, local gods, troublesome beings, etc

Make each of the four classes of guest happy.

Distinguishing clearly between object and subject, and then recognising that there is no actual basis for this, all outer and inner phenomena are seen to be illusory. Clearly experiencing that all possible appearances are the play of the mind, may we practise the profound offering assembly with our illusory bodies and thus make each of the four classes of guest happy.

བླ་མ་རྡོ་རྗེ་སེམས་དཔའ་སྤྱི་བོར་བསྒོམཿ

LA MA	DOR JE SEM PA	CHI WOR	GOM
guru	Vajrasattva	crown of head	meditate

Meditating on the guru as Vajrasattva on the crown of our heads

གཉེན་པོ་སྟོབས་བཞིའི་བཤགས་སྡོམ་རབ་བྱས་ཏེཿ

NYEN PO	TOB	ZHI	SHAG	DOM	RAB	JAE	TE
antidote*	strength	four	confess	vows	fully	do	then

*witness (image of Lord Buddha or our guru), feel regret, confess the sins, promise to never do them again

May we confess with the four strong antidotes and keep our vows well.

བྱིན་བརླབ་ཀུན་འབྱུང་ཀུན་བཟང་ཧེ་རུ་ཀཿ

JIN LAB	KUN	JUNG	KUN ZANG	HE RU KA
blessing	all	source	Samantabhadra, always good	heruka, anger form

Glorious guru, you who are not different from the source of all blessings,

བཅོམ་ལྡན་འདས་མ་མཆོག་དང་དབྱེར་མེད་པའི༔

CHOM DEN DAE MA CHOG   DANG   YER MED PAI
Parambhagavati (wife of Heruka, sunyata)   and   inseparable

Kunzang Heruka and Chomden Dema Chog,

དཔལ་ལྡན་བླ་མའི་སྐུ་གསུང་ཐུགས་གསུམ་གྱི༔

PAL DEN   LA MAI   KU   SUNG   THUG   SUM   GYI
glorious   guru's   body   speech   mind   three   of

The excellent yoga of the secret inconceivable vajras of

གསང་བ་བསམ་མི་ཁྱབ་པའི་རྡོ་རྗེ་ཡི༔

SANG WA   SAM MI KHYAB PAI   DOR JE   YI
*secret   inconceivable *   vajra #   of*
*i.e. very rare and excellent good qualities   # undeceiving, indestructible

Your body, speech and mind —

རྣལ་འབྱོར་མཆོག་ཉིད་འབྱོང་བར་བྱིན་གྱིས་རློབས༔

NAL JOR   CHOG   NYID   JONG   WAR   JING GYI LOB
yoga   excellent   itself   get   as   bless

May we gain this blessing.

Meditating on the guru as Vajrasattva on the crown of our heads may we confess with the four strong antidotes and keep our vows well. Glorious guru, you who are not different from Kunzang Heruka and Chomden Dema Chog, the source of all blessings — may we gain the blessing of the excellent yoga of the secret inconceivable vajras of your body, speech and mind.

ཅེས་པ་འདི་ནི་གསུམ་ལྡན་རྡོ་རྗེ་འཛིན་པ་ཆེན་པོ་མཆོག་གི་སྒྲུབ་བརྗེས་བི་མ་ལ་

མི་ད་འི་རྣམ་སྤྲུལ་ཚུལ་ཁྲིམས་བཟང་པོ་ཡེ་ཤེས་རོལ་པ་རྩལ་གྱི་བཀའ་བཞིན་ཉིད་

ཀྱི་སློབ་འབངས་ཐ་ཁལ་བདག་ཟ་ཧོར་གྱི་རྒྱལ་ཁམས་སུ་གནས་ཆེན་མཚོ་པདྨར་

པོ་གསུམ་བླ་དྲག་ལས་མེད་སོས་དལ་དུ་བཅད་རྒྱར་སྒྲོ་སྐྱབས་ཟ་ཧོར་རྒྱལ་པོ་རྫོ་

ཀེན་དར་སིང་ནས་འཚོ་བའི་མཐུན་རྐྱེན་སྤྱར་བྱུང་ཞིང་༔ ཚོགས་མཆོད་དང་མར་

མི་ཞལ་ཟས་བཅས་པར་མེད་མར་དུ་འབུལ་རྒྱུ་ཡོད་པའི་གོ་སྐབས་བྱུང་ཚེ་སེམས་

ཅན་སྤྱི་འི་བདེ་སྐྱིད་དང་ཁྱད་པར་མཆོག་སྤྲུལ་རིན་པོ་ཆེ་ཚུལ་ཁྲིམས་བཟང་པོ་འམ་

གཏེར་ཆེན་ཡེ་ཤེས་རོལ་པ་རྩལ་གྱི་དགུང་གྲགས་དྲག་ཅུ་རེ་གཅིག་པ་བརྗོག་ནས་

སྐུ་ཚེ་བསྐལ་པ་རྒྱ་མཚོར་བརྟན་པར་བཞུགས་པའི་དོན་དུ་དམིགས་ནས་ཏེ་སྐབས་
ཐབ་ཞིག་བདེ་ཆེན་རང་ཤར་ལས་ཟིལ་གནོན་ཡེ་ཤེས་ཀྱི་མཁའ་འགྲོ་མ་སེང་གེ་
གདོང་པ་ཅན་གྱི་ཆོས་སྐོར་ལ་བརྟེན་པའི་མར་མེའི་སྨོན་ལམ་ཞིག་བྲིས་ཡོད་པ་དེ་
ག་གཞིར་བཞག་ཕྱིས་སུ་རང་ལོ་ང་བདུན་པའི་ཐོག་བལ་ཡུལ་གྱི་གནས་ཆེན་བྱ་
རུང་ཁ་ཤོར་གྱི་མདུན་དུ་གུ་རུ་པདྨའི་རྒྱལ་ཚབ་ཆེན་པོ་བདུད་འཛོམས་འཇིགས་
བྲལ་ཡེ་ཤེས་རྡོ་རྗེ་མཆོག་གི་ཞབས་དྲུང་དུ་བགའར་གཏེར་གྱི་དབང་ལུང་རྣམས་ཞུ་
སྐབས་བར་མཆམས་སུ་ཚེས་བཅུ་དང་ཉེར་ལྔ་རེ་བྱེད་དུས་ཁ་ཅུང་ཟད་བསྒྱུར་ནས་
ཆག་གང་ལའང་སྒྱུར་དུ་རུང་བར་རྗལ་གནོན་སྐྱིང་པའམ་འཚེ་མེད་རིག་འཛིན་གྱིས་
བགྱིས་པའོ༔

Regarding this text, the great tantrica having Hinayana, Mahayana and Vajrayana vows who gained the excellent result, the incarnation of Vimalamitra, Tsultrim Zangpo Yeshe Rolpa Tsal (Tshul Khrims bZang Po Ye Shes Rol Pa rTsal) ordered me to stay at the great pilgrimage place of mTsho Padma in the kingdom of Zahor. While living there without work in a loose retreat for a period of three years and six months the King of Zahor, Joginder Sen, was my sponsor providing all necessities. He generously gave offerings and butterlamps and food, as much as I wished. At that time for the general benefit and happiness of all sentient beings and in particular for the supreme precious incarnation Tsultrim Zangpo or as he is known Terchen Yeshe Rolpa Tsal (gTer Chhen Ye Shes Rol Pa rTsal), whose most ordinary disciple I am, in order to remove the difficulties of his sixty-first year (that being a dangerous year to be), so that he would stay for an ocean of kalpas, I wrote a prayer of aspiration for lamps to be joined with the Zab Thig Dechen Rang Shar Lae, Zilnon Yeshe Kyi Khandroma Senge Dongpa Chan Gyi Choekor (Zab Thig dDe Chhen Rang Shar Las, Zil gNon Ye Shes Kyi mKha' 'Gro Ma Seng Ge gDong Pa Chan Gyi Chhos sKor). With that as a basis, later on when I was fifty-seven years of age, before the great pilgrimage place of Bodhanath Stupa (Bya Rung Kha Shor) in Nepal, at the feet of the great representative of Padmasambhava,

Dudjom Jigtral Yeshe Dorje (bDud 'Joms 'Jig Bral Ye Shes rDo rJe), from whom I was receiving initiations of Kama (bKa' Ma) and Terma (gTer Ma), during the intervening period when doing the tenth (Tsechu) and twenty-fifth day (Nyernga) practices I, Zilnon Lingpa (Zil gNon gLing Pa), (C.R. Lama), changed it slightly so as to make it suitable to join with any puja of the four schools.

དགེ་བསྔོ།

DEDICATION OF MERIT

དགེ་བ་འདི་ཡིས་མྱུར་དུ་བདག །

GE WA   DI   YI   NYUR DU   DAG
virtue   this   by   quickly   I

By this virtue may I quickly

པད་འབྱུང་གནས་འགྲུབ་གྱུར་ནས། །

PAD MA JUNG NE   DRUB GYUR   NAE
Padmasambhava,   established become,   and then
Guru Rinpoche   attain

Attain the state of the Lotus Born and then,

འགྲོ་བ་གཅིག་ཀྱང་མ་ལུས་པ། །

DRO WA   CHI KYANG   MA   LU PA
beings   one even   without   exception

All beings without exception,

དེ་ཡི་ས་ལ་འགོད་པར་ཤོག །

DE   YI   SA   LA   GOE PAR   SHO
that   of   state,   into   place, lead   may it happen
level

May I establish them in that state.

By this virtue may I quickly attain the state of the Lotus Born. Then may I establish all beings without exception in that same state.

སྤྱོད་འཇུག་ལས།

FROM THE BODHICARYAVATARA

ཕན་པར་བསམས་པ་ཙམ་གྱིས་ཀྱང་།

PHEN PAR	**SAM PA**	**TSAM GYI**	**KYANG**
benefit	*think*	*only*	*also*

When merely the thought of helping others

སངས་རྒྱས་མཆོད་ལས་ཁྱད་འཕགས་ན།

SANG GYE	**CHO**	**LAE**	**KYA PHAG**	**NA**
buddhas	*offering*	*than*	*excellent*	*thus*

Is more excellent than the worship of the Buddhas,

སེམས་ཅན་མ་ལུས་ཐམས་ཅད་ཀྱི།

SEM CHEN	**MA LUE**	**THAM CHE**	**KYI**
sentient beings	*without*	*all*	*genitive*

It is unnecessary even to mention the greatness of striving

བདེ་དོན་བརྩོན་པ་སྨོས་ཅི་དགོས།།

DE DON	**TSON PA**	**MOE CHI GOE**
benefit	*do*	*not necessary to mention*

For the happiness and welfare of all beings without exception.

When merely the thought of helping others is more excellent than the worship of the Buddhas, it is unnecessary even to mention the greatness of striving for the happiness and welfare of all beings without exception.

བསྟན་པ་རྒྱས་པའི་སྨོན་ལམ།

ASPIRATION FOR THE FLOURISHING OF DHARMA

ཉེར་འཚེ་མ་ལུས་ཞི་བ་དང་།

NYER TSE	MA LUE	ZHI WA	DANG
difficulties,	*without*	*pacify*	*and*
troubles	*exception*		

All difficulties without exception being pacified and

མཐུན་རྐྱེན་ནམ་མཁའི་མཛོད་བཞིན་དུ།

THUN	KYEN	NAM KAI	DZO	ZHIN DU
harmonious	*situations,*	*sky's,*	*treasure*	*like*
	reasons	*infinitely vast*		

With harmonious conditions like the treasure of the sky,

རྒྱལ་དབང་པདྨ་འབྱུང་གནས་ཀྱི།

GYAL	WANG	PAE MA JUNG NAE	KYI
Jina, Victor	*lord*	*Padmasambhava*	*of*

The powerful Victor Padmasambhava's

བསྟན་པ་ཡུན་རིང་འབར་གྱུར་ཅིག

TAN PA	YUN RING	BAR	GYUR CHIG
doctrine	*long life*	*shining*	*must*

Doctrines must live long and shine brightly!

ཨོཾ་ཨཱཿཧཱུྃ་བཛྲ་གུ་རུ་པདྨ་སི་དྡྷི་ཧཱུྃ༔

OM	AA	HUNG	BEN DZA	GU RU	PAE MA	SID DHI	HUNG
Body	*Speech*	*Mind*	*indestructible*	*guru*	*Padma-*	*accomplishment*	*give*
					sambhava		

Indestructible three kaya guru, Padmasambhava, grant us accomplishment!

All difficulties without exception being pacified, and with harmonious conditions like the treasure of the sky, the powerful Victor Padmasambhava's doctrines must live long and shine brightly! Indestructible three kaya guru, Padmasambhava, grant us accomplishment!

(All texts translated by C.R. Lama and James Low.)

Part 3

Radiant Aspiration

A Commentary
by
James Low

on

The Butterlamp Prayer
Lamp of Aspiration
by *Chimed Rigdzin, Zilnon Lingpa*

PRELIMINARIES

རང་རིག་ཀྱི་དམར་མོ་ཁྲི་ཐོད་འཛིན༔

དེའི་ཐུགས་ལས་སྤྲུལ་པའི་མཁའ་འགྲོ་མ༔

དཀར་གསལ་བཞིན་མཛེས་སྤྱན་གསུམ་ནམ་མཁར་གཟིགས༔

ཕྱག་གཉིས་ཐུགས་ཀར་ཐལ་མོ་སྦྱར་བའི་ནང༔

ཡིད་བཞིན་ནོར་བུ་དགོས་འདོད་ཀུན་འབྱུང་ལས༔

བགྱང་ཡས་འོད་ཟེར་དཔག་མེད་རབ་འཕྲོས་ཏེར༔

མཆོད་པའི་ལྷ་མོ་གྲངས་མེད་བགྱང་ལས་འདས༔

རབ་མཛེས་རྒྱན་ལྡན་ལྷ་མོ་རེ་རེ་ཡི༔

ཕྱག་ཏུ་ཕྱི་ནང་གསང་བའི་སྦྱིན་མེ་འཛིན༔

ཏྲིང་བུའི་ཆད་ནེ་མཁའ་ཡི་ལྷུགས་རེ་དང༔

མར་ཁུའི་ཆད་ནེ་རྒྱ་མཚོ་ཆེན་པོ་མཉམ༔

སྡོང་བུའི་ཆད་ནེ་རི་རྒྱལ་ལྷུན་པོ་དང༔

མེ་ལྕེའི་ཆད་ནེ་སྲིད་རྩེའི་བར་དུ་ཁྱབ༔

འོད་ནེ་ཕྱིམ་དང་ཕྱུར་འཕུམ་ལས་ལྷག༔

ནུས་པས་ཕྱི་ནང་སྣུན་པ་ཀུན་བསལ་ནས༔

འགྲོ་ཀུན་འཁོར་བའི་ཆད་ཚོང་རབ་བསྒྲིག་གྱུར༔

My awareness is the red dakini holding a curved knife and a skull cup. From my heart emanates a radiant white dakini who has the most wonderful face with three eyes looking at the sky. The palms of her two hands are joined together at her heart and hold the wish-fulfilling jewel, Source of all Satisfaction, from which numberless rays of light radiate out endlessly spreading countless offering goddesses.

These goddesses have the most beautiful ornaments and each holds one of the outer, inner and secret lamps in her hands. The lamp pots are the size of the ring of iron mountains that contains the world. Their quantity of oil equals a great ocean.

Their wicks are the size of Mt. Meru and their flames reach the top of the world. Their light is brighter than a million million suns. By their power all outer and inner darkness is cleared away and thus the fuel of samsara belonging to all beings is completely burned up.

Aspiration is a method for changing circumstances; it is a way of working with the energy which is our world. This particular aspiration commences with a visualisation in which we remove ourselves from identification with our habitual body of limitations, our personal identity determined by past events, cultural frames like race, age, and gender, and by the fixed beliefs about us held by ourselves and others. The infinity of creative imagination, the root of all manifestation, is accessed by transforming the site of our identity into a divine form. The divine forms are not constructs; they are not built up from ingredients, or from processes of cause and effect. Rather, they are the natural effulgence of the awakened state, and by entering into their dimension, we experience ourselves as an energy freed from conceptual reification. This is the basis for engaging in the practice, for it allows us to experience the immediacy of whatever is being described rather than just developing thoughts about it.

The first line describes how, in an instant, we become divine, *my awareness is the red dakini holding a curved knife and a skull cup.* That is to say, between our ordinary existence and our existence as the red dakini there is no gap. Awareness, which has no form, displays the activity form of the red dakini, symbolising the force which produces manifestation. The potential of the nature of the mind to manifest different forms is activated by reciting the text which operates as a secondary condition. The red dakini is dancing her freedom and joy. Her aroused expression shows her passionate connection with all that lives. The dakini holds a curved knife in her right hand for cutting-off ignorance and a skull-cup in her left to catch the blood. The idea implicit in this is that the life force which we all have, our basic potential, is trapped in attachment. Blood represents life; it is moving through our body all the time. Without blood in our body we are dead. Moreover, if we forget the blood flowing in our body we deaden ourselves by taking our body to be a fixed entity, a thing which exists in itself. The ceaseless energetic movement of life can be trapped by our habitual assumptions, so that we lose touch with the freshness of the flow of movement. The dakini, the vital energy force of movement, cuts off the head of our familiar conceptual body, freeing us to experience the myriad forms of our responsive becoming. She represents the freedom of desire, of energetic connection with the world, and in becoming her we are immediately transformed from our ordinary existence centred in our karmic body of flesh where we are trapped in self-referential hopes and desires.

As ourselves, in our own bodies, we each find that there are many things we have to protect. We want to make sure, for instance, that when we go out our car is still where we parked it; when we go home we hope that burglars have not gone into our house. So in our fixed identity, necessarily we must protect things, because we cannot maintain ourselves and our function in the world without some degree of protection. However, in order to develop an infinite gesture, such as offering many butterlamps and spreading universal compassion, we have to move from the profane state of a physical material body, an ego-identity, into the sacred space of the red dakini where this transformatory work is possible.

Here we are making an immediate change, like a fish leaping in a river, and in this we practice according to anuyoga where there is no gradual development. The simultaneous dropping of our ordinary identity and arising in the form of the red dakini is just like one wave falling back into the ocean while the next wave rises up.

Then out of the heart of myself as the red dakini, there arises a white shining dakini, hence *from my heart emanates a radiant white dakini*. The centre or heart of the dakini is emptiness. Forms always arise out of emptiness. Emptiness is the mother of all forms. Dakinis move in the sky, they are inseparable from the sky, and with that nature, they are the energy of the sky. The sky indicates the unborn, open dimension, the natural state without beginning or end. It rests on nothing, never changes and is beyond limit or conditioning. When we shift our ground from the narrow concerns of the ego to the infinity of space, our potential is freed to manifest whatever forms are fitting. The white dakini is the purity and freshness of awareness. She is standing and her body sways as she opens herself to all that appears. Manifesting from emptiness, she is the infinite richness and fecundity of space.

Padmasambhava has eight manifestations yet the real nature of each of these forms is the same. The unborn, undivided dharmakaya is the source of all he shows. The different forms arise as a response to different situations in the world. This is the same in our own lives. We often think that we are just ourselves, 'I'm just me,' but then somebody says, 'Oh, yesterday you were so angry.' 'Was I? Well, I'm not angry now.' The anger is gone, yet when we were angry we were angry. This is because the ego also slips through different identities in response to changing circumstances. Or rather each shift in our changing identity is appropriated by the ego as something real. So we end up manipulating images of ourselves rather than enjoying the play of possibilities.

The white dakini *has the most beautiful face with three eyes looking at the sky.* When we rest our gaze in the open blue sky, the infinite expanse before us reveals the infinite expanse within us. We gaze from sky to sky without the interruption of cloud-like thoughts. This unveils the clarity which is not based on effortful interpretation. Being open it reveals what is there and frees an immediate response which is fresh and fitting and not over-invested.

Opening to this experience requires that we relax our reliance on ourselves as the necessary, central agent, the one who has to control situations and ensure that things are done properly. Trusting our openness requires the releasing of the habitual knots which would tie us back into our familiar predictive patterns.

The palms of the white dakini's hands are joined together at her heart in the same manner as Chenrezig who also holds the wishfulfilling jewel in his two central hands. When our hands are held in this way the energetic circle running through the heart is completed and we feel energised. The body of the dakini is always an energetic body, a body of light and energy, just as our own bodies are bodies of light and energy. The trouble is we are so used to seeing our bodies as heavy, solid, and material. But that very materiality is itself a quality of energy; it is just a particular resonance or vibration.

Between the fingers of the dakini's hands she holds *the wish-fulfilling jewel, Source of all Satisfaction,* which provides whatever is needed. Many cultures have some notion of a cornucopia, the horn of plenty, or Annapurna ('Full of Grain') the goddess of grain and abundance, or the cow that always gives a plentiful supply of milk, or some other magical phenomenon that will supply whatever is required. In terms of the practice of this text, we need to remember that *everything* is the gift of the wishfulfilling gem, the fruitfulness of the inseparability of awareness and emptiness. Everything arises from emptiness, remains within emptiness, and then vanishes back from manifestation into the ground emptiness.

Being held at the heart in this way, the gem evokes awareness itself, for awareness, the relaxed, open nature of the mind, is the source of all that we need. Everything arises in awareness, and when we learn to relax and be present as awareness, everything we ever wanted is just there. The nature of our mind is open yet our habitual concerns generate a narrow focus that hides our own potential from us. This potential is not a personal possession but is the quality of our own awareness beyond appropriation. Yet our own beliefs easily disguise what is actually the case. This is why there are so many practices that help us to examine our reliance on concepts.

For example, if I really believe that I am *me,* that I am James, even if I spend many, many years doing tens of millions of mantras and dharanis and 'become' somebody else, even Padmasambhava or Arya Tara, I will not be liberated. This is because I will not have surrendered into the practice and become one with it. The practice will remain something that 'I' am doing. It will be ego-centred and the central point of reference will remain my sense of truly existing as myself. In this way all the energy of the practice can be wasted.

This is why we have to know that we are arising from emptiness and the white dakini is arising from emptiness: we both have the *same* nature. For if we think that we are real while the white dakini is a fantasy of our imagination, or a hope, or a symbol, we will remain in our limitation. So we have to investigate who we are and see if we can find any substantial basis for our own sense of having an individual, personal identity. Every day, all day, we attend to objects that seem to exist in themselves. Tables, chairs, tea-cups and so on, all seem to be separate entities that are defined by something within them. We then apply the same kind of identification to ourselves, believing that I am this specific entity which endures through all sorts of changes and experiences. 'I have my own essence and this is me.' Such a statement rings true for us most of the time – no matter how circular and self-serving it is. The imputed essence and the emergent moment of identity seem to be always the same despite the fact that the latter is always changing. Our constructs generate the world we know, including ourselves, and in the state of ignorance we take these constructs to be self-existing, just there by themselves.

In buddhism, awakening means to awaken from this hallucination, this fantasy that the world is full of real objects, of separately existing things. From the buddhist point of view, what I, as a reflecting self, as a thinking subject, have access to are mental events. The mind sees the mind's experience; within our usual frame of reference we have no capacity to have a direct experience with worldly things, because what we take to be 'things' are actually concepts, constructs.

Chimed Rigdzin Rinpoche often used to say to me, 'Don't mix your food with your shit'. This is very good advice. It is very important because in our ordinary perception, food, the fresh moment, and shit, the stale assumption, are mixed together. Moment-by-moment we have beautiful, wonderful, alive, fresh experience, but we mix it with the shit of our ignorance, our reification, our habitual patterns of belief. One of the powerful beliefs we have is that 'it is all up to me'. 'If I don't do it, it won't happen.' 'I have to become enlightened.' This creates the sense that enlightenment itself is a construct, something which is produced by effort. Yet even in the story of awakening of Shakyamuni Buddha, his breakthrough occurred when he just sat and stopped trying. He sat under the bodhi tree, and let go of all the practices he had learned. He stopped striving, and without collapsing found his balance and this in itself released all the obstacles and obscurations.

For six years he had been trying and trying, doing every kind of yoga and meditation, but he gained the result when he saw that he was not going to get the result. So, the result came to the one who was not waiting for the result, who was not trying to get the result. In the same way, when we relax our concepts the world is transformed.

Buddhist prayers often say, 'Please bless me by cutting the root of ignorance'. If we see the problem as existing in each of the objects we encounter in the world, then we have to change each object as it arises. This is like cutting the leaves off a tree one by one in order to kill the tree. But it is a very, very big tree! Whereas, if you recognise that the root of all the phenomena you experience is your own mind, then, through meditation, by directly seeing the nature of your own mind, you recognise it as infinitely open. Then all thoughts, feelings, memories and projections are recognised to be the dream-like appearances of emptiness, for out of emptiness only emptiness can come. The mind is empty and it is clear, a clarity which reveals manifold forms, none of which has ever been born as a truly existing real entity.

When you look for your mind you can't find it, and all the stuff that fills it is empty of true nature, being ephemeral and ungraspable. Emptiness is inseparable from awareness and clarity; everything has the quality of clarity, even headaches or depression and despair are clarity. But from the point of view of the ego I don't want despair, I don't want to be depressed; I want to be happy. This is the ordinary position of the ego: it wants always to be happy. Then because we like some experiences and we don't like others, we think that the experiences we don't want are bad, while the others are good. Therefore we continue with our dualistic conception, trying to attract the things we like, while pushing away the things we don't like. But from the point of view of meditation, everything that arises, arises from the mind and is not different from the nature of the mind. Therefore, to make discriminations, and say *this* is good, inherently good, especially good, and *that* is bad, inherently bad, especially bad, is to experience false or mistaken perception.

So, to return to the text, it describes how *numberless rays of light radiate out endlessly* from the wish-fulfilling gem, each giving rise to *countless offering goddesses*. This style of offering takes inspiration from the aspiration of the bodhisattva Samantabhadra. He imagined that on each grain of sand in the River Ganges, there were as many buddhas as there are grains of sand in the whole of the River Ganges. Each of them, in turn, is surrounded by as many bodhisattvas as there are grains of sand in the Ganges. This infinite multiplication causes every construct to collapse, encouraging a limitless participation. *Samantabhadra's Aspiration* is given in its brief form earlier in this book (see page 20).

This meditation practice evokes an infinite view of countless world systems and huge expanses of time, in order to take the closed sense of self and stretch it out so much that it pops like a balloon, and a new kind of sense of presence arises. Usually you can only stretch the ego so far, for it keeps trying to spring back to its familiar sense of self. At a certain point, however, the ego collapses and there is a new form of knowing, an awareness which is a completely different mode of experiencing, one which is not self-reflective or self-reflexive and so avoids all invitations to entrapment. Dzogchen points the way to being present with how things are: whatever comes, comes; whatever goes, goes. Awareness does not settle into things as they arise but remains relaxed and present and allows them to move. That is very, very different from our usual anxious involvement. The role of the teacher is to give knowledge of the path of immediate experience that is not limited by the many different kinds of events. So without worrying about our current capacity we are encouraged to trust the practice and enter the domain of this infinite generosity.

When we offer the lamps we are entering into a transaction with those to whom we offer them. The prayer and the actual lamps we might burn are a means or a method for experiencing a dynamic dialogue with the divine beings, the enlightened ones. We offer up the lamps and they respond by fulfilling our wishes for universal awakening. They are happy to help, that is why they manifest, and when we make an offering it opens a track of communication through which they can rapidly meet our request.

They are happy to do this. It is their function. There is no uncertainty or chance in the process as long as it is done with full faith and focused attention. We are not making a humble request to a figure much more powerful than ourselves, one who may be indifferent to our needs. Our wishes will be fulfilled because they are in harmony with the intentions of the enlightened ones. The act of offering is not merely symbolic – it has an actual direct impact on what occurs. It is a practice of effective participation in the non-dual energy field which is our world. We are working with circumstances by mobilising forces which are always available. We are not mere passive supplicants.

When we do the practice in a group setting it is important that we stay in rhythm, all on the same beat, as this harmony not only increases our sense of collaboration as sangha, it also strengthens the power of our intention. The beneficial synergy helps fulfil our aspiration; our practice increases our faith and our faith deepens our practice. Faith contains us, helps us settle, trust and open. It also protects us from distraction because faith is a focus that orients our energy, aligning it with the practice so that we are not looking for anything better or more interesting. We become fulfilled and satisfied in what we are doing.

We cannot stop bad things happening, for we are in samsara, a domain of chaos where life is not fair. But we can learn to work with circumstances so that we optimise the potential of any situation. Although we want light to prevail over darkness, goodness to prevail over evil, we cannot do this by getting rid of the dark, the bad, the frightening. By not running away, by not trying to cut off from or suppress the things we do not like, we can face them, see how they operate, and then learn to work with them as they are. Collaborating with their energy we remain active, dynamic, flexible and thereby able to change and adapt creatively without feeling overwhelmed or trapped. Fear increases the sense of duality, of the fundamental split between subject and object, self and other. But when we work with circumstances we participate in the undivided field of manifestation and in working for the welfare of all, our own fulfilment comes automatically.

These goddesses have the most beautiful ornaments and they are very attractive, so that when they offer their gifts, whoever sees them will be charmed by them. This is not the heroic path of sacrifice; they are not burning their hands or their bodies. This is much more charming, seductive, and joyous, creating a mood of expansive radiance, in harmony with *the outer, inner and secret lamps in their hands.*

The *outer* lamp is the kind that we burn in a house, ordinary butterlamps or any kind of illuminating lamp. The *inner* lamps are the lamps of the practices that we do, which bring illumination to us and connect our awareness to our being in the world. And the *secret* lamp is the unborn lamp of our own awareness, the quality of clarity and luminosity, which is the nature of the mind itself. We imagine the pots of these lamps are huge, *the size of the ring of iron mountains that contains the world.* Each contains an infinite supply of fuel, as *their quantity of oil equals a great ocean.* Effortless bounty and ease of giving are the mood of these goddesses who are the radiance of our own unborn awareness.

These huge lamps burn up all the outer darkness, which can bring fear and danger, as when you are walking on your own through the forest in the night. They also dispel the inner darkness of not recognising your own mind. All this is cleared by the brightness of the lamps, whose *wicks are the size of Mt Meru*, which is described as being over two hundred kilometres high. *Their flames reach the top of the world* illuminating every kind of terrain so there is no place for darkness to hide, for *their light is brighter than a million million suns.* This light also penetrates all beings, bringing illumination that ends ignorance, hence *by its power all outer and inner darkness is cleared away.* Due to this, *the fuel of samsara belonging to all beings is completely burned up.* The karmic fuel of each sentient being, the accumulations of pent-up energy which keeps them revolving in samsara, is burned up leaving them unburdened, at peace, and able to relax into their own natural awareness. The light of these millions of suns burns up habitual reliance on concepts as the determinants of reality, freeing the space for spontaneous clarity free of impulse, patterns and fixation.

ན་མོ་རཏྣ་ཏྲ་ཡཱ་ཡཿ ན་མོ་བྷ་ག་ཝ་ཏེཿ
བཛྲ་སཱ་ར་པྲ་མ་རྡ་ནེཿ ཏ་ཐཱ་ག་ཏཱ་ཡཿ
ཨཪ་ཏ་ཏེཿ སམྱཀ་སཾ་བུ་དྡྷ་ཡཿ ཏ་དྱ་ཐཱ
ཨོཾ་བཛྲེ་བཛྲེ་མ་ཧཱ་བཛྲེ་མ་ཧཱ་ཏེ་ཛོ་བཛྲེ
མ་ཧཱ་བི་དྱཱ་བཛྲེ་མ་ཧཱ་བོ་དྷི་ཙི་ཏྟ་བཛྲེ
མ་ཧཱ་བོ་དྷི་མཎྜོ་པ
སཾ་ཀྲ་མ་ཎ་བཛྲེ་སརྦ་ཀརྨཿ
ཨ་ཝ་ར་ཎི་བི་ཤུ་དྡྷ་ནེ་བཛྲེ་ཡེ་སྭ་ཧཱཿ
ཨོཾ་བཛྲ་དྷརྨ་ར་ཎི་ཏཿ པ་ར་ཎི་ཏཿ
སོ་པ་ར་ཎི་ཏཿ སརྦ་བུ་དྡྷ་ཀྵེ་ཏྲཿ
པ་ཙ་ལི་ཏཿ པྲ་ཛྙཱ་པཱ་ར་མི་ཏཿ
ནཱ་ད་སྭ་བྷཱ་ཝེ་བཛྲ་དྷརྨ་ཏེ་ཧྲི་ད་ཡཿ
སནྟོ་ཥ་ཎི་ཧཱུྃ་ཧཱུྃ་ཧོ་ཧོ་ཧོ་ཨཱཿ སྭ་ཧཱཿ

Salutation to the Three Jewels. Salutation to the Perfect Ones. Vajra essence. Great gift. All Tathagatas, Arhats, Samyak Sambuddhas are like that. Om. Vajra, vajra, great vajra, great shining vajra. Great vidya vajra. Great bodhicitta vajra. Great enlightenment's meaning.

Coming out by stages, all deeds like vajras. Experience becomes very pure and strong. Om Vajradharma jewel. Long life. Excellent life. All buddha realms. Knowledge. Transcendent wisdom. Sound naturally has vajra dharma essence. Satisfying all, they rise out endlessly filling the sky.

Then we come to this long dharani, a long, complex mantra of purification. It is a sequence of powerful images, symbols of great value which
empower and validate the practice that is to follow. It is important
to recite this mantra in a loud, clear voice so that its energising vibration can create its full effect. This effect is both on the environment
around us, the infinity of the world system, and on ourselves as the
white dakini, further establishing us in the power and simplicity of the
fulfilment of the practice.

We are not reciting these words in the ordinary sense of talking *about*
something, but rather, the saying of the words gives rise to a direct *felt*
presence which we inhabit. From emptiness sound arises; the sound is
not different from emptiness. It has no essence, no innate meaning.
Whatever meaning we experience sounds as having, arises from our
own attribution. The true meaning and value of this recitation arises
from the potential released by its sound. The cognitive meaning is
secondary yet useful since it gives us an anchor that we are familiar
with. Firstly we evoke the Three Jewels, the Buddha, the Dharma and
the Sangha assembly, along with all the aspects of refuge and protection
including the guru, the meditation deities and the dakinis or communicative goddesses. In particular we evoke the great refuge of our own
enlightened nature, dharmakaya, sambhogakaya and nirmanakaya:
salutation to the Three Jewels. Salutation to the Perfect Ones.

Vajra essence! Great gift! All Tathagatas. Vajra essence means the quality
of emptiness, the indestructible heart of all things. Great gift indicates
expansiveness; emptiness is everywhere, a gift that awaits us wherever we turn. All the Tathagatas, the Buddhas, the *Arahats,* and the
Samyak Sambuddhas are like that. By this we evoke the presence of the
ones who are awakened to their inseparability from emptiness. We use
these powerful presences to ensure the purest of dharma motivation
and understanding so that the offering will be devoid of our usual ego
concerns.

Om. Vajra, vajra, great vajra, great shining vajra. Emptiness is the
unchanging basis of all forms, the root of wisdom and compassion.
Emptiness is not a new kind of super-entity or a metaphysical truth. It
is not something that can be or needs to be established by proposition,
analysis or belief. Rather 'it' is what is there when we stop creating
things, when we cease from the mental activity which creates our outer
and inner worlds and fills them with stuff. This vajra or indestructible

nature shines forth as all the realms of experience, the moments of radiance. *Great vidya vajra. Great bodhicitta vajra.* Awareness itself (vidya) is inseparable from emptiness (vajra). When we exist as a self referential consciousness we feel ourselves to be 'something', me, myself, something that is here. But the root of this is awareness which is not a thing and which cannot be located anywhere. Bodhicitta, our minds intrinsic presence, the basis of an all encompassing compassionate response, is also inseparable from emptiness and cannot be found anywhere as a thing to be appropriated. All arising phenomena, everything which has a beginning, will inevitably come to an end. Only emptiness, our open unborn ground is unchanging and unconditioned. It is the great source of all purity; it is never mixed with anything else as all arisings are always already integrated in its non-duality. This is *great enlightenment's meaning.*

When we relax our preoccupations and judgements and attend to what is actually occurring we can see a natural ordering, an autopoiesis, bringing pattern and function. *Coming out by stages, all deeds like vajras.* There is no need then for us to struggle to be in control, for we are moving easily in this emergent field of non-duality, hence *experience becomes very pure and strong.* In experiencing our nature, our source, as indestructible, we have freedom to enjoy the ungraspable flow of moments. This jewel-like radiant wisdom is free of birth and death. *Om. Vajradharma jewel. Long life.* Although we tend to be focused on the details of our daily lives, the awareness which illuminates this has the capacity to illuminate infinite possibilities, *excellent life. All buddha realms.* In not limiting ourselves to the familiar intoxication of the details of life maintenance, there is a door to knowledge of infinite realms, a knowledge which simultaneously reveals the infinity of awareness. *Knowledge. Transcendent wisdom.*

Sound links infinite silence to infinite noise, the commotion of manifestation. We don't have to choose one or the other, it is not an either/or, for manifestation is empty. *Sound* is the energy of emptiness, it *naturally has vajra dharma essence.* The pure sound of the heart beat of all the buddhas is always with us. This nurturing guide which satisfies us and leads us home is here symbolised by an endless stream of HUNGs and HOs rising out and filling the sky, *satisfying all, they rise out endlessly filling the sky.*

In samsara there is always a danger that we will lose our openness to events and become small and self-protective. For example, when we become angry or sad our world shrinks, and we shrink, becoming obsessed and caught up in the upsetting situation. The best release from this retraction is to be able to instantly recollect our innate spaciousness which is unchanging. This presence immediately reveals the transient and illusory nature of the troubling event. It cannot catch you in your true nature, and so there is no basis for being limited by it. When we imagine the infinite sky, full of offering goddesses with rays of light and infinite offerings, we are opening our mind to its own ground. The nature of the mind is infinite awareness within which all kind of appearances are arising. With this practice we experience our mind as vast and rich in the treasures of its wonderful display. This is a powerful way of avoiding collapsing into identification with narrow ideas.

When a person, a subject, becomes involved with an object there is always disappointment for no object can be caught. Objects, appearances, are inherently transient and elusive. What seems to be stable is only our concept. The actual object, which is only accessible to us as an experience, is ungraspable.

In fact it is the object that always 'gets' the subject, for the subject keeps turning around the object giving more and more of its power to it. Thus we become caught-up in the things that we become attached to. They catch us. When objects catch us we develop intentions based on our hopes and fears. These intentions lead us to perform actions which have immediate effects as well as consequences which manifest later. The karmic potency of these actions gives rise to further thoughts and feelings, and this turbulence leads to rebirth again and again in samsara.

Reciting this mantra and entering the dimension of its sound relaxes our pre-occupation with, and reliance upon, conceptual meaning, and allows us to rest in infinite awareness free of attachments. This is the state in which we recite the rest of the prayer. Our words arise as self-liberating sound, the radiance of the mind of all the buddhas.

OFFERING THE LAMPS

ཧཱུྃ༔ ཆོས་དབྱིངས་ཀུན་ལ་ཁྱད་པའི་སྣོད་དུ་རུ༔

དོན་དམ་བྱང་ཆུབ་སེམས་ཀྱི་མར་ཁུ་འཁྱིལ༔

མི་རྟོག་ཏིང་ངེ་འཛིན་གྱི་སྡོང་བུ་ལ༔

རིག་པ་རང་བྱུང་གསལ་བའི་མེ་ལྕེ་འབར༔

ཉོན་མོངས་གཏི་མུག་རྟོག་པ་རང་སར་གྲོལ༔

མ་སྤང་ཆོས་ཉིད་དེ་བཞིན་སྐྱོང་དུ་ཞིམ༔

ཆོས་དབྱིངས་ཡེ་ཤེས་རང་བཞིན་འོད་ཟེར་འཚེར༔

འགྲོ་བའི་མ་རིག་མུན་པ་སེལ་ཕྱིར་དུ༔

བླ་མ་སངས་རྒྱས་རིགས་ཀྱི་ལྷ་ཚོགས་ལ༔

འབུལ་ལོ་བཞེས་ནས་མཆོག་ཐུན་དངོས་གྲུབ་སྩོལ༔

Wonderful! In the pot of all-pervading hospitable space swirls the oil of non-dual awareness. On the wick of absorbed contemplation free of dualistic thoughts the flame of the self-existing clarity of awareness burns bright. Thoughts arising from the affliction of stupidity are liberated in their own place. Without being rejected they dissolve in the vastness of the actuality of what is.

Original knowing as hospitable space manifests as shining rays of light. In order to dispel the darkness of ignorance of all sentient beings we offer this to the guru and the gods of the Buddha clan. Please accept and then bestow supreme and general accomplishments.

'Ho', wonderful!, is a vocative. It evokes our availability, opens us up; it has a kind of joyous tone to it. All the verses that follow have the same structure as this one. They each take the image of the butterlamp and use it to reveal different aspects of dharma by giving each part of the lamp different symbolic associations. This is a common literary style in Tibetan, one that is seen as being very polished because of its pattern of repetition and minimal structural variation. In modern English poetry and novel writing, repetition is rarely admired. We do not want to see the same adjective used twice on the same page; that is judged to be poor style. Whereas, in this kind of composition, repetition and variation on a theme build up meaning through resonance and this is felt to intensify the impact. It is similar to a musical composition where a phrase is repeated with nuanced variation. The idea is not to free associate into new pathways but to bring the reader into the state of simplicity that, paradoxically, arises from ever deepening complexity.

In this first verse the first line describes the lamp-pot as being *all-pervading hospitable space*. The containing vessel is the dharmadhatu, the infinite hospitality which welcomes each appearance just as it is. This spaciousness has no beginning and no end, no top and no bottom, and is without limit of any kind. Everything everywhere is the pot. Within it *swirls the oil of non-dual awareness*. The swirling clarified butter of pervasive absolute truth bodhicitta, pure awareness, is present everywhere as there is no limit to non-duality.

Absolute truth bodhicitta is the direct experience of the fact that no beings have ever come into existence nor has any suffering, for all appearance is an illusion. Absolute truth refers to what is there when all judgements, projections, interpretations and so on are cleared away. No object that we encounter, including ourselves, has any true inherent self-essence. All that appears has no intrinsic essence for it is an illusion. The actual nature of all phenomena is emptiness, the absence of a substantial existence. Yet, clearly, many 'things' arise. The absence of entities is not just an absence, for there is the presence of nothing, a presence which takes the form of all that we are familiar with. These appearances are like rainbows – they are there yet are ungraspable, being without any substance. Any substance that we experience them as having is an attribution made by us; it is the manifestation of the delusion we hold that the world is full of separate, internally defined things. Due to our belief in duality we concretise our experience, generating the felt sense of being an individual subject inherently separate from the environment which surrounds us. This belief is shared by all beings in samsara; it is the basic cause of our suffering and confusion.

To recognise and abide in the open, empty nature of all phenomena is to be free of suffering. To see, to directly experience, the emptiness of all beings is true compassion for it offers no confirmation of the delusion which torments them. Not only do sentient beings not recognise their own nature but they impute a causal force to events which are actually like a dream. Taking the dream to be 'real' we imagine that our suffering is created by actual 'real' events – and so we feel persecuted and become determined to control the flow of events. In trying to control situations which cannot be controlled we become unhelpfully busy and endlessly frustrated. If I see you suffering, and I affirm the true existence of you and your suffering, then my attitude, even if it shows compassion towards you in your suffering, is not very helpful. Paradoxically, if I *don't* take your suffering seriously, that is actually more helpful! Moments of pain and difficulty pass but when we affirm their 'real' existence this ensures that our dualistic view continues. It is this limiting attitude which is the basis of the present and future suffering of all beings.

The true quality of compassion lies in offering space to sentient beings; a relaxed spaciousness which resolves all the tensions, hopes and fears that arise from the habitual thought that 'I truly exist'. However, we generally take each other very seriously. We worry if our actions or our words will upset others. Then we become uptight and so does the other person, causing a mutually confirming vibrational movement, the best outcome of which is that one 'person' tries to help another 'person'. Whereas the natural state of absolute truth bodhicitta is very open and relaxed. It is not careless, but is carefree, an attitude of non-reification and non-solidification. This is the butter or fuel without any limit. The term bodhicitta – literally mind of awakening or awakening mind – has many meanings, from the dualistic, or relative truth, intention to help beings, through the sense of vitality of our potentiality, to the infinite unborn awareness, a simple presence devoid of characteristics.

What is being referred to here is a compassion where you engage in saving all sentient beings with the understanding that, from the very beginning, not one sentient being has ever really existed. This is "compassion arising in the manner of a dream", a compassion free of activity. Our experience of ourselves and others as separate, individual beings is a delusion. Sentient beings arise from ignorance, from not seeing how it is. A mistaken perception becomes the basis of their identity. Generally speaking, it is very difficult to get other people to change their minds. This is particularly true regarding the core beliefs a person has about their character, qualities, and autonomous existence. The only way to 'save' them is to know that they do not exist as entities. Then we are not limiting ourselves or others, or blocking the potential for integration. As is said in the Prajnaparamita literature, a bodhisattva saves sentient beings by knowing there are no sentient beings to be saved.

Into the nurturing butter of non-dual awareness is set *the wick of absorbed contemplation free of dualistic thought*. This does not mean that there are no thoughts, but rather that the arising and passing of thought does not determine or condition the continuity of absorbed contemplation.

It is not thought itself that is the problem, but how you stand in relation to it. When you recognise the emptiness of your own mind, you don't stand in relationship to thoughts, because non-duality is not a relationship. That is why the text says, 'without thought', yet there are thoughts! So often we look to thoughts for the answer to our problems as we struggle to think of a solution. Yet since our problems are created from our reliance on thoughts, a solution composed of thoughts tends to create its own problems – and so we go on, wandering in samsara, asking the causes of our problems to provide the solution.

As is often the case with this kind of text the language is very subtle because it is trying to describe experiences which are really on the other side of language, beyond expression. So, it is important to try to understand the function of the words correctly, but without becoming an expert intellectual taking a narcissistic delight in knowing what is what. Rather, we need to allow these profound words, full of the wisdom of the tradition to move inside us and give our mind a gentle massage to help it relax.

In this pot you have a stick, the wick, which here is said to be composed of absorbed contemplation, *ting nge dzin*, in Tibetan. *Ting nge* means deep, undisturbed, and *dzin*, which usually means to hold, here means aligned with. So *ting nge dzin* means just calm and clear, going deep, not being disturbed, without attachment to thoughts, so that whatever arises just passes through.

On this wick *the flame of the self-existing clarity of awareness burns bright.* This clarity arises by itself, for it is the mind's nature to shine. Two examples are often used to illustrate this. When a young person is active and healthy, the skin on their face glows and you can feel the health radiating from it. It is also compared to the rays of light which flow ceaselessly from the sun. The rays are not called forth by second-ary causes or anything else. The self-existing, self-arising radiance of our mind is inexhaustible and effortless.

Awareness is always youthful, always fresh, for it is relaxed and open to how things are, whereas, the ego is always old, being burdened with karma from the distant past. Our ego is conditioned by the events of this life so that by the time we are old enough to take responsibility for ourselves we are already full of attitudes, beliefs, habits, and assump-tions which we have taken in and incorporated from our environment. What we take to be 'I, me, myself' is always co-created with the world. In absorbing so much information at home, at school, with friends, we are simultaneously empowered and limited. The more we learn, the more difficult it can be to trust our relaxed spontaneity which functions between the extremes of impulsivity and thoughtful consideration.

Generally speaking, life will provide what we need if we stay close to the basics. But if we feel too responsible, if we feel that it is all up to us, we actually lose contact with the source of our energy. Of course we need to make an effort, but we can make the effort with the energy which is naturally flowing out of our own awareness by staying in non-dual participation. This is very different from mobilising an individual, personal will-power.

When the three aspects described in the first three lines are in place and ignited, their collaborative synergy gives rise to the brilliant flame of the radiance of the self-arising clarity of awareness. Each of us has this clarity which reveals everything we experience, including ourselves. Each of us has all beings in our mind. This might seem like a logical impossibility since we can seem so small, locked in our little skin bag, while the world is so big. Yet the infinite hospitable space, the ground of our own presence has room for everything. Each mind contains everything yet it is not awakened to this due to pre-occupation with the limiting concerns of being this and that. Actually, each of us is the container, or field, or ground of all beings and also, simultaneously, an arising within the minds of all beings. Each of us is both the centre-less centre of the spontaneous richness of all possibilities, and just this precise, unique moment of arising. The integration of these three modes: infinite, rich and precise, frees us from the sense of being a limited vulnerable entity anxiously concerned about what others think of us. Awareness is inseparable from unborn emptiness, the ever-open ground. Its clarity is effortlessly arising, revealing the entire field of experience in an instant. And within this field, rays of energy radiate as our activities of walking, sitting, speaking, sleeping; infinitely vital, present, alive yet ungraspable, beyond being an object of thought. And here is the paradox of dharma teaching, that so many words are used to say the unsayable. Yet, the speaking or the writing is not a mere transfer of concepts from one mind to another but the evoking of the always already present, awakening to it in this shared moment of non-dual experience.

Usually, we are trapped in busy self-preoccupation, the felt sense of me-in-here-inside-myself-with-my-thoughts, a private, personal world with a high threshold over which we may or may not move in order to be with others, who are also essentially isolated monads pursuing their own private visions. When we relax out of that foreclosure and return to our actual nature, we are automatically less estranged from the world. Then we can allow our free participation – letting words and gestures flow into the emerging field of which we are an inalien-able part. The open ground is the basis of our capacity to respond and it requires little conceptual elaboration. We are part of the world; it is the current site of our activity and so we can be at ease. The more we relax the more we find ourselves here.

With the clarity just described, *thoughts arising from the affliction of stupidity are liberated in their own place.* What is the troubling attitude of stupidity? The Tibetan term, *ti mug,* carries the idea of dullness and heaviness. It is the quality of stupefaction and thickening which arises in the process of becoming a separate self, of becoming dependent on assumptions to make sense of what is going on. We can be intelligent and know lots of things, yet still be 'stupid', for this term points to our habit of taking our usual frame of reference for granted. It points to being confused and deluded so that one takes the familiar and stale to be fresh and new. Due to this one can be ceaselessly excited about things which have little true value – like watching the news on the TV all the time. This attitude, this positioning and all that arises from it, is liberated in its own place when we awaken to where we are.

The thoughts that arise from stupidity are not truly bad or dangerous. They themselves are the radiance of awareness, but when *mis*-taken, when taken via reification and identification, they function in a limiting manner. As soon as we directly experience their own ground, their actual source, they are seen for what they are and they self-liberate i.e. they go free where they are without leaving a trace. Normally, thoughts are sticky, they stick to each other in chains of signifiers and they leave a slimy trace linking past, present, and future. When they are recognised as momentary arisings they go free, they vanish and leave no impact, conditioning or mark.

We are not seeking to purify stupidity and its thoughts; it is not as if something has to be changed into something else. Rather, by relaxing into the natural state there is no basis for attachment or identification and also no entity to be harnessed by these thoughts. They come and go without causing trouble. They don't need to be purified or liberated – so no effort is required as they go free right where they are. This is an experience we can have directly in the meditation. It is not abstract philosophy to be thought about nor a dogma to be believed. It is a path to be entered on.

Each thought, feeling or sensation has arisen in the mind, out of the mind, and when it goes, it goes back into the mind. A traditional example used to illustrate this is the ocean and the wave. Out of the ocean, a wave arises. The wave looks different from the ocean; it has a particular shape with spray coming off it. But it has the same nature as the ocean. When the wave comes back into the ocean, it merges into the ocean without difference, because the nature of the wave and the ocean was always the same. But in the moment that the wave was a wave it appeared to be something existing in itself. 'Look, there is a wave!' The wave, by itself, without effort being applied by anything else, goes back into the ocean. Thoughts arise and pass away. If you truly observe your mind, you can see that each appearance that arises goes free by itself.

This is the deep meaning of impermanence. On the outer level, we study impermanence through thinking of the waxing and waning of the moon, the changes of the seasons, the fact that we get older, and so on. But on the subtle level, when we truly observe our mind, we see that moment-by-moment everything is changing. This applies to all that we take to be the subject, and all that we take to be an object. The one we take to be the thinker, our felt sense of self, is just another transient thought. The thought that arises passes, and when it passes, if we allow it to pass, it will leave no trace. Usually, however, we are attached to the thoughts that arise and so we interfere and block the natural self-liberation of arisings. That is to say, one mode of transient energy, the thought, adheres to another mode of transient energy, the thinker, the subject. My sense of myself is itself just a thought, a thought that needs other thoughts to create a 'self'. The quality of this attachment is stupidity, the dullness which obscures the actual nature of the knower, the thinker: unborn, radiant awareness. It is this habit of mistaking which is let go of through the actualisation of the meaning of this verse.

When we experience a thought as being self-existing, as existing as a substance, we simultaneously constitute ourselves as an individual self-referential subject. Then towards the various thoughts that arise we have a reaction of attraction or aversion. We want to hang on to the 'good' thoughts, the good sensations, the good experiences, and we want to get rid of the 'bad' thoughts and bad experiences. Because this process of attraction-repulsion is going on all the time it seems completely natural and habitual to us. We never, therefore, get the chance to experience the self-liberation of phenomena; we are always too involved in trying to influence what is going on.

So, that is why self-liberation is such an important term. On an outer level, we might say we want to renounce samsara. That can mean, becoming a monk or a nun; turning our back on the 'outer' pleasures of the world. At a deeper level, though, to renounce samsara means to let go of attraction and repulsion, to drop them as an unnecessary interference in the natural self-liberation of all phenomena.

Thus by releasing our need for control, previously problematic tendencies cease to trouble us, hence *without being rejected they dissolve in the vastness of the actuality of what is*. Without having to sort them out or push them away, when there is no unnecessary activity, all thoughts effortlessly dissolve by themselves. They melt back into the space of unchanging actuality. The actuality of objects free of any conceptual elaboration is spacious emptiness itself. When we stop interpreting, describing, making sense of things, when we stop telling them what they are, there is space for manifestations to reveal what they are. And what they are is beyond speech, thought or expression. There is nothing for the mind to do so it relaxes and opens like a flower. It opens until it is open like the sky, just as it has always been. As all the busy activity subsides mind is revealed as it is, as ungraspable awareness. The great renunciation is the renunciation of ego's central role in the drama of existence. So in the meditation the key instruction is to stay relaxed and open. Whatever comes, comes. Whatever goes, goes. Stay relaxed and open. Do not edit your experience. Don't try to improve it. Without having to get rid of thoughts or entities they will dissolve by themselves, through their own nature, into the natural state.

The light rays arise spontaneously from the unchanging state of original knowing which is inseparable from hospitable space. The capacity to be present in knowing the source, the field of experience, and the movement of one's energy, is light and clear and illuminating. Hence *original knowing as hospitable space manifests as shining rays of light.* The preoccupation and foreclosure of stupidity, assumption and habit has been let go of, revealing the primordial space of knowing. It is a state of knowing, not of fixed knowledge. Alive and present, it is naked, raw, and unconditioned. This is the opening of the central area of the mandala, as poison and impediment are transformed into wisdom. When the function of stupidity is liberated on its own natural ground, it reveals the effortless quality of original knowing. Limitation is transformed into relaxed openness. The former operated without awareness of its own ground while the latter is always already integrated with that ground.

In order to dispel the darkness of ignorance of all sentient beings, we further enrich the quality of this radiance by offering it *to the guru and the gods of the Buddha clan.* The Buddha clan or family are the deities residing in the section of the mandala arising from the purification of stupidity. We offer it to them because we want all beings, including ourselves, to awaken to our natural condition.

We offer the radiance of the natural state to our guru, the one who shows us this nature as our own nature. We offer it to the deities associated with this wisdom. Although we say *please accept and then bestow supreme and general accomplishments*, there is no doubt that they will accept and be available. That is the very nature of their being. The offering immediately brings their response, which arises in the form of rays of light spreading out to all beings, removing their obscurations and awakening them to the accomplishment of liberation. This is not an accomplishment built up on the basis of activity but is the revelation of the natural purity of their own nature.

If you have time you can recite each verse very slowly so that the meaning of each line comes alive in you, and you experience it directly. Through this you come to inhabit a field of light in which everything you know is there but without the sense of solidity that hooks our usual assumptions, judgements, and projections. This is the experience we wish for all sentient beings.

ཧྰུྃ༔ ཕྱོགས་མེད་མཐའ་དབུས་བྲལ་བའི་གོང་བུ་རུ༔

ཞེན་པ་གཞི་ལ་གྲོལ་བའི་མར་ཁུ་འཁྱིལ༔

བདག་གསལ་རང་ངོ་ཤེས་པའི་སྡོང་བུ་ལ༔

རིག་པ་རང་གསལ་འཁར་བའི་མེ་ལྕེ་འབར༔

ཉོན་མོངས་ཞེ་སྡང་རྟོག་པ་རང་སར་གྲོལ༔

མ་སྤང་གསལ་སྟོང་གཉིས་མེད་ཀློང་དུ་ཐིམ༔

མེ་ལོང་ཡེ་ཤེས་རང་བཞིན་འོད་ཟེར་འཆོར༔

འགྲོ་བའི་མ་རིག་མུན་པ་སེལ་ཕྱིར་དུ༔

བླ་མ་རྡོ་རྗེ་རིགས་ཀྱི་ལྷ་ཚོགས་ལ༔

འབུལ་ལོ་བཞེས་ནས་མཆོག་ཐུན་དངོས་གྲུབ་སྩོལ༔

Wonderful! In the pot free of bias, without centre or circumference swirls the oil of the liberation of attachment on the natural ground. On the wick of knowing one's own nature of happiness and clarity, the flame of the arising of the natural clarity of awareness burns bright. Thoughts arising from the affliction of anger are liberated in their own place. Without being rejected they dissolve in the vastness of the non-duality of clarity and emptiness.

Original knowing as mirroring manifests as shining rays of light. In order to dispel the darkness of ignorance of all sentient beings we offer this to the guru and the gods of the Vajra clan. Please accept and then bestow supreme and general accomplishments.

In this verse *the pot* has no tendency, bias or prejudice, *being without centre or circumference.* Usually, we enter a situation with a bias, a preference which we maintain by selective attention. Our orientation is often as basic as, 'I know what I like and I like what I know.' This generates a kind of safety because we can act to avoid being consciously in contact with anything we don't like. It is as if we have already chosen before we enter a situation and so we avoid the open potential of the new moment. What is happening? What shall I do? The anxiety that this uncertainty can generate is diminished if we rest in our prejudices. However, there is a price to pay for this. We remain cut off from the full richness of the evolving situation and miss out on experiencing new aspects of our potential. To be without bias is to remain open, to be fresh to what arises without maintaining or defending a pre-established position. This is only possible when we relax into the natural state of awareness, for ordinary mental activity is prone to bias. Of course, in daily life, choices have to be made, but they can be context-based rather than prejudice-led. Awareness is without centre or circumference. When we look for it we cannot find any core or essence, for it does not exist as a thing, as a definable entity. Nor can we find any limit or edge, for whatever we encounter is already within our awareness.

When we enter this state, we experience it as having no fixed location in space, for it goes everywhere without moving. Similarly, it has no beginning or end. So why do we experience an end to our meditation? We sit for a while, relax and open and then we come out of it. Perhaps it is because we have a fixed period for practice or perhaps because we get distracted. Where do we go when we leave the meditation? Back to our usual world of assumptions. But where is this in relation to awareness? Is it really outside it? Or is it an illusion occurring within awareness? These are essential questions for us to explore in our own practice, for only the direct experience of the limitless natural condition will allow us to integrate whatever occurs and enter the state of dzogchen. Whatever appears to be a limit, if left by itself, will self-liberate, going free without leaving a trace. Then everything that is arising just unfolds back into the openness so there is no interruption to the continuity of presence.

In this state subject and object, self and other, are experienced as waves of energy arising and passing, and there are no divisions or hard edges to disrupt infinite effortless integration. This is why it is often described as 'the unconditioned'. Being itself unconditioned, and free of tendencies to interfere with or condition whatever arises, natural clarity reveals things as they are. This is the basis of optimal responsivity, direct participation in the ever-changing flow of experience.

However, we also need to understand how conditioning functions, as our current capacity to relax into the natural state is limited by our own conditioning. Once we release the conditioning by not identifying with it and not expecting it to perform functions it cannot, then we see that the unconditioned is the unchanging actuality of existence.

On a simple level, if we go for a walk in the fields, some people will attend to what is there, the flowers, a sudden flock of birds, everything. While someone else will just keep talking about their own life, their concerns and preoccupations. They will be untouched by the beauty around them.

Our conditioning determines our focus and our capacity, and this determines which world we live in. When the results of conditioning are intense, for example in the experience of chronic depression, our experience of the world may be such that we are never interrupted in the enclosure of our own limited experience. Selective attention and fixed attitudes can make our world very small.

The process of conditioning has been going on for millions of lifetimes and yet it is difficult to recognise. Sometimes, as we get older, we look back on our life and recognise that for many years we were caught up in particular activities, maybe raising children or making music. We can see this because we are no longer doing it, whereas when we were in it, it was our existence, we were fully identified with it.

For a period of time we were inside a kind of bubble created by our conditioning, and we lived according to that. Inside that conditioning, what we were doing felt very real and very important. Then, after a while, it was not so important. You can see this with children as they grow up. For many years a particular doll or toy might be very important to a child and they can't get to sleep without it. Then, later, you find it has been pushed to the back of the toy cupboard. Conditioning is an aspect of identification. Our own identity is generated out of the arisings that we identify with. The objects we relate to determine the way our subjectivity and sense of self evolve.

At an outer level, we are conditioned by the summer and the winter.

We wear specific clothes in summer, we also walk in a particular way in sandals and we eat different food. It is not the adaption to the changes in weather that make the conditioning but our identification with it, our believing that a transient situation is something truly real. We become taken in by it, and it becomes the limit of our experience and of ourselves. The first line of this verse is describing a different possibility, the experience of the state of dharmakaya, which is fresh, raw, pure.

Within that limitless pot *swirls the oil of liberating attachment on the natural ground*. This is the freedom from longing, hope, and attachment, which occurs once we are at home in the ground or field or dimension free of bias.

Longing points to the presence of a lack, the sense of absence that we all have in our lives. This is the sense that something is not quite complete in our world, an absence in the object that gives rise to a sense of lack in the subject. This then gives rise to a kind of hunger, something which is always there and which keeps us moving out towards the environment in search of things to be appropriated and consumed. It is this which is liberated on the ground. When the mind relaxes into its own natural state of awareness it does not stand in relation to anything else, and because it is not into relation to anything else it has gone beyond duality and so is free of the desire for something else. Longing is the flavour of duality.

Right from birth babies are moving outwards towards the environment and from birth they begin to make eye-contact and engage in responsive interaction. This is part of the longing that we have to connect, yet in the connection we *lose* connection. You want to make connection because you feel you don't *have* connection, so every time you make connection, you simultaneously affirm to yourself the importance of connection and the feeling of being disconnected. In the tradition it is said that satisfying a desire is like drinking salt water; the gratification creates even more thirst, more longing.

When we look to an object to complete ourselves, to make us whole, we are opening a door to great suffering. Our true nature is not a thing. It is not limited in any way, it is naturally complete. It is the unchanging state of dzogchen. However, in the dimension of manifestation we arise as energy in the dynamic field of appearance. In this domain the particularities of manifestation are very important, for how one person is co-determines how another person can relate with them. That is, two ranges of energy, two repertoires of vibration meet and the unique specificity of the moment determines what will be possible. This is not in itself conditioning. There are two possibilities here. If one is present in awareness then the momentary fit of the connecting energy arises and passes without trace. But if we fuse with the energy, taking the momentary form to be our true identity, awareness of the ground is lost, and then whatever is happening is taken as happening to me, and through this conditioning occurs.

Now we insert *the wick of knowing one's own nature as happiness and clarity*. This is the clarity and happiness that arises from being yourself, from re-integrating with your own nature, with what you have always been. This is a deep contentment and satisfaction that endures, rather than a transient moment of bliss.

This brings further relaxation and with it an openness to whatever arises and so our manifestation expresses an open, easy, connective responsivity. From this state you can see that the longing and existential emptiness you felt before, a feeling of being 'less than', of being inadequate, of being a failure, of not realising your full potential, was just a painful illusion. The experience which felt like a kind of core-definition of who you were, was really just the bitter taste of not recognising your infinite openness, inseparable from awareness, clarity and contentment. From this, energy flows out as an inexhaustible wave of compassion to liberate beings from the delusion that you are now freed from. The experiences of clarity, happiness and absence of thought need to be integrated into the ground by releasing them. As meditation experiences they can be a dead-end if we attach to them and identify with them. If we do that our desire for 'good' experiences will lead us to a bias, a tendency, and a new kind of longing. As with any experience, whether it seems good or bad, relax the habit of attachment; by not interfering, energy will change and vanish. The only aspect which remains is unborn presence.

Within this experience, *the flame of the arising of the natural clarity of awareness burns bright*. This flame is spontaneous clarity, it is not a construct produced by effort. The flame of awareness burns up all attachments, habits and obscurations so that everything is shown clearly. This flame removes the basis for seeing self and other as truly separate.

Abiding like this, *thoughts arising from the affliction of anger are liberated in their own place.* All the thoughts, feelings and sensations connected with anger go free by themselves without causing trouble. In tantra anger is transformed into the mirror-like wisdom or original knowing. When we look in a mirror we see ourselves and others, self and environment, and both have equal status as reflections. But when we get angry we look at the other through the lens of self and become irritated that the other has hurt us by not fulfilling our wishes and expectations. We feel ourselves to be pulled out of shape by the actions of others and our anger is a way of re-asserting our basic familiar shape – the sense of 'this feels like me'. Our basic bias is our sense of our own importance, of being essentially unique and special. This leads us to privilege our own patterns and ways of doing things, and this fixed shape is often at odds with the surrounding shapes in the dynamic context which we inhabit but cannot control. By entering the state of the mirror there is an immediate freeing from this limited point of view. Self and other appear as transient patterns with the same status as illusory reflections.

Resting in non-identification with the forms of anger, *without being rejected they dissolve in the vastness of the non-duality of clarity and emptiness.* When we are at ease they dissolve into the infinity of clarity and emptiness. Everything is seen clearly, including oneself, but there is nothing to cling to, nothing to grasp. This includes all our limiting qualities. It is vital not to get too angry with oneself when meditation does not go well or when we get lost in an interaction with someone and then think that after all these years of practice we should have done better. Mistakes are part of the path, and learning to use them creatively is also part of the path. We are moving into unknown territory, stepping out of our familiar frames of reference, so it is reasonable to suppose that we will get lost quite frequently. Just be with whatever occurs, including self-blame, disappointment, regret, and let them go free by themselves.

When you practice according to tantra, it is like sailing round the coast. The boat is on the sea, the big sea, the big ocean, but you can always see where the coast is. Padmasambhava is always there. When you enter dzogchen meditation, you turn the boat out to sea, you go over the horizon and you don't know where the land is. At that point, you cannot look for comfort or reassurance from the structure of a ritual practice. What you have to rely on is yourself and the transmission.

With the feel of the wind on your face, the sense in your body of the movement of the waves, reading the stars, reading the clouds in the sky, it is vital to be in the state of immediate presence. So, it is really important to practice observing yourself, learning to live without guarantee as you work with circumstances.

Our natural state is unchanging yet it can show many aspects. Here *original knowing as mirroring manifests as shining rays of light*. Although this light is self-existing, we can make use of it by developing a clear intention *to dispel the darkness of ignorance of all sentient beings*. The mirroring quality of awareness is both the antidote to the poison of anger and the fruit of its transformation. The mirror of awareness also reveals the spontaneous display of whatever is required by beings. This flow is the potential of the open state which is the actual condition of all of us. Direct perception of the illusory nature of phenomena cuts the root of anger, revealing clarity and energy that liberates all reified structures. Tantra offers us the sense of the certainty, the predictability of the sambogakaya structures, and in particular, as in this prayer, the structure of the mandala with its five sections for the five buddha families or clans. Although they have the same nature, these five families perform different functions with precision and clarity. By relating to the energy of the different families we become empowered to respond skilfully to the diverse situations we experience in life. Everything that occurs is within the mandala of these five buddha families. There is nothing which can overwhelm or confuse one who abides in integration with openness.

We offer this to the guru and the gods of the Vajra clan, the gods in the section of the mandala associated with anger. These gods manifest effective action that stops troublesome situations yet is free from a sense of retaliation or a wish to punish. Karma itself inevitably delivers to us the consequences of our actions. Bias, prejudice, domination and so on do not help. Nor does the notion that life is somehow 'not fair'. What happens to us is the result of our own past actions – accepting responsibility for this frees us to get on with working with circumstances. By linking with the compassionate energy of the enlightened ones, benefit for all is revealed, hence *please accept and then bestow supreme and general accomplishments*.

ཧོ༔ ཆོས་དབྱིངས་མཉམ་པར་བཞག་པའི་ཀོང་བུ་རུ༔

ཀུན་རྟོག་བྱུང་ཆུབ་སེམས་ཀྱི་མར་ཁུ་འཁྱིལ༔

སྣང་སྟོང་ཟུང་དུ་འཇུག་པའི་སྡོང་བུ་ལ༔

རིག་པ་རྗེན་པར་རྟོགས་པའི་མེ་ལྕེ་འབར༔

ཉོན་མོངས་ང་རྒྱལ་རྟོག་པ་རང་སར་གྲོལ༔

མ་སྤང་མཉམ་པ་ཉིད་ཀྱི་ཀློང་དུ་ཐིམ༔

མཉམ་ཉིད་ཡེ་ཤེས་རང་བཞིན་འོད་ཟེར་འཚེར༔

འགྲོ་བའི་མ་རིག་མུན་པ་སེལ་ཕྱིར་དུ༔

བླ་མ་རིན་ཆེན་རིགས་ཀྱི་ལྷ་ཚོགས་ལ༔

འབུལ་ལོ་བཞེས་ནས་མཆོག་ཐུན་དངོས་གྲུབ་སྩོལ༔

Wonderful! In the pot of hospitable space that is the same everywhere swirls the oil of dualistic altruism. On the wick of the union of appearance and emptiness the flame of actualising naked awareness burns bright. Thoughts arising from the affliction of pride are liberated in their own place. Without being rejected they dissolve in the vastness of perfect equality.

Original knowing as identity manifests as shining rays of light. In order to dispel the darkness of ignorance of all sentient beings, we offer this to the guru and the gods of the Ratna clan. Please accept and then bestow supreme and general accomplishments.

The pot of hospitable space is the same everywhere, the same in all directions, the same in all places and at all times. Whatever we find anywhere is already inseparable from this open, spacious nature and so there is no basis for establishing one 'part' as being essentially different from any other 'part'. It is described as being pervasive. This could imply something spreading out, like the smoke of incense spreading out and filling a room. It has the sense of expansion from a particular point, just as smoke rises from a stick of incense. But of course, according to this tradition, space is not expanding from a place. It is always already there, the way we see the colour blue pervading the sky. As the sky is full of blueness so the dharmadhatu is full of equality. And since this infinite spaciousness is the source of all, every arising has the same nature wherever it appears.

Within this pot *swirls the oil of dualistic altruism*, the butter of relative truth compassion. This comprises both the bodhicitta of aspiration, the intention to save all sentient beings, and the bodhicitta of practice, actually working to save sentient beings. Relative truth, the experience of duality, has two aspects. There is *impure* relative truth in which you see objects as separate and inherently real, and then react to them with the five poisons or afflictions of stupidity, desire, aversion, jealousy and pride. With *pure* relative truth you see objects as separate but with less inherent reality so that there is very little basis for the afflictions to arise. Thus, I might see you suffering and feel it to be terrible and definitive of who you are, or I could see you suffering and feel compassion but in the manner of a dream. In the latter case there is the arising of suffering but without a truly existing sufferer. In the former case there are real sentient beings to be saved while in the latter there are illusory forms to be awakened from their dream of truly existing as this or that. Both of these approaches are forms of compassion but the former has more hooks for us to get over-involved and attached.

Compassion is not a gesture from a 'higher' person to a 'lower' one. All sentient beings are equal in their buddha nature, their innate potential to awaken, their inalienable natural state. They are also equal in wandering in samsara under the power of ignoring or mistaking. Although they will experience an infinite variety of situations due to the particularities of their karmic accumulations, the root of this type of experience is the same for all beings.

The wick is the union of appearance and emptiness, the arising of appearances from within and into infinite emptiness. Emptiness is not a thing yet it is the source of all appearance. Due to ignorance we see appearances as being self-existing yet they are mere patterns, momentary constructs of multifold causes, all of which are the energy of emptiness. In terms of meditation, relaxing into the open state is not so difficult. The real work is in manifesting as its unborn energy within the illusory field of everyday experiences. Manifesting the nirmanakaya is more challenging than awakening into the dharmakaya or sambhogakaya. They may have higher status and seem more spiritual, yet integrating our manifestation with its own ground and maintaining this under diverse conditions is very challenging, since there are so many hooks and provocations for old habits and conditioning. Nothing is more difficult than epiphany.

From this wick *the flame of actualising naked awareness burns bright*, free of any obscuration or confusion. This is referring in particular to the subtle obscuration of thinking that because awareness burns with a bright light, it must show itself in only happy primary colours.

When I was a child, I liked painting with bright colours, and when I was a teenager I liked Matisse very much, for his paintings seemed so vibrant and alive. Then I started to be interested in the Spanish painter, Zurburan, who used a lot of brown and grey. At first these did not look like colours to me, they just looked dull and dirty. Yet, gradually I came to see that when a great artist balances light and dark, the darkness can be luminous. This is one of the great joys of Rembrandt's painting. This example might give a sense of what the text says here. The naked radiance of the mind includes *all* colours, all moods. It doesn't mean just happy and lovely. Guilt, shame, confusion, all of these, are also the radiance of awareness and so can be integrated without having to be improved first. If you understand this, then the path of dzogchen is open to you. If you don't understand this then you can easily be caught by the thought that, 'Only when I have purified my mind will I be able to practice dzogchen.'

If you have taken the bodhisattva vow and opened your mind to other beings and their suffering, then their karma has become yours. This becomes most obvious when we do the practice of exchange, tonglen, where we give our happiness and virtue to others, and take their suffering into ourselves. You can spend all your life cleaning butterlamps, transferring the dirty soot from the butterlamps to your fingers, and likewise you can transfer all the difficulties of other people to yourself. This commitment to benefit others is very beautiful but it can easily place too great a burden on even the most heroic of ego shoulders. Linking ourselves to all beings can intensify the sense that the path to enlightenment will take a very long time and after a while the inspiration and energy of the original intention can fade. In order to stay buoyant and not burdened we need to integrate with the actuality of our situation. However, if you don't open to your own natural purity, there will always be a tendency to believe, 'I am not ready', 'I am not pure enough to recognise my nature.' This can become an obstacle for meditators. Awakening to your own nature will not block compassion but allow it to flow freely in the world as it is. Chimed Rigdzin always taught that you should take the easy way, the quick way, the direct way. Giving yourself a hard time has no inherent value.

It is very important, therefore, that first of all we enter the practice of being present with our own nature. Don't start from an assumption that you are a bad person, that you are a stupid person, that you have a huge burden to get rid of because you have committed so many sins, otherwise enlightenment will always seem very far away.

Naked awareness means that our presence in the natural state is not covered by conceptualisation, even in the midst of the movement of experience. Awareness is naked and unchanging even as it reveals the complexity of this world. It does not get covered over by the concepts that are passing through it. Thus we are able to be with each situation precisely, opening to all its details but not getting hooked by and caught up in them. The one who is aware is not a personal identity, not the constructs 'I, me, myself'. Awareness is the open clarity which reveals the contingent arising of the moments of 'I, me, myself'.

Awareness is free of a sense of personal agency, for there is no self-referential feedback loop, just naked presence. Due to this, *thoughts arising from the affliction of pride are liberated in their own place.* Pride is the sense that, 'I am here, I am special and I can help you.' This has no ground or basis in open awareness and so it self-liberates. But if we stay trapped in our ego identity it is easy to select situations that affirm our pride. The world is like candyfloss. As soon as our ego-stick goes in, pride gets swirled around it and when we take a bite it is very tasty, but it sticks to our face! When activity arises effortlessly there is no sense of special achievement – it is just the natural flow. Any prideful thoughts dissolve because there are no ego-hooks to keep them. Hence, *without being rejected they dissolve in the vastness of perfect equality.*

From this open state the wisdom of equality arises as the transformation of pride, thus *original knowing as identity manifests as shining rays of light*. This generates an immediate sense of connection with all who suffer, hence *in order to dispel the darkness of ignorance of all sentient beings, we offer this to the guru and the gods of the Ratna clan*. Knowing that all phenomena, including ourselves and all sentient beings, are inseparable from the open state of emptiness, we experience them whilst sharing a basic identity with them. This identity is different from the usual sense of identity created by similarity of appearance or representation. There is no basis for seeking an intrinsic difference between self and other. All our qualities arise from the open ground; there is no personal essence to the action or quality, nor to the one who is perceived as their doer or possessor. This is the quality of identity, or sameness, or equality inherent in all arisings, and it is the basis of the automatic availability of the welcoming compassion that receives our request, *please accept and then bestow supreme and general accomplishments*.

ཧྃཿ ཆོས་ཀུན་རྣམ་པར་འབྱེད་པའི་ཀོང་བུ་རུཿ
ཟག་མེད་བདེ་བ་ཆེན་པོའི་མར་ཁུ་འཁྱིལཿ
བདེ་སྟོང་ཟུང་དུ་འཇུག་པའི་སྡོང་བུ་ལཿ
རིག་རྩལ་སོ་སོར་རྟོགས་པའི་མེ་ལྕེ་འབར
ཉེན་མོངས་འདོད་ཆགས་རྟོག་པ་རང་སར་གྲོལཿ
མ་སྤང་གཉིས་མེད་བདེ་ཆེན་ཀློང་དུ་ཐིམཿ
སོར་རྟོགས་ཡེ་ཤེས་རང་བཞིན་འོད་ཟེར་འཚེརཿ
འགྲོ་བའི་མ་རིག་མུན་པ་སེལ་ཕྱིར་དུཿ
བླ་མ་པདྨ་རིགས་ཀྱི་ལྷ་ཚོགས་ལཿ
འབུལ་ལོ་བཞེས་ནས་མཆོག་ཐུན་དངོས་གྲུབ་སྩོལཿ

Wonderful! In the pot of attention to the distinct features of all phenomena swirls the oil of undeclining great happiness. On the wick of the union of happiness and emptiness, the flame of the energy of awareness revealing each appearance as it is burns bright. Thoughts arising from the affliction of desire are liberated in their own place. Without being rejected they dissolve in the vastness of non-dual great happiness.

Original knowing as precise discernment manifests as shining rays of light. In order to dispel the darkness of ignorance of all sentient beings we offer this to the guru and the gods of Padma clan. Please accept and then bestow supreme and general accomplishments.

The pot of attention to the distinct features of all phenomena is free of distraction and obscuration. This points to not categorising, to not putting phenomena into the pigeon-holes of our assumptions and concepts, but rather, focusing on what is actually there both as object presentation and as its simultaneous concomitant, subjective experience. Neither homogenised nor strongly differentiated, the flow of experience is offered a sharp, clear, attention that allows each moment, each situation, to reveal itself to the viewer in all its particularity. This reveals our capacity for discernment, so that events can be savoured as displays of unique, unrepeatable radiance. Meditation practice should make you more intelligent, it should make your mind light and quick, like mercury, like quicksilver. Just as mercury poured on a flat surface will form a rounded shape without edges or corners, so awareness has no pre-existing shape or predisposition and thus reveals what is there without conceptual elaboration. Because there is no conditioning there is no carry-over to the next moment and with this, awareness is always fresh and open to the detail that is present now.

In this pot *swirls the oil of undeclining great happiness,* a happiness that is generated by each event. Usually, we have things we like and things we don't. If we encounter things we don't like we find dissatisfaction arising. That seems quite a reasonable response. How could we find happiness in everything if some things are awful? This question contains its own answer. There is nothing which is awful in itself. By remaining open to what is actually occurring rather than being merged in our fantasy about how things should be there is an ever-fresh surprise at the intensity of experience. Basic aliveness, our presence beyond conceptualisation, is the ground of all experience, and each moment, whatever it might be interpreted as being, is the happiness-generating interaction of subject and object, the primordial and uninterrupted intercourse of Kuntu Zangpo and his partner Kuntu Zangmo.

Within this experience is planted *the wick of the union of happiness and emptiness.* Happiness is not a thing; it is ungraspable, seemingly fleeting. Yet when held in union, in inseparability, with emptiness, it is unchanging as the immediacy of all that occurs. Ordinary subject-object intercourse cannot provide lasting happiness since both subject and object are changing, and the object of delight will pass away. Only if, through open non-judgemental, non-reifying attention, we are fully present in each moment, will we enjoy the union of happiness and emptiness. This is a relaxed, open and appreciative state; neither merged nor held apart, it is simply present.

When these three factors are operating together, *the flame of the energy of awareness revealing each appearance as it is burns bright.* The natural energy of awareness is free of projection, labelling and appropriation. It effortlessly, immediately, illuminates each moment with an equal light. This is the energy of our mind's actual nature, of our living presence. By relaxing we come to appreciate all that we experience as the energy of our own awareness. This brings both a freedom from the sense of there being fixed, self-existing objects 'out there', and, a vital freshness to our engaged participation which is not 'in here'. There is a heightened, deepened, aesthetic appreciation through which each moment reveals its infinite value, a value obscured by the foreclosure embedded in prejudice. Awareness is available, available for everything. There is no entry ticket, no separation of chosen and not chosen. It is always already available as an immediate presence inseparable from hospitable space. Never bored, never looking ahead to something else, nor caught up in the past, it is instantly present with whatever arises, big or small, near or far, good or bad.

When we are relaxed and content in this open enjoyment of everything, *thoughts arising from the affliction of desire are liberated in their own place.* Generally, desire arises from making something special; we desire what we like or what we feel we need and that is not everything. Desire involves a dualistic discrimination between good and bad, lovely and unlovely. It also involves a further move of wanting the lovely and discarding the unlovely in whatever way this is experienced by an individual. Thus aversion is not far from desire. In saying 'yes' to Mary we necessarily say 'no' to Bob. We can't want everything. Furthermore, we don't always get what we want. Dissatisfaction is never far from desire. Yet when we remain open to everything that arises, when we focus on the immediacy of each moment unwaveringly, there is no opportunity for desire to enter the dimension of reification. Desire is thus an aspect of clarity.

This doesn't mean we are indifferent to the unique patterns of our own existence. Clearly, we might prefer tea to coffee and therefore desire a cup of tea more than a cup of coffee. Yet integrating in the open state, tea is just as it is, not over-invested, and does not become a defining signifier of 'who I am'. Therefore, if it comes, it comes, and if it is not available, it is not available. Thus, one can be with whatever occurs without pre-occupation. In this state we experience the wonder of attention, for when we fully, freely attend to anything it will start to glow, to appear brighter. This reveals the mutually supportive interaction of attention and phenomena. Full value is received in each instant and so there is no need to attempt to hang on to that which is inherently transient, hence *without being rejected they dissolve in the vastness of non-dual great happiness.* How amazing it is that by letting go of the small yet intense longings we have for objects of desire, we find unending, non-circumstantial happiness awaiting us. 'I' sits at the crossroads for it is used to refer to both our limited ego and to our open awareness. This can be very confusing but for meditators that confusion is helpful. It is a call to relax, to open to the clarity of presence free of identification. The ego builds its house on sand, it is always in the process of vanishing. Without changing anything, the simple non-conceptual awareness inseparable from the self liberating of arisings is itself always already free. The inseparability of samsara and nirvana is ceaselessly unfolding for and as us.

Original knowing as precise discernment manifests as shining rays of light, illuminating the world as a dynamic, relational field. Original knowing connects us directly with what is going on because it is not a constructed, artificial knowledge and it does not rely on concepts. It is immediate, simple and precise as the quality of our participation. It is this aspect that manifests as rays of light. Our altruistic intention *to dispel the darkness of ignorance of all sentient beings,* is itself an aspect of this wisdom, a commitment to be with each being as they are.

We offer this to the guru and the gods of Padma clan. The lotus family is the family situated in the section of the mandala arising from the transformation of desire, so when we make the offering, it is accepted without desire or selection. *Please accept and then bestow supreme and general accomplishments.* The lotus represents purity as it arises unsullied from the mud. Desire for one or two 'special' things is transformed into the power to connect with everything and appreciate the unique specificity of each appearance. We make this offering so that the recipients will in turn offer their light in order to free all beings from the darkness of not attending to what is there.

རྃ༔ བྱ་བ་ལས་ཀྱི་འཁོར་ལོའི་ཀོང་བུ་རུ༔

ཚོལ་མེད་ལྷུན་གྱིས་གྲུབ་པའི་མར་ཁུ་འཁྱིལ༔

གསལ་སྟོང་ཟུང་དུ་འཇུག་པའི་སྡོང་བུ་ལ༔

རིག་པ་ཐོག་མཐའ་བྲལ་བའི་མེ་ལྕེ་འབར༔

ཉོན་མོངས་ཕྲག་དོག་རྟོག་པ་རང་སར་གྲོལ༔

མ་སྤང་རྩོལ་སྒྲུབ་བྲལ་བའི་ཀློང་དུ་ཐིམ༔

བྱ་གྲུབ་ཡེ་ཤེས་རང་བཞིན་འོད་ཟེར་འཚེར༔

འགྲོ་བའི་མ་རིག་མུན་པ་སེལ་ཕྱིར་དུ༔

བླ་མ་ལས་ཀྱི་རིགས་ཀྱི་ལྷ་ཚོགས་ལ༔

འབུལ་ལོ་བཞེས་ནས་མཆོག་ཐུན་དངོས་གྲུབ་སྩོལ༔

Wonderful! In the pot of the wheel of continuous activity swirls the oil of effortless accomplishment free of striving. On the wick of the union of clarity and emptiness the flame of awareness free of beginning and end burns bright. Thoughts arising from the affliction of jealousy are liberated in their own place. Without being rejected they dissolve in the vastness of freedom from work and effort.

Original knowing as effective action manifests as shining rays of light. In order to dispel the darkness of ignorance of all sentient beings we offer this to the guru and the gods of the Karma clan. Please accept and then bestow supreme and general accomplishments.

The outer and inner activity of this world is like a wheel which keeps turning. Just as the environment or the field of our activity keeps changing, so our responses keep manifesting in new forms. When we walk down the street our breathing, our gait, our flexibility will all be affected by what we encounter. These events are not pulling us out of our 'normal' state. We don't have a normal state for we are responsive beings inexorably articulated into the turning world. This is the energy of the natural condition – it never ceases. The only thing that is truly still is the natural state itself.

In this *pot of the wheel of continuous activity, swirls the oil of effortless accomplishment free of striving.* Very often the tasks that face us are in the future so we have to prepare for them. This involves organising, mobilizing, striving towards our goal. Yet at each step of the way, in each moment, there is just this, instantly arising. If we are fully present in the moment, effortless activity arises as the flow of the energy of awareness and what is required for that moment is accomplished without striving. That does not mean that there are no difficulties but, rather, that each difficulty is a chain of moments, each of which can be responded to immediately from a state of relaxation. When we get caught up in problems and worry about them, they become 'our' problems; they seem to grow bigger, and in thinking about them we become disheartened and then need to force ourselves to face them and to strive. In that situation there is the subject, 'me, the troubled one', the object, 'the actual problem' and thirdly the relation between them. When all three seem very real and pressing we easily get stuck. Yet if we see that all three are the energy of our own awareness rather than fixed entities, they can be reintegrated into the flow of experience and will start to resolve without the effort of 'me' having to act on 'that'.

The wick of the union of clarity and emptiness provides the basis for the activity. Inexhaustible emptiness inseparable from infinite awareness provides the potential out of which activity arises, while clarity provides the fine tuning of the fit with the emerging situation so that energy is not wasted. With these united factors, *the flame of awareness free of beginning and end burns bright* protecting us from slipping into anxiety and the need to be in control. This allows us to stop planning in terms of the maps in our head, as if they indicated how things actually are, and instead to respond precisely to what is arising while utilising the full repertoire of our skills and knowledge that are to hand. This capacity manifests naturally with the non-differentiation of meditation and post-meditation experience. Then everything is the energy of awareness, everything is integrated into the open ground, the source of all. Everything can be accomplished for there is no other ground for manifestation and activity. Thus we are not operating on a field of fixed entities that are apart from us but, rather, participating in a dynamic co-emergent field where our activity is so much more effective because it is already part of the field.

When the object is not over-invested, there is no basis for jealousy. Jealousy arises with the sense that something, and especially someone, of mine may be lost to another. I will not be able to keep them although I feel that they are mine. I look on them as my sphere of operations and feel entitled to have access to them. This is very solid, very heavy; a web of concepts and beliefs that binds everything very tightly. I am attached to the object and even more attached to my map, to my belief, my sense of what is mine and of how things should be. In this there is little room for manoeuvre and one quickly feels trapped, desperate and powerless. Yet when we rest in spacious awareness all these thoughts that wriggle and tickle and torment go free by themselves, hence *thoughts arising from the affliction of jealousy are liberated in their own place.* They are seen to be just ideas which never had any way of controlling what arises, and *without being rejected they dissolve in the vastness of freedom from work and effort.* In that way we see how close jealousy is to pride, to the sense that this shouldn't be happening to me because I am special and I should be able to get what I want; my life should be safe and secure. As long as we are looking for a predictable outcome we are attempting to control situations rather than freely participating. The fact that I love someone is no guarantee that they will love me in return. That is why open awareness offers gifts, gestures into the flow, rather than seeking to bind transient arisings into a contract. Being grounded in its own source it is not looking to any arising to provide the meaning of existence or validate a fixed sense of self.

With the previous factors in play, *original knowing as effective action manifests as shining rays of light.* Effective action is the capacity to respond to a situation without seeking to control it in terms of your own ego gratification. Your action fits the potential for general benefit inherent in the situation as it arises from a vast intention: *to dispel the darkness of ignorance of all sentient beings.* It is about finding the workability of a situation, identifying the key points that can unlock whatever is stuck, rather than a divine omnipotence that always gets its own way. One works with what is there, not what one would prefer to be the case. The many factors present in a situation have to be taken into account, since our own wishes are not the central hub. When we see how things are, the workability or not of the situation will be revealed. Trying to change things when we lack the resources is not wisdom, nor is ignoring the current capacity of others. Modifying the well-known *Serenity Prayer*, we can say:

> May I rest in the serenity
> To accept the things I cannot change,
> Free the courage to change the things that I can change
> And awaken the wisdom to know the difference.

We offer this to the guru and the gods of the Karma clan or activity family who manifest as the transformed energy of jealousy. Their capacity to accomplish all things without effort brings the immediate fulfilment of our request, *please accept and then bestow supreme and general accomplishments.*

ཧྃ༔ ཀུན་གཞི་འཁྲུལ་པས་བཅིངས་པའི་ཀོང་བུ་རུ༔
ཉེ་ཉོན་རྟོག་པའི་ཚོགས་ཀྱི་མར་ཁུ་འཁྱིལ༔
མ་རིག་བདག་ཏུ་འཛིན་པའི་སྡོང་བུ་ལ༔
བདག་མེད་ཡེ་ཤེས་ཆེན་པོའི་མེ་ལྕེ་འབར༔
ཉོན་སྒྲིབ་ཆ་དང་བཅས་པ་རང་སར་གྲོལ༔
མ་སྤངས་ཆོས་ཀྱི་བདག་མེད་ཀློང་དུ་ཐིམ༔
ཕྱོགས་མེད་ཡེ་ཤེས་ཆེན་པོའི་རང་འོད་འཆོར༔
འགྲོ་བའི་མ་རིག་མུན་པ་སེལ་ཕྱིར་དུ༔
བླ་མ་མཆོག་གསུམ་རྩ་གསུམ་ལྷ་ཚོགས་ལ༔
འབུལ་ལོ་བཞེས་ནས་མཆོག་ཐུན་དངོས་གྲུབ་སྩོལ༔

Wonderful! In the pot of the ground of all bound by delusion swirls the oil of the many thoughts arising from the minor afflictions. On the wick of belief in self-existing entities that arises from ignoring, the flame of the great original knowing free of reification burns bright. The obscuration arising from the afflictions is liberated in its own place. Without being rejected it dissolves in the vastness of the absence of inherent self-nature in all phenomena.

The great impartial original knowing manifests its own shining light. In order to dispel the darkness of ignorance of all sentient beings we offer this to the guru, the three jewels, the three roots and all the deities. Please accept and then bestow supreme and general accomplishments.

The ground or basis of everything is not itself a thing and so it gives rise to no things. Yet this very openness of the ground, its inexpressibility, its indeterminacy, its ungraspablility, means it is like space. And from one point of view space needs to be filled; it is not appreciated for what it is and appears to require something to be done to it. Just as when explorers went from Europe to America and Australia they often took the land to be empty and requiring settlement. This was inseparable from ignoring the fact that there were already people living there, people whose way of life was very different from that of the settlers. After quite a short period of time the settlers began to feel at home and with that, they experienced the original inhabitants as an intrusion as if they were the outsiders occupying land that really belonged to the new inhabitants.

When thoughts establish themselves as the guarantors of meaning, they start to fill the space and take it over with a sense of 'natural' entitlement. They map out the territory, they say what is what, they determine planning, management, problem-solving and their busy activity and self-preoccupation leave no time or space for considering where they come from and what their own ground is. Thoughts, the energy of radiant awareness, come to take themselves as self-existing. When we meditate we can feel the seductive power of thoughts, how easily, quickly, 'naturally', they hook our attention so that we fuse with some of these arisings, merging into them, becoming them, taking ourselves to be them. Then, identified with a thought, from that position we have to manage and control the other thoughts that we take to be 'not us'. Duality is the dividing of arisings into self and other and taking both as inherently real. The ground itself, our own actual source, is never divided, conditioned or changed. The task of awakening is to reintegrate thoughts and their own ground. In fact, thoughts have never actually separated from this ground, for such a separation is a dream, an illusion. As our ordinary selves we are part of the illusion, and, not recognising this, we continue being busy trying to build a better illusion. All of this activity is actually the radiance of the open state of our own awareness.

The first line in this verse describes the pot as being *the ground of all bound by delusion*. The source, the openness, is itself never actually bound yet it appears to be so when we ourselves are merged in the delusion of duality and reification. For then, infinite creativity, the ceaseless waves of light and sound which are the basis of our actual existence are mis-interpreted, mis-taken, as being a multitude of things, a whole lot of stuff requiring endless attention. This is overwhelming, so we develop maps in order to cope. But the maps don't quite fit, so, in our attachment to concepts we deny the actual territory and trust our maps. While actually getting more lost, we feel we are finding the right way, doing the right thing. This is because thoughts chase each other. If you don't know the nature of thoughts, you might think that you are freeing yourself, and that you are gaining clarity and moving towards a state of awakening while, actually, you are making yourself more stupid. There is no end to thinking, for it is actually the flow of the unborn nature. Yet while believing in thoughts we do not see this nature and so what is naturally free is recruited into the task of binding us, we who are not different from the pure openness.

Inside this pot *swirls the oil of the many thoughts arising from the minor afflictions,* the many different kinds of small, confused thoughts and emotions, such as worry, anxiety, ambitions, fear and doubt. These are the qualities that arise very quickly and automatically once subject and object are separated out in the experience of duality. They are subtle and generative of further thoughts and feelings. They are part of our on-going busyness, our always-being-caught-up- in-something; the waterfall of daily stuff that hides us from ourselves.

Into this oil is placed *the wick of belief in self-existing entities that arises from ignoring.* When the actual ground is ignored there is reification, the taking of all appearances to be self-existing entities, whether they arise as subject or object. When any appearance, that is, anything arising and passing, is taken to be truly real, it is, as it were, cut off from its ground. It has not *actually* been cut off yet it appears to be so. Who is the one who does this? I, me, myself. Why? Because I, me, myself, are themselves reified moments. That is to say, the actual evanescent flow is not opened to as it is, but is engaged with from a position within the flow, the position of an illusory construct, the ever changing ego which presents itself as stable and enduring. Then the flow is interpreted in terms of concepts, concepts which come to be taken to be the actual reality. So an abstraction comes to appear concrete, as a real entity, while the actual, the presenting facticity of ungraspable moments, is experienced as an unwarranted intrusion into my concept of my stable world.

Ignoring what is actually the case we imagine ourselves, others, and the phenomena of our world to all be truly existing separate entities. This is not a sin, not something bad, rather it is like a spiralling, an intoxi-fication, an enfolding of energy within energy that creates a realm of illusion. No one is to blame, for there are no true entities. Yet when we awaken to the actual nature of the dimension in which we are, we find we need to learn to let go, to stop weaving the fascinating threads of our own entrammelment. When we loosen our grasp on our sense of self we can see that rather than being a fixed thing, a secure base, it is a communicative gesture, a quality of energy as participation in the unreified, ungraspable field of co-emergence. Thus we don't have to renounce our daily existence, everything can continue as before. Yet everything is changed, for every arising is now integrated with the ground; it is no longer cut adrift from its source. Thus our body, voice, and mind are relaxed and at ease as part of the flow, and no matter how complex our life situations are, by resting in integration, the hooks to and of objectification and control are self-liberated.

Paradoxically from the limiting factors described in the first three lines *the flame of the great original knowing free of reification burns bright.* This is primordial awareness which is itself never an entity. When the obscu-rations are seen for what they are, when we directly experience that they have no other ground than natural openness, the full presence of open knowing which illuminates everything appears effortlessly. The presence of this awareness reveals that all the obscurations that arise from the afflictions are vanishing without trace. Hence, *the obscuration arising from the afflictions is liberated in its own place. Without being rejected it dissolves in the vastness of the absence of inherent self-nature in all phenom-ena.* They don't have to be changed or worked on with some antidote. No effort is required. They go free by themselves – just as they have always done. It is our own grasping at dharmas, at phenomena, at entities, that goes free in its own place. The word dharmas here indi-cates the fundamental building blocks of the universe; whatever one would take to be the basic core ingredients of whatever diverse arisings manifest. This basic materialism dissolves because it was never truly existing in its own right, rather, it has been created by the intensity of our own conceptualisation. As the obscurations of the afflictions vanish without trace, so all seemingly real separate entities effortlessly integrate into the open infinity in which they have always resided.

When arisings, appearances, experiences, are no longer turned into things, we ourselves relax more, and *the great impartial original knowing manifests its own shining light.* There is just one undivided flow. Yet it is not a homogenized flow, for all the unique details of each arising are there. There are no hooks for grasping, comparing, judging, and so there is impartiality and openness to everything just as it is. It is easy to see how pride can make us feel superior to others but we also need to recognise that feelings of inferiority, self-hatred and the tendency to placate others also serve to reinforce dualistic experience. The ego is created by splitting and operates to enforce further splitting on a moment-by-moment basis. This is profoundly unhelpful for all concerned as there is no end to this interplay of action—reaction. Awakening to the impartiality of awareness free of ego is a great relief, a dropping of burdens which then releases a loving intention: *in order to dispel the darkness of ignorance of all sentient beings we offer this to the guru, the three jewels, the three roots and all the deities.*

It is offered to the guru, and to the deities we have access to thanks to the guru, and to the dakinis, the communicative forces that connect all appearances to the ground. The offering is a connection, as is the response. This is the matrix of co-emergence. *Please accept and then bestow supreme and general accomplishments.* On receiving these offered rays of light they amplify them for the sake of all beings so that all can awaken in, and as, the unborn ground.

When we make these offerings we are involving our emotions, generating a warmth in our heart towards the kindness of those who help us and towards the suffering of those we wish to help. Apart from its own value as a practice, this emotional aspect of the offering helps to vitalise the other lines of the prayer. Many of the lines are full of technical terms which can function as an inspiring mnemonic if you are familiar with their meaning and use. But they can also create a wall of incomprehension if we are not familiar with them. The power of faith and devotion can help us to keep struggling with these views which are so radically different from the ones most of us have been raised with. Gradually the ideas will become familiar and supportive and then they will become true allies in our meditation practice.

ཧོཿ ཆོས་དབྱིངས་བརྟལ་ཁྱབ་ཆེན་པོའི་ཀོང་བུ་རུཿ
ཕྱ་བའི་རྟོག་ཚོགས་བྱུན་འབྱམས་མར་ཁུ་འཁྱིལཿ
ཤེས་པ་རང་འོད་གསལ་བའི་སྡོང་བུ་ལཿ
དུག་ལྔ་ལྷག་མེད་འཇོམས་པའི་མེ་ལྕེ་འབརཿ
ཤེས་བྱའི་སྒྲིབ་པ་ལྷག་མེད་རང་སར་གྲོལཿ
མ་སྤང་གང་ཟག་བདག་མེད་ཀློང་དུ་ཐིམཿ
ཀུན་ཁྱབ་རང་གསལ་དག་པའི་རང་འོད་འཚེརཿ
འགྲོ་བའི་མ་རིག་མུན་པ་སེལ་ཕྱིར་དུཿ
བླ་མ་མཆོག་གསུམ་རྩ་གསུམ་ལྷ་ཚོགས་ལཿ
འབུལ་ལོ་བཞེས་ནས་མཆོག་ཐུན་དངོས་གྲུབ་སྩོལཿ

Wonderful! In the pot of infinite hospitable space swirls the oil of many small thoughts that appear ceaselessly. On the wick of the radiant natural light of knowing, the flame of the traceless destruction of the five poisons burns bright. Obscuration by and to knowledge is liberated in its own place without residue. Without being rejected it dissolves in the vastness of the absence of inherent self-nature in all beings.

The all-pervading natural clarity manifests as the purity of its own shining light. In order to dispel the darkness of ignorance of all sentient beings we offer this to the guru, the three jewels, the three roots and all the deities. Please accept and then bestow supreme and general accomplishments.

The pot of infinite hospitable space admits everything, allows everything, contains everything. Being infinite there is nothing outside of it. Everything that arises, arises from it, in it, and returns to it. This is the ground we share with everything, the source and field of our experience. No thought can limit this state; it cannot be caught, defined, divided by any concept. Yet, although all of samsara is within it, within samsara it is not recognised. Every year many people come to their limit, they feel they can't go on, and so they kill themselves. Suicide is an effect of limitation, of individuals feeling defined by factors which are felt to be implacable, overwhelming and unbearable. This is most tragic since each person who kills themself is naturally spacious and free. However, they were unable to see this because their gaze was caught by the conditioning limitations of their existence. Not examining who is the one who can't bear it, having no knowledge of who that is, they are trapped in narratives that bind them on a path of duality that is endless in its permutations. Samsara is dangerous; happiness quickly turns to sadness, wars suddenly erupt, economies collapse, and the sense of self we have developed can become unsustainable. Relaxing into hospitable space offers a radically different view that points to the actual situation, not further into illusion.

In this pot *swirls the oil of many small thoughts that appear ceaselessly.* They are always there but it is often only through meditation that we start to be aware of them. Arising and passing, they are part of the dynamic flow. When we feel solid and established they subtly impact us, affecting our mood, tolerance, capacity and so on, yet they rarely reveal themselves directly to our conscious mind.

The wick of the radiant natural light of knowing is inserted, bringing a great transformation. For the oil, the small thoughts, is revealed as being inseparable from the natural light of the mind. These thoughts are both the energy or light arising from awareness and also the fuel or secondary causes which evoke the radiant potential of awareness, keeping it shining brightly. Thoughts have no other source than our own mind, not our personal ego mind, but our unborn awareness. When this is realised there is a great sense of relief which might seem strange as there is now no one to blame, for neither self nor other truly exist. Yet in accepting the ephemeral contents of our experience as our actual experience, our existence, we are able to respond and participate with what is always already within our sphere of influence. The dropping of ego's need to control, the awakening to the fact that it is merely movement chasing movement, reveals the rich display of the energy of awareness, the unborn source of samsara and nirvana. This is the non-dual field in which our participation is the spontaneity of infinite connectivity rather than a personal task we perform. The infinite dharmadhartu is empowering not overwhelming – for we, our natural condition, our awareness, are the infinity of the openness as well as the infinity of the arisings. Within this, *the flame of the traceless destruction of the five poisons burns bright*. The five poisons are the fuel or the raw material of the five wisdoms. The very roughness and intensity of our limitation is actually energy which, when we are open to it non-judgementally, reveals, in its vanishing, its own source, the natural state of openness. In this way, without applying effort, the very energy of the five poisons brings about their own traceless destruction, just as if they had encountered a great master of aikido.

In not being caught up in the agitation of the poisonous afflictions, we have more capacity to see what is going on. Through this, *obscuration by and to knowledge is liberated in its own place without residue*. That is to say, conceptual knowledge, which was blocking true knowledge, is seen for what it is. Knowledge about things, which actually obscures the things themselves, is dropped and clarity radiates forth.

Conceptual knowledge of things reinforces the sense of the 'thingness' of the thing. It hides the actuality which is that thoughts relate to thoughts. Thoughts identify and develop other thoughts; they have no access to anything else. Yet, they do this while pretending that the thoughts refer to real, separate entities. Due to this, much worry, anxiety and planning is carried out trying to solve problems that don't actually exist. The real problem is the meta-problem of mis-construing what is going on. This is the buddhist sense of ignorance – the ongoing activity of ignoring, of mis-taking.

With the vanishing of the obscurations, the belief in truly existing beings dissolves in unborn space without having to be rejected or transformed. That belief is the obscuration of seeing people as people, birds as birds; effortlessly, thoughtlessly taking living beings as self-defining autonomous systems. All beings arise from causes and conditions, from endless chains of causal events, and this is inseparable from their simultaneously arising from the unborn ground from which they have never separated. Hence, *without being rejected it dissolves in the vastness of the absence of inherent self-nature in all beings*. When we open to ourselves and the environment, we experience the undivided field of light: clear, precise, yet without individual essences. Everything and everyone is in flow, constant change but not chaos, for the radiant hospitality is spontaneously self-organising.

As discriminations of good and bad, liking and not-liking and so on, cease, and there is no pre-occupation with trying to work things out, to make sense of what is going on, natural clarity illuminates everything. Thus, *the all-pervading natural clarity manifests as the purity of its own shining light.* We make use of this light to fulfil our intention *to dispel the darkness of ignorance of all sentient beings,* an intention arising from the light itself. *We offer this to the guru, the three jewels, the three roots and all the deities. Please accept and then bestow supreme and general accomplishments.* When this is offered, all the enlightened ones are happy and send more light to remove all darkness and awaken the enlightened potential of all beings. It is terrible to be cut off from your buddha nature, to be profoundly alienated from who you actually are. It is terrible to be a refugee, to have to live in a foreign country where you don't understand what is going on. In samsara, we are all refugees. Our ego is like a forged passport; it doesn't say who we really are and it brings with it the fear that we could be found out at any time.

ཧོཿ འཁོར་བ་ཤེས་བྱ་ཡུལ་གྱི་ཀོང་བུ་རུཿ

ལས་ཉོན་གཟུང་འཛིན་འཁྲུལ་པའི་མར་ཁུ་འཁྱིལཿ

བདེ་སྡུག་གཉིས་སུ་མེད་པའི་སྡོང་བུ་ལཿ

ཡེ་ཤེས་རང་ལས་བྱུང་བའི་མེ་ལྕེ་འབརཿ

འཁྲུལ་པའི་སེམས་ཅན་ཚོགས་རྣམས་རང་སར་གྲོལཿ

མ་སྤང་གཟུང་འཛིན་གཉིས་མེད་ཀློང་དུ་ཐིམཿ

འཛིན་མེད་ཡེ་ཤེས་ཆེན་པོའི་རང་འོད་འཚེརཿ

འགྲོ་བའི་མ་རིག་མུན་པ་སེལ་ཕྱིར་དུཿ

བླ་མ་མཆོག་གསུམ་རྩ་གསུམ་ལྷ་ཚོགས་ལཿ

འབུལ་ལོ་བཞེས་ནས་མཆོག་ཐུན་དངོས་གྲུབ་སྩོལཿ

Wonderful! In the pot of samsaric objects of knowledge swirls the oil of dualistic confusion which generates karma and the afflictions. On the wick of the non-duality of happiness and sorrow the flame that arises from original knowing burns bright. All confused sentient beings are liberated in their own place. Without being rejected they dissolve in the vastness of the non-duality of graspable object and grasping mind.

The great original knowing free of grasping manifests its own shining light. In order to dispel the darkness of ignorance of all sentient beings we offer this to the guru, the three jewels, the three roots and all the deities. Please accept and then bestow supreme and general accomplishments.

The pot of samsaric objects of knowledge is constituted from all the cultural knowledge of the universe. All that relates to the experience of beings who take themselves to be truly existing, and which becomes a support for their limited sense of self, is gathered here: history, geography, science, beliefs, operas and so on. All that is known by beings anywhere is the sphere of operation of the ego. In this pot *swirls the oil of dualistic confusion which generates karma and the afflictions.* This is the oil of taking oneself to be a needy subject in a world of objects that must be appropriated or rejected. This gives rise to the afflictions, the five poisons and so forth and to the accumulation of karma, some good and some bad. We need to remember that the exit ticket from samsara cannot be purchased with karma, no matter how good.

The wick is the non-duality of happiness and sorrow. That is to say, happiness and sorrow are not separate phenomena. Not only are they mutually defining but the binary opposition that seems to keep them apart is a kind of glue. They are not two different phenomena nor are they just one phenomenon. They are part of the vast interweaving of co-emergent factors which create the moment by moment experiences of our lives. They are also inseparable from the awareness within which they arise. This awareness is like a mirror that reflects exactly what is put in front of it. It doesn't pick and choose. It has no preferences and also no anxiety, for it is not marked or conditioned by any arising whatsoever. The mirror itself cannot be seen. When we look at it, all we see are reflections. In the same way, when we look for ourselves we cannot find ourselves as a definite entity. The mirror itself is not a thing, there is nothing that can be grasped, yet its open awareness is constantly showing itself through the reflections which arise; they are its own energy, its potential for manifesting. Similarly, moment by moment our body, voice and mind arise as an illusory appearances displaying new forms, new patterns of gesture, posture and so on. All of that is us, our richness, our range, yet its source, our awareness itself, is never to be found as an arising; it is never a possession that we can have.

It is on this level, the level of the mirror, that happiness and sadness are the same. However, on the level of manifestation happiness and sorrow are not the same. As energy, their vibration and impact are different. Not to notice the difference would be to not be manifesting on the level of participation. Thus, from the point of view of wisdom, happiness and suffering are not different. But from the point of view of manifestation, of compassion, they are. Yet, since wisdom and compassion are inseparable, the difference is illusory.

The flame that arises from original knowing burns bright. This flame arises of itself, it has no cause or conditioning, it is the natural quality of radiance which is available when the obscurations self-liberate. Usually, we are prone to dullness and sleepiness and see these as enemies of the light. But here every arising is not other than the natural light. In its presence *all confused sentient beings are liberated in their own place,* waking up without effort from the phantasy of separation. Confusion, delusion, bewilderment, and obscurations all fall away so that every sentient being awakens to their own natural state of open, luminous emergence. *Without being rejected they dissolve in the vastness of the non-duality of graspable object and grasping mind.* The mind that grasps and the objects that are grasped dissolve into their own ground without there being any need to work on them or get rid of them.

When the turbulent energy of the mind relaxes, the personal subject, I, me, myself opens to its own ground of intrinsic openness and thus primordial integration is revealed as, *the great original knowing free of grasping manifests its own shining light.* All the grasping and dualistic involvement vanishes leaving things as they are – the forms of natural luminosity. This light radiates out as the offering. If ignorance was truly real, if it was the defining characteristic of our nature, then it could never be removed – and certainly not by rays of light. But ignorance itself is an illusion, the illusion of delusion. It is like stumbling in a dark room and trying to guess what is there. As soon as the light of wisdom is shining, the darkness of beginningless samsara vanishes. Darkness, not seeing, fantasy – all such mental creations were always conditional, contextual. They never had one iota's worth of true self-substance. And yet, how powerful this delusion has been, how much unnecessary suffering has been created! Awareness itself acts to *dispel the darkness of ignorance of all sentient beings.* Although the text sets out the intention to offer, the object offered and the recipients of the offering, these three are empty and the whole interaction happens in the manner of a dream. *We offer this to the guru, the three jewels, the three roots and all the deities. Please accept and then bestow supreme and general accomplishments.* By living in and as this light we are able to abide with the natural perfection of all beings however they manifest, and however they define themselves.

ཧོཿ བྱམས་པ་ཚད་མེད་སྣོད་འདས་ཀོང་བུ་རུཿ

སྙིང་རྗེ་ཚད་གཞུང་མེད་པའི་མར་ཁུ་འཁྱིལཿ

བཏང་སྙོམས་ཚད་མེད་རྣམ་དག་སྡོང་བུ་ལཿ

དགའ་བ་ཚད་མེད་རྒྱས་པའི་མེ་ལྕེ་འབར༔

ཉོན་མོངས་དུག་ལྔའི་རྟོག་པ་རང་སར་གྲོལཿ

ཚད་མེད་ཁྱབ་གདལ་ཆེན་པོའི་ཀོང་དུ་ཐིམཿ

གཉིས་མེད་སྒྲོ་ལས་འདས་པའི་རང་འོད་འཚེརཿ

འགྲོ་བའི་མ་རིག་མུན་པ་སེལ་ཕྱིར་དུཿ

བླ་མ་མཆོག་གསུམ་རྩ་གསུམ་ལྷ་ཚོགས་ལཿ

འབུལ་ལོ་བཞེས་ནས་མཆོག་ཐུན་དངོས་གྲུབ་སྩོལཿ

Wonderful! In the pot of inconceivable measureless love swirls the oil of immeasurable compassion. On the wick of very pure immeasurable equanimity the flame of spreading immeasurable joy burns bright. Thoughts arising from the five afflicting poisons are liberated in their own place. They dissolve in the vastness of the great infinitude of the immeasurable.

Inconceivable non-duality manifests its own shining light. In order to dispel the darkness of ignorance of all sentient beings we offer this to the guru, the three jewels, the three roots and all the deities. Please accept and then bestow supreme and general accomplishments.

The pot of inconceivable measureless love offers warm good wishes to all without any restriction. This is expressed in the wish: 'May all sentient beings be happy and have the cause of happiness.' Such a view of love doesn't have any connection with the western notion of romantic love. In Tibetan buddhism the focus is on making universal the intense love that a mother has for a small child. It means wanting the other to be happy, and being able and willing to put the other first. This goodwill towards others is proactive and is offered irrespective of how others behave. It is not just a fleeting thought but a complete reorientation of our existence, a tilt towards being for the other that rectifies the damaging imbalance of our habitual being for ourselves. From this openness our energy radiates out, so that we feel ourselves to be part of the world rather than locked in the box of self-concern.

In this pot *swirls the oil of immeasurable compassion*, the attitude that fuels beneficial activity. This is expressed in the wish: 'May all beings be freed from suffering and the causes of suffering.' What affects others affects me. My existence is part of infinite interconnectivity. This is how it is. It is therefore not just selfish to be only concerned for oneself but a cause of much suffering as one is denying the actuality of interbeing. *The wick of very pure immeasurable equanimity* stands straight and without bias. This is the capacity to make the same quality of response, according to actual need, whether I like someone or not, whether they are family or not. This is incredibly difficult because of the intensity of our habitual prejudices. We are born into groups and are encouraged to have loyalty to them, privileging their members over anyone else. Although, in daily life, we necessarily, contextually, give a lot of time to a few people, the function of this line is to help us remember all beings while we perform our specific daily tasks. It is expressed in the wish: 'May all beings abide in the great equanimity free of privileging friends and attacking enemies.' The fact that we consider some people to be friends and others enemies is purely contextual. All these beings have the same nature, which is the same nature that we have. To be deeply for some and against others is to fall under the sway of concepts and forget who we and they are.

The flame of spreading immeasurable joy burns bright, expressing the wish: 'May all beings abide in the joy that is free from suffering.' Joy is an expansive feeling, an uninhibited trust that life is OK, more than OK, fulfilling, satisfying. We feel light of mood, relaxed, contented and 'hopeful' in this state. In his first teaching Buddha Shakyamuni set out the Four Noble Truths: the Truth of Suffering, the Origin of Suffering, the Ending of Suffering and the Path to the Ending of Suffering. All the teachings radiate out from this. Immeasurable joy is the fruit of the ending of suffering.

These four states or qualities or experiences are said to be immeasurable because they are grounded in emptiness. They are not just human aspirations, something beautiful that we can offer to the world. They are the qualities that flow effortlessly out of the heart that has awakened to its own infinity. They are the ultimate protection from accumulating bad karma for they locate us in an awareness free of duality. We become attentive to what is going on, truly open and participative, alive to the common good. We experience being alive as a subject in a world of subjects – a living inter-subjectivity free of reification, objectification and all that demeans our potential for radiance. Due to this, *thoughts arising from the five afflicting poisons are liberated in their own place*, for the self referencing root of the poisons has been cut. Then *they dissolve in the vastness of the great infinitude of the immeasurable* whose nature they have always shared.

There is no difference between the illuminator and the illuminated, just the integrated field of experience beyond speech, thought and expression. *Inconceivable non-duality manifests its own shining light.* This is the union of wisdom and compassion. The less that is done by the anxious and controlling ego the more that is accomplished effortlessly. *In order to dispel the darkness of ignorance of all sentient beings* we offer this light so that hope, trust, relaxation, opening and awakening will manifest for all beings. *We offer this to the guru, the three jewels, the three roots and all the deities. Please accept and then bestow supreme and general accomplishments.* So many burdens have been taken on due to a misunderstanding of responsibility. The ego strives to accomplish tasks beyond its capacity, generating feelings of hopelessness, despair or defensive indifference. Awakening to our manifest existence as the flow of energy of the unborn dharmakaya allows us, as nodes of energy, to take our place and participate while integrated with the ground openness.

ཧོཾ༔ འགྲོ་ཀུན་ཕ་མར་ཤེས་པའི་ཀོང་བུ་རུ༔

རྗེན་གྱིས་བཀྱང་བར་དྲན་པའི་མར་ཁུ་འཁྱིལ༔

དྲེན་ལན་གསོ་བར་འདོད་པའི་སྡོང་བུ་ལ༔

ཡིད་དུ་འོང་བའི་བྱམས་པའི་རས་བལ་ཀྱིས༔

བརྩེ་བའི་སྙིང་རྗེའི་དམ་དུ་རབ་དཀྲིས་པར༔

ལྷག་བསམ་རྣམ་པར་དག་པའི་མེ་ལྕེ་འབར༔

བདག་གཞན་འབྲེལ་མེད་རྟོག་པ་རང་སར་གྲོལ༔

དམིགས་བཅས་དམིགས་མེད་ཆེན་པོའི་ཀློང་དུ་ཐིམ༔

རང་འབྲས་བླ་མེད་རྫོགས་བྱང་འོད་དུ་འཆེར༔

འགྲོ་བའི་མ་རིག་མུན་པ་སེལ་ཕྱིར་དུ༔

བླ་མ་མཆོག་གསུམ་རྩ་གསུམ་ལྷ་ཚོགས་ལ༔

འབུལ་ལོ་བཞེས་ནས་མཆོག་ཐུན་དངོས་གྲུབ་སྩོལ༔

Wonderful. In the pot of knowing all beings to be my parents swirls the oil of remembrance of the kindness with which they held me. On the stick of the desire to repay their kindness the cotton of very beautiful love is wound well with the binding of very strong compassion. The flame of the most excellent purity burns bright. Thoughts of the absence of connection between myself and others are liberated in their own place and dissolve in the vastness of great compassion with and without an object.

The light of our own result of unsurpassed complete enlightenment is shining. In order to dispel the darkness of ignorance of all sentient beings we offer this to the guru, the three jewels, the three roots and all the deities. Please accept and then bestow supreme and general accomplishments.

The pot of knowing all beings to be my parents is the recognition that all beings are known to me; they are not strangers but are beings with whom I have already shared many intimate moments. I have been born in samsara again and again and in each life I had parents, beings whose energy created the physical basis for my existence. Thus I am always already connected to all beings for they have each been so kind to me in my different lives, protecting me, feeding me, clothing me. In the pot *swirls the oil of remembrance of the kindness with which they held me.* Thus I have a debt of gratitude to all beings. I go towards them already in their debt, happy and willing to repay it. For not only did they sacrifice a lot to take care of me, but while helping me they performed actions with negative consequences and so the limitations they experience now arise from their actions for my welfare. *The stick of the desire to repay their kindness* is inserted. This is the profound desire we can feel to repay this kindness, to work constantly and forever for the welfare of all beings.

The knowledge that each being has been our own parent comes before any other knowledge about them. That is, it is more basic, more given than all other identifications that occur in samsara, such as friend, boss, child, French, German, old, sick etc. Our obligation towards them is not generated by their current qualities or circumstances but by this deep bond that is already in place. We are not helping others from a position of superiority or in order to gain something. We help them from the position of a servant; we enter a willing servitude supported by gratitude. This generates the loving tenderness which forms *the cotton of very beautiful love.* Love without limit, without expectation, love that is freely available and which opens us to the awareness of inter-dependence, of co-emergence, of inter-being. Through this our heart remains open, and our awareness vast. We become able to hold in mind all beings at all times so that we do not fall into the forgetfulness of self-preoccupation and blinkered identification with our limited life context.

It is very important to help children develop a sense of gratitude towards and respect for those who care for them. This antidotes the currently pervasive sense of entitlement, of taking everything for granted, by which children remain stuck in an unhealthy narcissism which annihilates any sense of the actual structure of their daily existence. To say, 'Well, I never asked to be born', is to be so out of touch with life, with the actuality of mutual exchange and dependence, that it expresses only a profound delusion. Angry indifference blocks the way to receiving help – for if we deny that we have ever been helped how will we make use of what is available now?

Love itself is charming, beautiful, attractive – we are drawn towards those who embody love and who express it easily. The cotton of this love *is wound well with the binding of very strong compassion*, compassion which does not give up on others no matter how testing and challenging they are. We vow never to abandon sentient beings. This means not retaliating, not getting so caught up in the moment that we forget our bodhisattva intention. Of course, our limited habits continue to arise, they are always available. Through meditation and being mindful in daily life we can come to see more clearly what we are up to; see the hooks, triggers and invitations to become small, petty, and over-identified. Seeing this in ourselves we can see it in others. We are not basically bad, and they are not basically bad – but we all get lost. Strong, great compassion is to never forget our natural openness even as we observe ourselves and others getting lost again and again. Gradually, all our patterns of lostness can be reintegrated into our open ground. They cease to be habits that grab us, patterns that seem to have a life of their own. We start to be able to see them as our own energy – egocentrically at first as we learn to 'own' them. Yet as we progress in the practice they are revealed as the energy of the ground, spontaneously arising and self-liberating.

With the happy collaboration of all these factors, *the flame of the most excellent purity burns bright*. It is unsullied by any narrow motives. There is just the openness of the moment itself – it is not being used as a means to an end. Self-less love and compassion radiate without seeking a reward. The paradox of this is that the less reward is sought the more it is gained both in terms of the lightness of our being and the warmth of the world. This is not an ideology, not something we want to convert other people to. Rather, it is a quality of awakening already present in all beings, one which will ripen in them when the conditions are ready. One of the functions of sending out rays of light is to facilitate the ripening process.

Thoughts of the absence of connection between myself and others are liberated in their own place. These are the thoughts of our own isolation and our deep feelings of autonomy. That is, we see these thoughts to be just empty arisings and, as they vanish, we find ourselves to be part of the living world. This connection is primordial, there from the very beginning, unaltered by any concepts, naming, defining and so on. The constructs of samsaric discrimination cannot condition the givenness of the fact that I and all beings have, from the very beginningless beginning, been the radiance of the unborn natural state.

All sense of non-connection *dissolves in the vastness of great compassion with and without an object.* 'Great' indicates that compassion is inseparable from emptiness. Compassion with an object refers to both the wish to help beings and the actions that flow from this intention. We can think of specific beings we know, of beings we don't know and of all sentient beings. In each case we have an object to focus on, to think about, to organise ourselves towards. They exist and we want to help them. Even if we have a sense of the emptiness of the entire field, our focus is on the being to be saved and our role in achieving that.

Compassion without an object arises when we rest in awareness, allowing whatever comes to come, open to everything without reification. There is only ungraspable luminous arising. There are no objects and no subjects engaging with objects, no entities out there and no fixed self 'who I am'; there is nothing that exists in itself. In this state there are no beings to be saved, for what we take to be beings are illusory energy modes, already fully integrated into the ground nature from which they have never strayed. This compassion is free from any collusion in the fantasies of samsara. It is not an absence of care for sentient beings, but rather that they are seen directly for what they are, the natural radiance of the open state.

The light of our own result of unsurpassed complete enlightenment is shining. This light arises from the result of all our effort, and it is also the effortless result for it is the return to the place we have never left. This state which is always there as our potentiality, arises clearly when, as a result of all our effort, we finally feel able to stop making effort, to stop interfering so that the natural state of great completion, dzogchen, is actualised; ever present where it has always been. This is the inseparability of ground, path and result, the natural light of awakening. With this, the intention *to dispel the darkness of ignorance of all sentient beings,* the method, *offering this to the guru, the three jewels, the three roots and all the deities,* and the result, *please accept and then bestow supreme and general accomplishments,* are simultaneous.

ཧོཿ ཚུལ་ཁྲིམས་རྣམ་པར་དག་པའི་ཀོང་བུ་རུཿ
སྦྱིན་པ་རྣམ་དག་འཛིན་མེད་མར་ཁུ་འཁྱིལཿ
བསམ་གཏན་རྣམ་པར་དག་པའི་སྡོང་བུ་ལཿ
བརྩོན་འགྲུས་རྣམ་པར་དག་པའི་སྲོས་སྦྲང་ཏེཿ
བཟོད་པ་རྣམ་པར་དག་པའི་རས་བལ་དཀྲིསཿ
ཤེས་རབ་རྣམ་པར་དག་པའི་མེ་ལྕེ་འབརཿ
རང་དོན་གཅེར་འདོད་གཞན་དོན་ཀློང་དུ་ཐིམཿ
ཕུགས་རྗེའི་ཐབས་དང་སྨོན་ལམ་སྟོབས་རྒྱས་ཏེཿ
ཡེ་ཤེས་པ་རོལ་ཕྱིན་པའི་རང་འོད་འཚེརཿ
འགྲོ་བའི་མ་རིག་མུན་པ་སེལ་ཕྱིར་དུཿ
བླ་མ་མཆོག་གསུམ་རྩ་གསུམ་ལྷ་ཚོགས་ལཿ
འབུལ་ལོ་བཞེས་ནས་མཆོག་ཐུན་དངོས་གྲུབ་སྩོལཿ

Wonderful! In the pot of very pure morality swirls the inexhaustible oil of very pure generosity. On the stick of very pure concentration, with the very pure attitude of diligence the cotton of very pure patience is tied. The flame of very pure true knowing burns bright. The desire to privilege one's own welfare dissolves in the vastness of benefiting others.

With the increase of power, compassionate method and aspiration, transcendent original knowing manifests its own shining light. In order to dispel the darkness of ignorance of all sentient beings we offer this to the guru, the three jewels, the three roots and all the deities. Please accept and then bestow supreme and general accomplishments.

This verse concerns the six paramitas, the six transcendent qualities which characterise the ripening bodhisattva. The path to realising one's own nature lies through the forgetfulness of self that comes with devoting oneself fully to the welfare of others.

The pot of very pure morality is composed of our capacity to follow the right path of conduct: firstly, to do no harm and secondly, if possible, to do some good. Rules provide helpful support for this, as they offer us a frame that exists prior to the heat of actual interactions. We can mobilise our will, our decisiveness, and our intention to resist the pull towards outer and inner behaviour which will bring no true benefit for self or other. Although our aim is to abide in the view of natural perfection, we also need to observe our capacity, our limits, and take care not to imagine we can manage or integrate more than we can. The practice of morality can also be integrated with instant presence. Morality here is a set of rules to be followed, and we can use these to review our own actual capacity as it reveals itself in each concrete situation. We may be able to perform the act, but can we deal with the consequences? Very often the aspect of ourselves which performs the action is not around to pick up the bill when it is all over. Morality helps to keep our eager, expansive, impulsive aspects in communication with the responsible, rational aspects, and also with the regretful, guilty and self-blaming aspects. In this way, we are challenged to hold ourselves together long enough to see what we are up to.

In this pot *swirls the inexhaustible oil of very pure generosity*. This is a generosity which responds to the actual needs of the situation. This does not necessarily mean giving people what they want but rather seeing the widest, deepest, potential of the situation and responding in a way that optimises benefit on all levels. That means balancing immediate and delayed gratification. For example, being able to determine how to balance a person's capacity for awakening, which might be aided by the gift of a strong confrontation, with the needs of their arising vulnerability, which requires tenderness and care.

The stick of very pure concentration is a concentration which is undisturbed, not because one is fiercely holding oneself together, but because of a complete immersion in the practice. Relaxing into the practice as if it was the whole of existence, all that there is, there is no basis for distraction. Thoughts arise and pass but absorption is undisturbed.

The very pure attitude of diligence is the capacity to keep going, to be undaunted. It requires the focusing of energy and the commitment to carry tasks through to the end, whatever outer or inner obstacles arise. Of course, worldly busyness can easily be a distraction. It is important to make time for rest and retreat. However, the view is not something to be picked up and put down as it suits us. To maintain the view, to rest in the practice, requires vigilance and diligence, spacious diligence that allows the naturally arising energy of the open state to flow as required. That is to say, diligence is not only about pushing ourselves but about being aware where our energy comes from so that what we take to be our own will is integrated into its own ground.

Diligence is about discipline, it binds us to the task and here it binds *the cotton of very pure patience*. Pure patience is the quality of being undisturbed, of feeling that there is time, that nothing is more important than maintaining the state of awareness, and that tasks take as long as they take. So often, the demands of daily life have us rushing ahead, multi-tasking, feeling there is so much to do and so little time. With this sense of pressure it is easy to feel impatient, to feel persecuted by trains being late, people who fail to phone us back and so on. Yet, on reflection, very few of the tasks which seem so pressing, so vital, are actually that important. Our lives would go on if they didn't happen. Yes, of course, our lives would be changed, but they are changing anyway. Part of the work of developing patience is to question our fantasy of being in control. When we see and accept that there is very little that we actually control, we become more able to collaborate with circumstance and that includes being patient, seeing the bigger picture. Other people may develop their meditation more quickly than us, may rapidly display finer qualities. If our envy drives us to try harder we can lose sight of our actual capacity, yet it is only by staying with that growing edge that true progress can be made. Patience allows us to resist acting on impulse, it lets us stop, look, listen, consider, so that the action is one that fits the situation rather than expressing a transient feeling.

On the basis of those five qualities, *the flame of very pure true knowing burns bright*. Wisdom, true knowing, discernment, is a quality of intelligence, not a cognitive intelligence based on developing information-processing skills but an intuitive intelligence that can quickly discern what is going on and what needs to be done. It requires optimal attention to the experiential field coupled with optimum availability free from assumption, pre-planning, expectations and all the myriad ways we foreclose. Wisdom is the capacity to remain grounded and balanced in the midst of life. It is centred without being centred in or on anything. Present and available, yet not off balance, it remains calm and clear whatever is going on, for it has the infinite stability of being inseparable from emptiness and of knowing that everything that occurs is similarly inseparable from emptiness. When this flame burns, *the desire to privilege one's own welfare dissolves in the vastness of benefiting others.* The desire to put ourselves first vanishes in the infinity of concern for the welfare of others, and one's own body, speech and mind arise in the service of others. How? Because with wisdom we are sorted, content, we have what we need, we are at peace, and so all our energy is available for the service of others.

The increase of power, compassionate method and aspiration refers to four further qualities: compassionate method, aspiration, strength, and power. Traditionally these constitute the four additional paramitas that make up the class of ten paramitas or transcendent qualities. When they are all fully developed our bodhisattva activity manifests with optimal effect. Compassionate method is the capacity to utilise any situation for the benefit of beings. Any event has the potential to aid awakening. Aspiration is the generation of a big hope, that of full enlightenment, letting ourselves be filled with a big breath so that our vision expands to reveal tasks that have true value. Strength is the capacity to take up a position of responsibility, to not be intimidated by what one has chosen to do. This is the strength of spaciousness, of not getting mired in the details but being resolute, unflappable and able to empower others. Through this one stays centred in the flow of one's intention and thus avoids slipping into feelings of, 'I have to...', 'I must...', 'I should...'. Duty and obligation are poor allies and sooner or later we rebel against them. Power is the quality of accomplishment, of being able to make things happen. It is not that one is necessarily a powerful person with a store of personal charisma. Rather, the power arises from the compassionate way with which we articulate ourselves in any situation.

As these four qualities collaborate with the previous six, their consummation, *transcendent original knowing, manifests its own shining light.* This is the non-duality of the qualities of the path, those that are developed by effort, and the quality of the result, which is presence in the actual-ity of the unchanging ground. The intention to benefit others, *to dispel the darkness of ignorance of all sentient beings*, is implicit within it. *We offer this to the guru, the three jewels, the three roots and all the deities. Please accept and then bestow supreme and general accomplishments.* This light spreads out as an offering to all the buddhas, to all the enlightened ones, calling on them to act for the benefit of all beings. They will do that anyway, and moreover all beings have been pure from the very beginning, yet this communication through the offerings keeps the interconnectedness alive for us, reminding us that we too have a vital role in the well-being of all.

ཧོཿ ལྡག་པ་ཆུལ་ཁྲིམས་གཙང་མའི་ཀོང་བུ་རུཿ

འཕགས་ལམ་ཡན་ལག་བརྒྱད་ཀྱི་མར་ཁུ་འཁྱིལཿ

གཡོ་མེད་ཏིང་འཛིན་བརྟན་པོའི་སྡོང་བུ་ལཿ

སེམས་གནས་དགུ་དང་ཡིད་བྱེད་བཞི་ཡིས་དཀྲིསཿ

སྟོབས་དྲུག་རྣམ་པར་དག་པའི་གྲུབ་འབྲས་ལཿ

ཐོས་བསམ་བསྒོམ་པའི་ཤེས་རབ་མེ་ལྕེ་འབརཿ

རྟོག་དཔྱོད་རྣམ་པར་མི་རྟོག་ཀློང་དུ་ཐིམཿ

བསླབ་གསུམ་རྣམ་པར་དག་པའི་རང་འོད་འཚེརཿ

འགྲོ་བའི་མ་རིག་མུན་པ་སེལ་ཕྱིར་དུཿ

བླ་མ་མཆོག་གསུམ་རྩ་གསུམ་ལྷ་ཚོགས་ལཿ

འབུལ་ལོ་བཞེས་ནས་མཆོག་ཐུན་དངོས་གྲུབ་སྩོལཿ

Wonderful! In the pot of the finest pure morality, swirls the oil of the noble eightfold path. On the wick-stick of unwavering, steady absorbed contemplation the nine methods of mind control and the four aspects of mental development are tied. With the result of the perfect attainment of the six powers, the flame of true knowing arising from study, reflection and meditation burns bright. Judgemental thoughts dissolve in the vastness of complete freedom from thoughts.

The completely pure three trainings manifest their own shining light. In order to dispel the darkness of ignorance of all sentient beings we offer this to the guru, the three jewels, the three roots and all the deities. Please accept and then bestow supreme and general accomplishments.

The pot of the finest pure morality is the basis for all spiritual progress. If we cannot trust ourselves, if we cheat ourselves and are unclear about what we do and why, then we lack a foundation for being able to see clearly. It is not that we will always please people or do what they want but we have to develop a clear capacity to see what we do and to work with the consequences – and this is aided by morality. Within the pot *swirls the oil of the noble eightfold path* which was set forth in the first teaching given by Buddha Shakyamuni. He set out what are known as The Four Noble Truths. The first, the truth of suffering, is a fact, an undeniable fact, although we often try to deny it: the suffering of birth, old age, sickness and death, the finite nature of our existence that conflicts with our dreams and fantasies. The second, the truth of the cause of suffering, names attachment arising from ignoring how things are. Attaching to concepts about self and other we step out of the living moment into a mental world of plans, interpretations and judgements in which we create the fantasy of a secure existence for ourselves. The third, the truth of there being an exit from suffering, points to the unchanging, the unconditioned, nirvana, that which is not like anything we know. The fourth truth is the path to freedom from suffering, the Noble Eight Fold Path.

This path covers all aspects of our existence. The first aspect is right view, looking clearly, seeing the impermanence of all things and their absence of inherent self-existence. This view illuminates all the places where we get trapped and provides the clarity necessary for practice. The next aspect is right understanding which is the capacity to apply the view so that it becomes an effective tool. Understanding involves looking at oneself, seeing how one functions and learning to avoid habitual limitation. Right speech is the capacity to be truthful and direct, to use language only for the welfare of others and to avoid generating complex narratives that hide the simplicity set out in the view. Right action involves control of our body so that our activity is both virtuous and harmonious. It means being careful about what we do so that we become skilful in avoiding the unwholesome, and effective in developing the wholesome.

Right living as right livelihood is about care in how we maintain our existence: what kind of work we do, what kind of relation we have to money, to power, to other people. It is about ensuring that our life, our being alive, is not a source of suffering to others but is rather a positive

contribution to the wellbeing of the world. Right exertion is applying our time, resources and energy to whatever is advantageous and
ethical to develop. It means not being lazy, not wasting time, not being
distracted by the fascinating ephemera of this world. Right recollection is holding the view in mind. It means being mindful, and attentive. Thus, we try to avoid getting lost, and again and again have to call
ourselves back to attending to the flow of impermanent phenomena.
Through this we resist the siren's call to hurl ourselves on the rocks
of belief in substantial, truly existing phenomena, ourselves included.
Right meditation is the development of calmness and clarity. By maintaining a focused attention in meditation we avoid distraction and the
mind settles as it lets go of the habit of busy involvement. By intro-
spection, observing what is actually arising, we develop clarity which
illuminates how we ourselves construct the prison we inhabit.

The wick-stick of unwavering, steady absorbed contemplation is inserted.
By means of this the object of focus and the one who is focusing are
perfectly aligned so that a deep tranquillity arises. What is occurring is
enough; there is no need to be interested in anything else. Satisfaction,
deep peace, replaces the need for excitement, the endless hope that the
next thought or emotion will bring some deep and lasting meaning or
satisfaction. It never does. In this way the development of samadhi or
absorbed contemplation is a form of renunciation of samsara. If you
are really focused in the practice you are saying no to all the tempta-
tions of worldly existence. You are developing the power to let go of
all that is fascinating without feeling a sense of loss. You don't have to
keep checking out whether worldly life has any value; you have seen
its nature and now have the confidence of knowing how empty it is.

To the wick *the nine methods of mind control and the four aspects of mental
development are tied*. The nine methods are progressive stages. You
start with learning to turn your attention inwards, to disrupt your
immersion in the turbulence of subject-object interaction. Then you
focus your mind on a simple object for a short period of time. This
leads to learning how to return to the focus when your attention slips
away. Then you have a close fixation where you are working to return
quickly to the fixation. This gives rise to a disciplined mind which
has less tendency to stray. When this is maintained for some time,
the arising of disturbing thoughts, feelings and sensations diminishes
so that there is more peace. Then when there are long periods of no

disturbance the mind is completely pacified, calm and clear. This gives rise to one-pointed attention where concentration can be maintained for extended periods of time. Finally, one achieves an even fixation in which the felt sense of a calm focus is maintained not just in meditation but in all aspects of life.

The four aspects of mental development are practices for keeping our attention primed as a tool for developing understanding. This is supported by reading sutra texts and learning how to apply analytical tools to understand and release oneself from problems. This approach focuses on maintaining an intentional attitude that resists fascination with transient objects, so that one avoids falling under the sway of whatever is arising. Looking at all things as being equal in nature, applying antidotes if one finds oneself being hooked in, returning again and again to purifying one's attitude and mental factors, and clarifying the difference between mind and whatever arises in the mind – these four aspects all lead to the capacity to live with the right view.

The result of the perfect attainment of the six powers ripens from the fulfil-ment of the previous stages of training. Although our aim is integra-tion in the natural state, it is important to learn other methods as they provide tools to benefit others. They weave a safety net, so that when we slip from the high-wire of dzogchen we have other methods to break our fall. Moreover it can feel helpful and reassuring to have other practices to utilise when our capacity is limited. However, in the dzogchen view, what we call 'my capacity', my felt sense of what I can cope with, is not the aspect to focus on. For if we become preoccu-pied with the vagaries of 'our own experience', there will be no end to adjusting and correcting. It will be all up to us and this noble struggle will create new obscuration. So relax, dis-identify and simply be the immediate presence that is present with whatever is going on.

The six powers are: firstly, to listen attentively, to be able to really listen and feel the impact of what is being said. This requires us to be open, interested and available. The second power is thinking, which means being able to attend precisely to what is presented and consider it without adding unnecessary concepts which would lead to everything getting mixed up. This involves the discrimination of only bringing to mind what is pertinent without rambling or free association. The third power is memory, the capacity to recall accurately what has occurred. This also entails not mixing things up, being respectful of the actual situation and so recalling it as it occurred. Very often interpretation and memory get mixed up together so that an event shared by six people gives rise to six opinions about what went on rather than a clear factual consensus. Knowledge, the fourth power, is the capacity to apply what has been learned so that knowledge becomes an effective tool, a powerful method for illuminating what is occurring. It involves the development of confidence and authority. Exertion, the fifth power, is the capacity to break through, to keep going long enough to allow radical change to occur. It is the capacity to not be moved from the task in hand. Finally, the sixth power is full understanding, the understanding of all things both as they are in their empty nature, and as they appear to be in all the unique particularity of their arising.

With all this preparation *the flame of true knowing arising from study, reflection and meditation burns bright.* Study means to really attend to whatever is heard or read. It means not falling into the three pot faults. Firstly, not to be like an upturned pot that cannot be filled with what is offered i.e. to pay attention. Secondly, not to be like a pot with a hole in it so that whatever is heard gets forgotten i.e. to focus on remembering accurately what is said. Thirdly, not to be like a pot with rotten food in it which corrupts whatever new food is added to it. This occurs when we mix dharma teachings with our own ideas and feel that our opinion is very important. Dharma understanding is hard enough to gain without confusing ourselves with ideas from other paths, and from our own chaotic experience.

When this flame burns brightly *judgemental thoughts dissolve in the vastness of complete freedom from thoughts.* All discursive thoughts, judgements, opinions and so on vanish in the infinite space free of the elaboration of dualistic thoughts. All the antidotes mentioned in the preceding lines help to lessen the intoxification we experience from our habitual reliance on the contents of our own mind. As with any addiction the substance, which is actually toxic, seems to be helpful and fulfilling, at least in terms of instant gratification. Thoughts are the greatest and most common addiction. There is no end to thinking for there is no end to the supply of thoughts. The drug dealer and the drug user live side by side inside us. Applying the methods of detoxification mentioned above brings a new sense of freedom and vitality. A life no longer dependent on thoughts allows in the freshness of each moment just as it is. There is a paradox here, for when we let go of our reliance on thoughts as the arbiters of value and meaning, our mind does not become empty and devoid of experience. Rather, as the clutter of habitual preoccupation declines there is more space for the arising of effective thoughts that support our compassionate being in the world with others. So freedom from thoughts means freedom from being dependent on dichotomising thoughts. Then their true nature as the radiance of the natural state is revealed and they are fully integrated with infinite hospitality.

The completely pure three trainings manifest their own shining light. The trainings in morality, in meditation and in wisdom, form the foundation of progressing on the buddhist path by which we move, stage by stage, from confusion and suffering to clarity and peace. Each of these stages can be integrated with dzogchen practice so that their value in increasing relative clarity and mental flexibility can be utilised without falling into a dualistic frame. Developing disciplined practice over time allows the wheel of offering to turn easily in the space of awareness. *In order to dispel the darkness of ignorance of all sentient beings we offer this to the guru, the three jewels, the three roots and all the deities. Please accept and then bestow supreme and general accomplishments.* These are repeated again and again, weaving samsara and nirvana back together. This offering evokes the blessing of the experience of non-duality which frees all beings from their endless dream-time.

ཏྲི༔ ཕྱི་སྐྱེད་ཞིང་ཆེན་གཡང་གཞིའི་ཀོང་བུ་རུ༔

ནང་བཅུད་ཤ་ཁྲག་རུས་པའི་མར་ཁུ་འཁྱིལ༔

གསལ་བྱེད་ཚིཏྟ་རྩ་ཡི་སྡོང་བུ་ལ༔

དོན་སྙིང་འབྱུང་བ་ལྔ་ཡི་རས་བལ་དཀྲིས༔

ཕུང་ཁམས་བཀྲག་མདངས་འཚེར་བའི་མེ་ལྕེ་འབར༔

སྙིགས་མའི་སྒྱུ་ལུས་འོད་ཕུང་ཀློང་དུ་ཐིམས༔

རིག་པའི་ཡེ་ཤེས་རང་རྩལ་འོད་ཟེར་འཚེར༔

འགྲོ་བའི་མ་རིག་མུན་པ་སེལ་ཕྱིར་དུ༔

བླ་མ་མཆོག་གསུམ་རྩ་གསུམ་ལྷ་ཚོགས་ལ༔

འབུལ་ལོ་བཞེས་ནས་མཆོག་ཐུན་དངོས་གྲུབ་སྩོལ༔

Wonderful! In the pot of the outer vessel of an entire human skin swirls the inner contents of flesh, blood and bones. On the wick-stick of the shining heart and channels is wound the cotton of the organs and entrails made from the five elements. The flame of all the radiant components of existence burns bright. The debased illusory body dissolves in the vastness of a mass of light.

The diversifying energy of the original knowing of natural presence manifests as shining rays of light. In order to dispel the darkness of ignorance of all sentient beings we offer this to the guru, the three jewels, the three roots and all the deities. Please accept and then bestow supreme and general accomplishments.

The pot is the outer vessel of an entire human skin, our own skin: we are this human being. This is the skin bag in which we live, the surface of which seems to separate us from the world. Within the pot *swirls the inner contents of flesh, blood and bones,* and all the other components of our biological existence. Often we live in a fantasy body, the ego's body that is just there, healthy and happy and not composed of flesh and blood. It is only when we get sick that the other body arises for us and then we take it to a doctor who knows about that sort of thing. To remember that we are our flesh and blood is to remember that we will die.

The wick-stick is our shining heart and channels, the functioning basis of our aliveness, the site of awareness and its energy. On a more general level, the eight-petalled chakra of the heart is the site of the eight consciousnesses through which we experience our samsaric existence. These are the consciousnesses linked to each of the five senses, plus the following three: the mental consciousness that organises the input from the sense consciousnesses, the consciousness that is the site of all the afflictions, and the ground consciousness which holds all memory and knowledge of things.

Around the wick *is wound the cotton of the organs and entrails made from the five elements.* They are composed of, or rather manifest from, the interaction of the five elements, earth, water, fire, wind and space. The uncertain balance, contingency and vulnerability of these elements mark our embodied existence. The whole body is an ongoing infinity of pulsations of dynamic communication which are constantly impacted by outer and inner forces.

The flame of all the radiant components of existence burns bright. These are the five heaps or skandhas and the eighteen constituents or dhatus. The five skandhas are a way of analysing all existence into five simple, seemingly irreducible, building blocks. The first is form, that is, shape and colour, the givenness of what we encounter prior to our naming and evaluating it. Then comes feeling-tone, the sense of positive, negative and neutral which forms the immediacy of the impact of whatever arises for us and leads to our moving towards it or away from it. Perception, the third skandha, is our organising of what comes through the senses into the patterns formed on the basis of our dispositions. This gives us our world, our particular take on the potential of what we encounter, organising our experience through the pathways of editing which pervade our perception. Then comes association, composing or conditioning, all the accumulated habits, assumptions and interpretations which we take to be true and valid and which shape our response to presented experience and formulate our reactions to it. These conditioned factors often operate outwith our conscious sense of the situation – they provide the unexamined 'giveness' of what we experience. Finally, there is consciousness, the capacity to organise thoughts about things, to engage in discursive thought, making sense of what is occurring through planning, linking, comparing and contrasting.

The eighteen constituents are another way of categorising, of giving order to the complexity of our experience. In this grouping there are the six sense organs: the skin, the eyes, the ears, the nose, the tongue and the heart as the organ of the mind. Then there are six conscious-nesses: touch, seeing, hearing, smelling, tasting, and mentation or mental activity. And finally, making up the eighteen, are the six sense objects: those which can be touched, seen, heard, smelt, tasted and entertained mentally.

These two ways of summing up the entirety of our embodied experi-ence, the five heaps and the eighteen constituents, blaze forth as the vibrancy of our moment-by-moment existence.

The debased illusory body dissolves in the vastness of a mass of light. How can it dissolve in this way? Because it has always been inseparable from the energy of awareness manifesting as light and sound. The body is described as a debased, illusory body, for although it has always been illusory, devoid of self-substance, of any kind of inherent self-exis-tence, this fundamental openness and freedom has been covered over by many afflicted thoughts and false beliefs. The material body is not a thing, it is not a solid, fixed, material entity. It is a flow of interweav-ing energies, a constantly changing manifestation whose changes are hidden from us by our own reifying interpretation. It is not that there are only two possibilities, that either we accept the material facticity of our existence – the biological basis of consciousness and so forth – or we are living in a fantasy world that cannot bear the truth. Dharma points to the middle way.

Of course the body exists as flesh and blood; if we are cut we bleed, if we are beaten we die. All this is true. Yet it is true from one particular point of view, that of ourselves as 'I, me, myself', someone who can be known, an active agent, the shaper of my own existence (which I own).

This is the ego's view. But what is the ego? As we have seen before, the ego is not some autonomous force but the ungraspable energy of the natural state, an energy which through its own rapidity has enveloped itself in the illusion of existence. Just as a glowing stick whirled round one's head on a dark night will create the illusion of a circle of fire so the vibration of energy creates the epi-phenomenon of the ego. Then that which is always emergent, always contextual and contingent, appears to be truly existing, stable, possessing a separate existence.

When the body, the consciousness and the sense of an individual self are examined they reveal themselves to be an illusion – for there is only movement, not substance. We appear yet are not the appearance of something else, of some essence somewhere else. Appearance is insep-arable from emptiness. We are ungraspable. When this is awakened to, the energy that was trapped in the spiral of self-reference and attach-ment is free to illuminate the world. We then participate in the field of becoming where nothing is ever secured, reliable or dependable. This is liberating not terrifying, for we are light and dynamic, moving freely in the energising moment; relating, not controlling, communicating not organising, collaborating not dominating.

The body is energy, the manifestation of light; vibrant, alive and insep-arable from the world which shares the same nature. It is the luminous site of the activity of awareness arising for the sake of all.

When the illusory nature of the body and all manifest phenomena is awakened to, the habits of reification and objectification dissolve in space allowing room to experience the radiant expression of the light that arises automatically, by itself, from the original knowing which is inseparable from awareness. Hence, *the diversifying energy of the original knowing of natural presence manifests as shining rays of light*.

Awareness never moves or changes, though it reveals all movement and change. Although it cannot be grasped or seen or measured, it shows many different aspects. One of these is the primordial or origi-nal or natural knowing, the noetic capacity to dynamically illuminate all that occurs. All that occurs is actually illumination. It is not that a light over here is illuminating something else over there. We ourselves and all that we experience are the play of light, a ceaseless display free of the duality of subject and object. Present in this openness, what shall we do? How to spend our time? Infinite possibilities arise and we are free to spontaneously engage with them. We can also turn the wheel of offering: *in order to dispel the darkness of ignorance of all sentient beings we offer this to the guru, the three jewels, the three roots and all the deities. Please accept and then bestow supreme and general accomplishments.* It is this light, the light of our true nature, that we offer for the sake of all beings so that they may recognise that this blessing light which illuminates them is not other than themselves, their own true nature.

ཧོ༔ ཀུན་གཞི་ཁྱབ་གདལ་ཡངས་པའི་ཀོང་བུ་རུ༔

ལྷན་སྐྱེས་ཀུན་བཏགས་རྟོགས་པའི་མར་ཁུ་འཁྱིལ༔

བདག་འཛིན་མ་རིག་པ་ཡི་སྡོང་བུ་ལ༔

ཉོན་ཤེས་སྒྲིབ་པ་གཉིས་ཀྱི་རས་བལ་དཀྲིས༔

ཀུན་ཁྱབ་རིག་པའི་རང་མདངས་མེ་ལྕེ་འབར༔

ལྷན་སྐྱེས་ཀུན་བཏགས་མ་རིག་དབྱིངས་སུ་ཐིམ༔

བདག་མེད་རིག་པའི་ཡེ་ཤེས་རང་འོད་འཆོར༔

འགྲོ་བའི་མ་རིག་མུན་པ་སེལ་ཕྱིར་དུ༔

བླ་མ་མཆོག་གསུམ་རྩ་གསུམ་ལྷ་ཚོགས་ལ༔

འབུལ་ལོ་བཞེས་ནས་མཆོག་ཐུན་དངོས་གྲུབ་སྩོལ༔

Wonderful! In the pot of the pervasive ground of all swirls the oil of simultaneous, discriminating and complaisant ignorance. On the wick-stick of the ignorant belief in inherent self-nature is wound the cotton of the obscurations arising from afflictions and false knowledge. The flame of the natural radiance of all-pervading awareness burns bright. Simultaneous and discriminating ignorance dissolve in the vastness of hospitable space.

Original knowing of natural presence free of reification manifests as shining rays of light. In order to dispel the darkness of ignorance of all sentient beings we offer this to the guru, the three jewels, the three roots and all the deities. Please accept and then bestow supreme and general accomplishments.

The pot of the pervasive ground of all has no limit. Nothing can occur which does not have this as its basis. There is nothing outwith or beyond it. Having no shape it is everywhere without border or limit. It is the source of all and having no self-essence it does not stand apart from phenomena and thus everything that arises also has that nature. It is the ground of both samsara and nirvana. It is always empty and always full.

In this pot *swirls the oil of simultaneous, discriminating and complaisant ignorance.* Within this ground, source, field, there arises, in an instant, simultaneous ignoring. This is the radiance of the ground ignoring the ground while abiding within the ground. There is no reason for this to happen; it is not part of a plan, not a divine intention. Energy folds back on itself creating an illusion which continues. Who experiences this? The illusion. What is experienced? The illusion. Because it is energy it is dynamic, it changes, develops, elaborates – each step of which is actually the energy of awareness being taken as something else.

For example, when you look in the mirror you see your face – but of course you don't. You see a reflection, a reflection you act towards as if it *were* your face. You both know and don't know that it is not really your face in the mirror. Yet, when you are shaving or putting on make-up it is as if what is happening in the mirror is what is really going on. Nothing has actually changed yet it is as if everything has changed. In taking the display of energy to be self-existing entities, things, a mis-taking has occurred and it continues to occur. This is ignorance. It is not a fixed state, but the on-going activity of mistaking what is not the case for what is actually the case. The one making the mistake is part of the mistake. There is no individual self who makes the mistake. There is no one to blame.

The mis-taking is a movement, an arising – and like all arising it is inseparable from the natural ground of all. Self and other are born together as the vibration of self-referentiality; we are both created by and taken in by this moment of illusion which is and always will be inseparable from the ground openness. Because of this there are no actual beings to be enlightened. Everything is always already the natural great perfection. Yet is does not appear that way when the interaction of illusory subject and object weave endless narratives.

How amazing that this felt sense that 'I am me' should not be true! We are taken in by our own story telling and yet the story teller has no true self-existence. This seems incredible – and how much easier it seems to go on believing the story we are in. That which is actually devoid of truth and should therefore be incredible – the experience of self-existing entities – becomes quite credible. We find ourselves and our world to be quite believable because we believe it, and the one who believes this is also just a belief.

Awareness becomes experientially absent due to intoxification with becoming, as the flow of energy is taken to be its own self-existing ground. From this, subject and object arise as seemingly discrete entities with separate identities. This develops as the second stage of ignorance, the identification and distinguishing of more and more entities. By naming, describing and marking differences between arising appearances, there develops the sense that there are truly separate phenomena. This brings with it an increasing degree of mental activity to manage relations with all this seemingly separate 'stuff', 'stuff' which is ceaselessly elaborated. This forms the basis of the multifarious environment we inhabit in our complexity. It is as if within the mirror there was a division between the subject-side reflections and the object-side reflections, and these two aspects, which have exactly the same ground, interact with each other as if they were truly separate and different.

This is not ignorance as a dull state of not knowing but, rather, it is a dynamic double move. On the one hand there is the on-going ignoring of what is actual while on the other there is the active attending to and developing of that which is not actual yet is taken to be actual. The energy of the source is giving rise to imaginary worlds. The potentiality or creativity or imagination, which is the radiance or display of awareness, is being mis-taken for real realms of existence.

Once the translucent, the evanescent, the illusory is taken as solid and substantial, energy is then recruited in the task of stabilising all these 'real' objects. By controlling them we can make a better life for ourselves. But since the basis of this control is our own mind, and our own mind is cut off from its own nature, our actions are often ineffective. Yet we rarely doubt the reality or validity of what is going on. This is the third level of ignoring; a complaisancy in which we accept the givenness of the situation we are born into. As humans we are taken in by the cultural beliefs that surround us. Something similar happens in the other realms of existence as each sentient being takes its world as a given. When we fully believe that 'I am me' and 'this is this' and 'that is that', our lived situation seems like a done deal. The only option for us seems to be to manipulate the situation as far as we can for our own benefit.

This way of ignoring is described as the stupidity of not knowing about karma, the fact that actions are causes having both immediate effects and long term consequences. When things are taken to be what they appear to be, this seeming givenness creates the sense of a static knowable world. For example, if I do something negative and there is no immediate painful result arising from the actions of others, then it appears that I have got away with it. There is no sense that actions are causes that have long term consequences quite apart from their immediate effects.

Karma arises on the basis of the subject being cut off from the ground source, of not experiencing one's true nature as an open, empty, radiant awareness. This is the first stage of karma in which one takes oneself and one's environment to be self-existing and separate. This gives rise to specific intentions, which require an intending subject and an object towards which the intention is directed. For example, 'I' might want to work for 'you'. My intention is always relational, as individualised subjectivity has no existence apart from its gestures of communication, connection and intention towards the object field from which it has been cut off. That is to say, although I experience myself to be an autonomous agent, my so called 'personal identity' is inseparable from my interactions with the world occurring through body, voice and mind. The third element is the act itself, the union of subject and object. I do the actual cooking and offer you the food, all of which I am taking to be real, to be how my life truly is – this is what is going on, this is what it is. Fourthly there is the fulfilment in which I am happy to have cooked for you; there is no doubt or regret or reservation. The four factors of karma are now in place, the event has been validated and it appears that that is the end of it. But a trace, a vibration, a spin, a tendency has been set up in my stream of consciousness that will later manifest as a new situation. This manifests partly on the object 'side', i.e. what is happening, and partly on the subject 'side', i.e. my experience of it. The consequence is not created by some external force; it is not a punishment by a god. Rather, our world is composed of patterns, of vibrations, of forms of energy all of which arise from the ground nature. Some of these movements of energy arise as what 'I' take to be 'me' performing 'my activity'. It is 'my activity' that generates the karmic consequence that 'I' will experience later.

These three aspects of ignoring constitute our world as we know it. They are the functional limit to our sense of who we are, what we could be, how we must live and so on. As long as we abide within them there is no experience of another way of being, no sense of the unborn ground nature. Recollecting this, gratitude arises for the buddhas who have taught the dharma and opened the possibility of awakening from the dream of phenomena to the actuality of luminosity.

The wick-stick of the ignorant belief in inherent self-nature is the fruit of ignoring, the belief in self and others as having a true existence. The sense of self, the sense of an essence, an internal defining core with inherent validity is very powerful. We see essences in everything we encounter: an apple, a man, a car... Each moment is full of things which seem separate and existing in and of themselves. When we refer to an object there is a sense of it being itself, for example, there seems to be a car-ness to the car, an apple-ness to the apple. When this is applied to a person we can identify Mary's way of speaking, walking, sitting and so on – but more than this, there is a Mary-ness to Mary. This we can take to be the expression of the person's ego, the unique shaping and patterning that each individual has.

Normally, we take it that the patterning and the behaviour and the choices arise from the individual's ego, which functions as a truly existing organising principle inside the person. Whereas, from a dharma point of view, this sense of separate existence is a product rather that a primary cause. The self as a 'product' in turn generates contextual secondary causes through its dualistic activity. When the causal chains are recognised as arising from the ground, the imputed self-essence vanishes like morning mist in the sun and the unimpeded, integrated flow continues.

Round the wick *is wound the cotton of the obscurations arising from afflictions and false knowledge.* These have been touched on in previous verses. The obscuration of the afflictions functions as our busy self-referential, affect-ridden involvement in what seems important and necessary in our daily lives. The intensity of this involvement means that there is rarely any time to pause and question our frame of reference and our emotional reactivity. This obscuration is intensified by our habit of being lost in knowledge about things, taking them to be truly existing and delighting in the details. This in turn feeds the development of strong emotional reactions to what is occurring. These mutually reinforcing patterns bring a narrow focus to our attention and an endless, provocative, sense of unfinished business.

All of these many factors arising together act as fuel, ensuring that *the flame of the natural radiance of all-pervading awareness burns bright.* Just as when we are healthy our complexion glows, so when awareness is unobscured it radiates clarity effortlessly. With this flame *simultaneous and discriminating ignorance dissolve in the vastness of hospitable space,* vanishing into the ground openness and source of all. As soon as the sun rises, darkness vanishes. Once we relax away from busy preoccupation with transient events we cease being confirmed as this or that by the thoughts arising in our own minds. A luminous spaciousness is revealed in which all-pervading awareness rests in its own ground and all forms of ignoring vanish without trace.

The wisdom which flows out of awareness is not tainted by any limiting conditioning or definable essence. It is not a thing to be gained or lost, for it is the effortless display of the enduring primordial state. We are always already inseparable from this, and it is this that we wake up into and as, when the illusion of separate entities is no longer grasped. As the pole of the subject who grasps relaxes so the pole of the object which is grasped starts to dissolve. Both poles merge into their own ground and the patterns of ignoring cease. *Original knowing of natural presence free of reification manifests as shining rays of light.* The light from this is offered so that all beings may relax and enjoy what is already present. Everything we experience is the light or expression of the source. Everything means everything, including all our activities, whether sacred or profane, exciting or habitual. This is the field of the repeated offering: *in order to dispel the darkness of ignorance of all sentient beings we offer this to the guru, the three jewels, the three roots and all the deities. Please accept and then bestow supreme and general accomplishments.* Integrating the ground and its myriad manifestations, all beings can see that all that kept them apart was energy's intoxification with the whirlpools and folds of itself.

ཧོཿ མིག་སོགས་དབང་པོ་ལྔ་ཡི་སྣོད་དུ་རུཿ
གཟུགས་སོགས་འདོད་ཡོན་ལྔ་ཡི་མར་ཁུ་འཁྱིལཿ
འཛིན་བྱེད་དབང་ཤེས་ལྔ་ཡི་སྡོང་བུ་ལཿ
ཀུན་བྱེད་འཛིན་མེད་རང་གྲོལ་མེ་ལྕེ་འབརཿ
ཐ་མལ་ཤེས་པ་ཟག་མེད་ཀློང་དུ་ཐིམཿ
གཟུང་འཛིན་གཉིས་སུ་མེད་པའི་འོད་ཟེར་འཚེརཿ
འགྲོ་བའི་མ་རིག་མུན་པ་སེལ་ཕྱིར་དུཿ
བླ་མ་མཆོག་གསུམ་རྩ་གསུམ་ལྷ་ཚོགས་ལཿ
འབུལ་ལོ་བཞེས་ནས་མཆོག་ཐུན་དངོས་གྲུབ་སྩོལཿ

Wonderful! In the pot of the five sense organs, the eyes and so on, swirls the oil of the five desirable qualities of form and so on. On the wick of the five grasping sense consciousnesses the flame of the self-liberating non-grasping performer of all burns bright.

Ordinary understanding dissolves in the vastness free of decline. The non-duality of subject and object manifests as shining rays of light. In order to dispel the darkness of ignorance of all sentient beings we offer this to the guru, the three jewels, the three roots and all the deities. Please accept and then bestow supreme and general accomplishments.

Here the pot is *the five sense organs, the eyes and so on,* the linking points between our sense of a world out there and a person inside. Within it *swirls the oil of the five desirable qualities of form and so on,* all the desirable objects that might delight the senses. This does not mean only the things that are normally taken to be beautiful according to our own culture, for individuals' dispositions are very different. It refers to whatever is pleasing to each being according to their own particular condition. Given the way different people find different objects pleasing, let alone what attracts animals and beings in different realms, one might imagine we would see the relativity of our own choices. Yet this does not appear to be the case. Whatever seems desirable and important to me seems to have these qualities built into it – no matter how other beings react to it. Awakening to the power of this limit, we open our minds to the fact that there is nothing in the universe that does not appeal to some being.

The wick is the five grasping sense consciousnesses which arise as they identify objects to latch onto. Consciousness always takes an object. The sense consciousnesses come into existence with the objects they arise with. According to the traditional buddhist view, if there is no sense object present there is no sense consciousness present either. They arise together as immediate co-emergence.

With this *the flame of the self-liberating non-grasping performer of all burns bright.* The 'performer of all' is the nature of the mind itself, unborn awareness. Everything that is experienced by day or by night, under all conditions whatsoever, is arising from this 'performer of all' as its automatic, effortless flow of display. All that arises is self-liberating. It is there and then gone – just as if you were to write your name on water with your finger. There is nothing to be grasped at and no one to do the grasping. The 'performer of all' does everything without doing anything. Of course, it does not appear like this when we are immersed in our stream of experience. If I don't wash the dishes, they won't get done. That is true. But who is this 'I', the one who is doing the dishes? The energy of the 'performer of all' arises in the form of me doing the dishes. The sense of 'I', as a personal identity and site of agency, is itself part of the flow of emergence or display of the one ground.

Integrating into the instant presence of openness, ordinary dualistic understanding dissolves in the infinity which never diminishes. *Ordinary understanding dissolves in the vastness free of decline.* The root of all our ordinary thoughts is the pure ground, and this is revealed when we stop being so responsible and let things happen, including ourselves. This is not the same as chaotic impulsivity, for relaxation finds us integrated in the self-ordering openness.

The non-duality of subject and object manifests as shining rays of light. Non-duality is not sameness or homogenisation. The phenomena of the world still manifest as they are, yet the seemingly inherent separateness linked to the sense of there being truly separate entities vanishes. The open ground gives rise to subject and object, like playful twins. They have never been apart and whatever forms they may show, they are never anything other than the energy of awareness. The easy interplay of subject and object turns the wheel of offering in the manner of a dream: *in order to dispel the darkness of ignorance of all sentient beings we offer this to the guru, the three jewels, the three roots and all the deities. Please accept and then bestow supreme and general accomplishments.* This is offered to evoke the awakening of all beings from their lonely illusion of isolation.

ཏྀ༔ ལྟ་བ་བློ་ལས་འདས་པའི་ཀོང་བུ་རུ༔

བསྐྱེམ་པ་དམིགས་གཏད་བྲལ་བའི་མར་ཁུ་འཁྱིལ༔

སྤྱོད་པ་ཆད་ལས་འདས་པའི་སྡོང་བུ་ལ༔

འབྲས་བུ་ཕྱག་རྒྱ་ཆེན་པོའི་མེ་ལྕེ་འབར༔

ཡུལ་གྱི་མདུད་པ་ཡུལ་ཅན་ཀློང་དུ་ཐིམ༔

ཐིགས་ཆད་ཕོད་རྐྱལ་ཤུང་འཇུག་སེམས་ཀྱི་ཀློང༔

གཞི་སྣང་གཞི་ལ་ཤར་བའི་རང་འོད་འཚེར༔

བཏོད་བྱའི་ཡུལ་ལས་འདས་པའི་དོ་བོ་ལ༔

བཏོད་བྱེད་ཚིག་ལས་འདས་པའི་རང་བཞིན་གྱི༔

ཐུགས་རྗེ་ཀུན་ཁྱབ་རང་བྱུང་སྦྱོན་མེ་འདི༔

འགྲོ་བའི་མ་རིག་མུན་པ་སེལ་ཕྱིར་དུ༔

ཁྱབ་བདག་རིན་ཆེན་བླ་མ་རྡོ་རྗེ་འཆང༔

མཆོག་གསུམ་རྩ་གསུམ་སྐུ་གསུམ་ལྷ་ཚོགས་ལ༔

འདུལ་ལོ་བཞེས་ནས་མཆོག་ཐུན་དངོས་གྲུབ་སྩོལ༔

Wonderful! In the pot of the view beyond the reach of thought swirls the oil of meditation free of preconceived objects. On the wick of immeasurable activity the flame of the result of mahamudra burns bright. The knot of object dissolves in the vastness of the subject as the depth of awareness unites releasing and immediacy.

The creativity of the ground arises within the ground, manifesting as shining rays of light. Openness is not an object that can be described; immediacy eludes the words it reveals; spontaneity is everywhere. This is the naturally occurring lamp. In order to dispel the darkness of ignorance of all sentient beings, we offer this to the pervading lord, our most kind guru Dorje Chang, and to the three jewels, the three roots, the three kayas and all the deities. Please accept and then bestow supreme and general accomplishments.

The pot is the view beyond the reach of thought, the vision that cannot be grasped by concepts. Whatever is said about it will be misleading. Traditionally, each of the nine major approaches to practice, each yana or vehicle, is described in terms of view, meditation, activity and result. A view is a way of seeing. It indicates how we position ourselves and what is revealed to us from that position. This line describes the view which is revealed when we don't take up a position, a view without limit. The view from nowhere is the view of everywhere. This is the view of non-viewing, the deconstruction of positioning revealed by the view from here, where here is always the immediacy of unconditioned openness. In samsara everything is up for grabs. Anything and everything can be appropriated, turned into a commodity and marketed. Even meditation techniques and profound teachings can be brought into the market place and exchanged for money. But this view will never be caught for it begins where concepts end. To enter it we need to relax our reliance on transient arisings and integrate with the state of presence that is instantly available because it is always here.

Within this pot *swirls the oil of meditation free of preconceived objects.* Usually we meditate on something, focusing on the breath, on a visualisation, a mantra or something else that we knew we would focus on even before we sat down. Having this means that if we get distracted we know what we should get back to. The pre-arranged focus allows us to determine what is and what is not meditation. This line, however, is referring to meditation where awareness merely attends to whatever presents itself. Resting in a state of presence everything is the object of meditation including all the problems and errors that can arise in meditation. Without presence it is easy to get lost in whatever is occurring. And when you get lost and have no clear frame of reference, confusion can easily become established. That is why entering the path of directly experiencing the state of presence is the vital first step and the purpose of the guru's transmission.

With this view and meditation comes the conduct or activity which is beyond measure, hence *on the wick of immeasurable activity*. This activity is not a form of mindful behaviour, or a specific tantric conduct. It is limitless, beyond measure because it includes all possible modes of behaviour not as a recipe or prescription but as whatever arises inseparable from context. All conditional responses, habits, limits are dropped and activity manifests directly as the energy of the open state co-emergent with fields of ceaseless display.

Then *the flame of the result of mahamudra burns bright*, heralding the ending of effort, as the limits to settling in awareness vanish and open presence continues as the actuality of our experience. This result is not produced by anything but is revealed by the falling away of all that is contrived.

With view, meditation, activity and result all aligned and effortlessly established, the knot of the object dissolves in the infinity of the subject. All the appearances that we once encountered as discrete objects are now revealed as the display of awareness. As the subject is freed from conceptual enmeshment through integration as awareness itself, there is no attachment to any object. All objects go free. The knots they created in the limited subject go free and the knots in the energy channels untie. *The knot of object dissolves in the vastness of the subject.* There is a free flow of the energy of awareness which is all there is, and the final exhaustion or ending of object and object-ness occurs. In this state of limitless freedom, the infinity of awareness is the union or inseparability of the dzogchen aspects of releasing identification and immediacy of presence, hence *as the depth of awareness unites releasing and immediacy*. This is the natural state beyond any method or focus of practice. It is the non-artificial uncontrived complete integration that is the state of dzogchen itself. Primordial purity and relaxed, immediate spontaneity are effortlessly present as they have been from the beginning.

The ground has no beginning or end, no top or bottom. Its own creativity, its expressiveness, manifests within it, though to say 'within' is confusing for there is no place without it. This is it, this is all there is, infinity displayed within infinity; nothing ever becomes limited because it is always integrated into this ground or field or dimension. Language collapses in its attempt to describe or 'capture' this. Language is the field of finite aspects, of this as opposed to that. The actuality of what is gestured towards here is beyond speech, thought and expression. The flow of spontaneity manifests as rays of light effortlessly shining out. Thus *the creativity of the ground arises within the ground, manifesting as shining rays of light.*

All that has been described in this verse so far is now presented as the natural lamp of the three modes of the natural state. Our true nature, *openness, is not an object that can be described.* The inseparability of infinite spaciousness and instant presence is just meaningless words until the experience occurs. It is not like anything else. It is not a thing. We are not things. All conditioned experience falls away in openness. Like a mirror, our nature is ungraspable in itself, empty of any content of its own, yet rich in its potentiality to display illusory images.

Openness reveals its own radiance, its creativity, this is the *immediacy which eludes the words it reveals.* This is like the reflection in a mirror. The reflection is immediately there and is the radiance or potentiality of the mirror. Without effort, without requiring to be created by some further or external source, spontaneous display occurs in response to the play of circumstances. This is the infinite richness of our experience beyond reification.

Within the immediacy of openness, spontaneous movement occurs everywhere: gestures, words, actions – precise moments of experience. Without requiring dualistic planning or conceptual structures, energy manifests within the field of emergence as specific gestures. *Spontaneity is everywhere. This is the naturally occurring lamp.*

These three modes, always integrated, free of all limitation and conditioning, are the naturally occurring lamp inseparable from the well-being of all, effortlessly *dispelling the darkness of ignorance of all sentient beings. We offer this to the pervading lord, our most kind guru Dorje Chang, and to the three jewels, the three roots, the three kayas and all the deities.* Dorje Chang is the fulfilment of the path to enlightenment, he is the union of the qualities of all the buddhas, the master of all the families in the mandala. Moreover, he is not different from our own root guru and not different from our own buddha nature. Our root guru is considered to be our root guru because he or she gives the transmission whereby we enter the path of integrating in our own true nature. This is the greatest gift of all, to give someone the means to actualise that from which they have always been inseparable, and so awaken to the supreme accomplishment. *Please accept and then bestow supreme and general accomplishments.* We make this offering, the offering of the radiance of our own nature so that the guru, the buddhas and all the other great beings will send their light to liberate all beings from the dream labyrinth into the wakefulness of their already awakened state.

ཧཱུྂ༔ རིན་ཆེན་སྣ་ལྔའི་རྒྱུ་ཡི་ཀོང་བུ་རུ༔
རྩི་བཅུད་འབྲུ་མར་འབྱུང་བའི་མར་ཁུ་འཁྱིལ༔
གཙང་མའི་རས་བལ་དཀྲིས་པའི་སྡོང་བུ་ལ༔
ཉི་ཟླའི་འོད་ལ་འགྲན་པའི་མེ་ལྕེ་འབར༔
མུན་པ་མ་ལུས་སྣང་བའི་ཀློང་དུ་ཐིམ༔
ཀུན་ཁྱབ་མུན་པ་སེལ་བའི་རང་འོད་འཚེར༔
འགྲོ་བའི་མ་རིག་མུན་པ་སེལ་ཕྱིར་དུ༔
ཕྱོགས་བཅུའི་རྒྱལ་བ་སྲས་བཅས་ཐམས་ཅད་དང་༔
བླ་མ་མཆོག་གསུམ་རྩ་གསུམ་ལྷ་ཚོགས་ལ༔
འབུལ་ལོ་བཞེས་ནས་མཆོག་ཐུན་དངོས་གྲུབ་སྩོལ༔

Wonderful! In the pot made with the five precious substances swirls the oil of butter coming from the concentrated essence of grasses and grains. On the wick wound with clean cotton wool the flame matching the light of the sun and moon burns bright. All darkness without exception dissolves in the vastness of light.

The illumination of darkness everywhere manifests as shining rays of light. In order to dispel the darkness of ignorance of all beings we offer this to all the buddhas and bodhisattvas of the ten directions and to the guru, the three jewels, the three roots, and all the deities. Please accept and then bestow supreme and general accomplishments.

The pot made with the five precious substances is an actual butterlamp made of gold and silver and decorated with turquoise, coral and pearls. It is beautiful, made in order to honour those to whom the lamp will be offered. Simple tasks, like offering a butterlamp, have great value if carried out with respect and dignity. Valuing what we do, we become more aware of ourselves moving in the world with others.

Within this lamp *swirls the oil of butter coming from the concentrated essence of grasses and grains* which represent the whole world, the play of the five elements, the seasons; the interconnectedness of all phenomena. *The wick wound with clean cotton wool* absorbs the butter, collaborating in the creation of the basis for the flame. The harmonious synergy of the various aspects of the lamp exemplifies dependent co-origination, the infinite matrix of interlocking cause and effect. When lit, *the flame matching the light of the sun and moon burns bright.* As a consequence of this flame *all darkness without exception dissolves in the vastness of light.* We are so used to having bright light available whenever we need it that it can be difficult to imagine what one butterlamp would be like in a dark room. As the flame gutters in the draught, so shadows move. It is so precious and so vulnerable, and needs to be tended well. The lamp means comfort, clarity, and the freedom to carry on activity. It brings, in its own small way, day time into the night. There is no darkness that can withstand the presence of light. All darkness without exception vanishes and disappears as soon as it meets light. Even darkness that has been there for centuries, for aeons, will be instantly dispelled by the presence of light.

This lamp gives light which transforms the dark into light. *The illumination of darkness everywhere manifests as shining rays of light.* Illumination is pervasive, an unobstructed flow of light that finds a way into every pocket of darkness. The shadows that hide secrets, that breed hopes and fears, fantasies and nightmares, are suddenly full of light, offering the clarity of seeing what is actually there. All outer and inner darkness, all obscuration, whether psychological or spiritual, is removed as this light *dispels the darkness of ignorance of all beings.* This is offered to the buddhas and bodhisattvas everywhere, to those who work constantly for the benefit of others. *We offer this to all the buddhas and bodhisattvas of the ten directions and to the guru, the three jewels, the three roots, and all the deities. Please accept and then bestow supreme and general accomplishments.* All the recipients of this offering, immediately and with pleasure, send forth more light which removes the darkness of ignorance from all beings everywhere. Now we can all see what is going on.

ཧོ༔ ཕྱི་ནང་སྒྲིབ་མེད་ཤལ་གྱི་ཀོང་བུ་རུ༔
མེ་ཆུའི་རྩལ་ཤུགས་ལས་བྱུང་མར་ཁུ་འཁྱིལ༔
དངས་མའི་རྩས་ལས་བྱས་པའི་སྡོང་བུ་ལ༔
གསལ་བྱེད་བཀྲག་མདངས་འཚེར་བའི་མེ་ལྕེ་འབར༔
འདྲེ་གདོན་བགེགས་རིགས་འོད་ཀྱི་ཀློང་དུ་ཐིམ༔
ཡ་ང་བག་ཚ་འཛིགས་སྐྲག་རེ་དོག་བྲལ༔
ཕྱི་ནང་ཟང་ཐལ་གསལ་བའི་འོད་ཟེར་འཚེར
འགྲོ་བའི་མ་རིག་མུན་པ་སེལ་ཕྱིར་དུ༔
སངས་རྒྱས་རྒྱུ་ཅན་སྐྱེ་དགུ་ཐམས་ཅད་དང་༔
བླ་མ་མཆོག་གསུམ་རྩ་གསུམ་ལྷ་ཚོགས་ལ༔
འབུལ་ལོ་བཞེས་ནས་མཆོག་ཐུན་དངོས་གྲུབ་སྩོལ༔

Wonderful! In the pot of glass free of outer and inner obscurations swirls the oil arising from the power of fire and water. On the wick made of glowing material the shining flame of radiant illumination burns bright. All demons, trouble-makers and obstructors dissolve in the vastness of the light which is free of fears, worries, terrors and fluctuating emotions.

Unimpeded clarity without and within manifests as shining rays of light. In order to dispel the darkness of ignorance of all sentient beings we offer this to sentient beings, all of whom have the cause of buddhahood, and to the guru, the three jewels, the three roots and all the deities. Please accept and then bestow supreme and general accomplishments.

The pot of glass free of outer and inner obscurations is translucent, free of dirt, and all outer and inner coverings. Within it *swirls the oil arising from the power of fire and water;* the fuel is electricity arising from the motion of the atoms which manifest as fire and water. When agitated in the generating station atoms release their power in a form we can direct and use. Like butter, electricity is the meeting place of the energy of the five elements. *The wick made of glowing material* is the filament of the bulb which glows in response to electricity as the various elements collaborate together. *The shining flame of radiant illumination burns bright* as a powerful illumination which can send light long distances. *All demons, trouble-makers and obstructors dissolve in the vastness of the light* as a stable source of illumination becomes available to us. With this we become *free of fears, worries, terrors and fluctuating emotions.*

Electricity has transformed modern life as cities glow with streetlights that are on all night. The dark places where demons might hide are gone for we can see clearly who or what is there. This light opens up a space which is free of our projected fears, worries, terrors and fluctuating emotions of hope and doubt. However, we only need to walk in a deep forest on a dark night to feel the presence of forces around us, forces which make us uncertain. A sudden noise and we are startled, 'What was that?' The root of this fear is our belief in duality, in the sudden sense of ourselves as being solely a small vulnerable subject, one who can easily be hurt, insulted, damaged and so on. As long as our primary site of identity is our over-invested ego, we will be vulnerable. Even in countries where there is plenty of electric light people can intentionally fantasize all kinds of terrors through reading crime fiction, watching horror movies or believing they are going to be abducted by aliens. There is no end to the narratives of the five poisons; they will run in the theatre of the ego forever. Yet if we awaken to the unborn non-dual light all such terror and agitation will vanish in the manner of being released from the absorbing power of a drama by the lights which come on at the end of the play.

Light from the bulb both fills the bulb and goes out in all directions. *Unimpeded clarity without and within manifests as shining rays of light.* There is no difference between outside and inside. In this sense it is a symbol of the light of the mind which is unimpeded, direct, immediate, already present wherever we go. This wondrous light, a light that brings freedom and relaxation, that generates a sense of confidence and ease, is offered to, and evokes, the buddha nature, the potential for enlightenment present in all beings. It *dispels the darkness of ignorance of all sentient beings. We offer this to sentient beings, all of whom have the cause of buddhahood.* There is no being who has ever been truly separated from the open ground nature. This is their buddha nature. It is not some wonderful essence hidden deep inside them; rather it is the fact that they are always already where they truly are, no matter what fantasies they are caught up in.

The light is also offered *to the guru, the three jewels, the three roots and all the deities. Please accept and then bestow supreme and general accomplishments.* Their acceptance and subsequent further effulgence brings an end to the illusory darkness benighting sentient beings in the midst of the eternal daytime of awakening.

DEDICATION AND GURU YOGA

དེ་ལྟར་མར་མེ་ཕུལ་བའི་བསོད་ནམས་ཀྱིས༔

འགྲོ་ཀུན་སྲིད་པའི་རྒྱ་མཚོ་ལས་བསྒྲལ་ནས༔

མ་རིག་མུན་པའི་གདུང་བ་རབ་བསལ་ཞིང༔

རྣམ་མཁྱེན་རྫོགས་པའི་སངས་རྒྱས་མྱུར་ཐོབ་ནས༔

འཕགས་པ་མར་མེ་མཛད་དང་དབྱེར་མེད་ཤོག༔

By the merit of offering these lamps all beings must be liberated from the ocean of samsara. Then, with the suffering of the darkness of ignorance completely removed, all must quickly gain omniscient perfect buddhahood and become identical with the noble Buddha Dipamkara.

Merit is true value. It is the power of virtue and is generated whenever good actions are performed. Not only does it arise from activity but it is an energetic resource that brings about benefit for others, so the text says *by the merit of offering these lamps*. The merit that arises from offering the lamps comes from all the aspects of the offering. The cleaning, filling and burning of actual lamps, the visualisation, the recitation and contemplation; all of this generates merit because it is done with the aim of benefiting sentient beings. What else could we do with our time? To practice dharma is to abide in merit and value, qualities which are increased by offering them again and again for the welfare of others. Merit has power, it is effective and here we focus its power with the intention *all beings must be liberated from the ocean of samsara*. That includes all those beings who are happy with their current situation. Part of their happiness is built on ignoring the fact that one day the happiness will end.   The ocean of samsara is infinite because it is co-terminous with the ocean of enlightenment. Samsara and nirvana are inseparable; there is but one ground for these two paths. When beings awaken to the fact that the turbulence, the great waves of the ocean in which they move, is not different from the infinity of the energy of awareness, liberation is immediately present. Due to this merit *the suffering of the darkness of ignorance will be completely removed* and each being will be fully centred in open awareness. With this panoramic vision comes omniscience, the direct knowledge of the actual nature of whatever arises and so *all must quickly gain omniscient perfect buddhahood*. There is no falling back from this state since all that was formally captivating is now recognised as the energy of our own mind effortlessly self-liberating the moment it arises.

In particular we wish that all beings *become identical with the noble Buddha Dipamkara*. His story is detailed in The Sutra of King Golden Hand that can be recited at this point in the Butterlamp Prayer (see page 8 and 65) There are many paths to awakening but all awakening has the same taste. The paths influence the kind of buddha activity that flows out after awakening occurs. For example, Buddha Amitabha created the pure realm of Dewachen, Sukhavati, out of the power of the intention he made as a bodhisattva. Due to his intention anyone who remembers his name and calls to him can be reborn in that happy realm where the path to enlightenment is made much easier. Buddha Dipamkara's offering of his body opens the path of offerings in a radical way, reminding us that something has to be at stake; we have to put our very sense of identity on the line. We offer all that we know, all that we are, so that a fresh space is opened in which we, and all beings, can recognise who we really are. *The Sutra of King Golden Hand* describes the many places and conditions under which beings live. Reciting the sutra reminds us of the many possibilities of existence, and that there are none unworthy of remembrance and compassionate inclusion. Enlightenment is not an add-on to the status quo, it is a fundamental shift in experience in which nothing changes and everything is changed. It is not a way to improve ourselves, to become better versions of ourselves, but a way of dropping all the constructs out of which our sense of self is created.

ན་མོ་གུ་རུ་དེ་ཝ་ཌཱ་ཀི་ནི་ཡེ༔

དེང་ནས་བཟུང་སྟེ་ཚེ་རབས་ཐམས་ཅད་དུ༔

ཁྱབ་བདག་དཔལ་ལྡན་བླ་མ་རྡོ་རྗེ་འཆང་༔

སྐུ་བཞི་ཡེ་ཤེས་ལྔ་ཡི་བདག་ཉིད་ཅན༔

ཁྱོད་དང་འབྲལ་མེད་བརྗེ་བའི་ཐུགས་བཟུང་ནས༔

མཆེས་པ་གསུམ་གྱི་སྒོ་ནས་ཁྱོད་བསྙེན་ཤོག༔

Salutation! I bow to the gurus, deities and dakinis. Pervading lord, glorious guru Vajradhara, embodiment of the four modes and the five original knowings, from this time on and in all my lives may I never separate from you, held by your compassion. May I serve and please you with my body, speech and mind!

We begin with a salutation, a greeting, as a way of reminding ourselves that we are always already connected with the divine. *Salutation! I bow to the gurus, deities and dakinis.* We remember the enlightened ones, the ones who shed all self-preoccupation so that they are now fully available for the service of others. We pay homage to them with our body, speech and mind, and recall their qualities. The gurus show the way through their embodied being. They teach, give initiations and transmission and can be present for us as an ongoing support and inspiration.

The deities are those who preside in the sambhogakaya realms and who reveal themselves to us when we practice. When we pray and do sadhana meditation we open ourselves to a different domain. We leave the sphere of complex interactions which constitute our daily life and enter the domain of vision in which symbolic forms manifest effortlessly from the open ground. In that dimension the deities show themselves, showering us with light that dissolves the solidity of our usual sense of self so that our bodies are radiant and translucent with the light of the three enlightened modes. Having become not different from the deity, the divine forms, we merge with them and enter the state of openness in which we integrate with our natural awareness. This is their gift to us.

The dakinis aid our path by energising us, calling into question the habits we get stuck in and actively linking us on to the path. They show many different forms but all have the same function of cutting off attachment to fixed ideas, habits and beliefs.

Having aligned ourselves with the refuge of these three roots of our practice we pray to our guru with an aspiration that goes beyond this life. The guru is vital in the lives of meditators for he or she is the living presence of the teachings. In them and through them the teachings go from being something we hear about, read about, talk about, think about, to becoming the vital wave of our own existence as we open to someone who is living in the dharma and expressing it in every gesture. We express the wish never to be separated from our own guru, not in this nor any other life, so that their presence can sustain us and revitalise us. Central to this is the fact that we don't need to do it all on our own, in fact we can't gain enlightenment on our own. Just as samsara arises from the illusory separation of subject and object which then interact, so, in the reversal, the seeming duality of student and teacher becomes the bond that leads through duality to the unchanging state of non-duality.

Awakening is not done by oneself nor is it done by another. Awakening arises when self and other dissolve as entities and are integrated into their own ground. Opening ourselves to the guru's compassion, feeling that he or she is truly there for us, helps us to settle in the practice of the path which is our refuge, secure in the fact that if we falter the guru's compassion is still there. The feeling that it is all up to oneself is very limiting for meditators. The bubble of self-concern and self-reliance has to burst to allow the experience of non-duality. For this reason we desire to serve the guru with our body, speech and mind. By doing whatever he or she says we align ourselves with another vision of the world and gradually break free of the assumptions and habits on which we have built our existence. He has the key to the door of freedom. Try as we might, we will not find it for it is not hidden in the places where we always look. It is not hidden in our possessions, in our achievements, in our qualities, in our feelings, nor in our thoughts.

Our own nature is hidden by the very activity that we mobilise to try to find it. Relating to the guru will cut through that and reveal us to ourselves.

Who is this guru? She is the dharmakaya, *pervading lord, glorious guru Vajradhara*. Resting on nothing, depending on nothing, the dharmakaya or natural mode is the spaciousness of awareness abiding in its own ground. This is located everywhere, and there is nothing outwith it. This is Vajradhara, unchanging integration with the indestructible natural state. This is the fulfilment of all practice, being that which is not a construct and is never created by practice. Our own guru is complete, lacking nothing, *the embodiment of the four modes and the five original knowings*.

The first three modes are as follows: the natural mode, the radiant mode, which is the immediacy of the display of the natural mode, and the revelatory mode which appears in the domain of manifestation for the benefit of beings. These three modes are inseparable and this co-presencing is the fourth mode, the inseparable mode which is the presence of the guru. The five original knowings were described in the earlier verses dealing with the five sections or families of the mandala. Faith is necessary for practice, for without it we will become bored and mechanical or get lost in our dreams of power. Samsara is vast. There are so many forms that life takes, so many places to be reborn – and therefore so many places to be lost. At this time we have a precious human birth. How long before we gain this opportunity again? Being mindful of this, of the dangers of transient existence we pray *from this time on in all my lives, may I never separate from you, held by your compassion*. In order to strengthen the bond with the teacher we offer whatever we have, being ready to step out of the pseudo-security of our habitual self concern. *May I serve and please you with my body, speech and mind!* Through relying on and serving the guru we enter the family of the mandala, becoming part of the intentional energy that keeps the possibility of awakening fresh.

ཐོབ་དཀའི་དལ་འབྱོར་མི་ལུས་རིན་ཆེན་འདིཿ

ཅི་ཚེ་འདུག་དབང་ཡོད་པར་མི་ཤེས་པསཿ

བསྐུ་མེད་ལས་འབྲས་ཁྱད་དུ་མི་གསོད་ཅིངཿ

འཁོར་བའི་འདམ་རྫབ་འདི་ལས་བསྒྲལ་དུ་གསོལཿ

Regarding this jewel-like human body possessing the freedoms and opportunities that are so difficult to gain, we do not know how long it will remain. Therefore always keeping aware of the non-deceptive nature of karma, may we all be freed from this foul swamp of samsara.

At this time we have the *jewel-like human body possessing the freedoms and opportunities that are so difficult to gain*. We live in a place where there is some dharma, and where our family background is not too extreme, for example, not being trained from an early age to slaughter animals. It means being able to practice because we are healthy in body and mind, and it means that we are connected with and interested in dharma, and that practice is possible. The eighteen factors are listed in many texts, and you can find them, for example, in Chapter 1 of *Simply Being* (For details see www.simplybeing.co.uk).

In the last hundred years, many countries where dharma had flourished for a thousand years or more underwent turbulent change and the old patterns of study and practice were destroyed or severely weakened. Dharma has come to new countries but its presence is still fragile and easily corrupted and commodified. The chance we have now for study and practice will not last long, for even if we live for a long time, old age, sickness and death will influence our capacity. We do not know how long it will remain. We are also easily distracted and our modern lives are full of fascinating ways to pass time. There are so many dharma books to read, and so much that we don't know, that it is easy to feel lost and overwhelmed. We are used to being busy, running from one thing to another with short bursts of enthusiasm. But dharma is a marathon not a sprint. We need to stay on track and persevere with courage and determination so that we gain the optimal benefit of this rare opportunity.

Given the fragility of this situation it is important to practice virtue and to be conscious that within duality our actions are likely to generate karmic consequences. We must be careful in everything we do, looking to the long term, to the big picture and focusing on the benefit of all beings. *Therefore always keeping aware of the non-deceptive nature of karma, may we all be freed from this foul swamp of samsara.* Samsara is like a swamp because the more you move within it, the more you sink. Subject and object lock together with great intensity and it is easy to take each passing circumstance as the limit of our existence. Integrating with the dharma path and never forgetting our commitment to all beings will empty this swamp by bringing all beings to awakening within their own natural state of openness.

འཇིགས་ལས་སྐྱོབས་བྱེད་བླ་མེད་དཀོན་མཆོག་གསུམ༔
སྲོག་ལ་བབ་ཀྱང་ཡལ་བར་མི་འདོར་ཞིང་༔
རྒྱུ་འབྲས་མན་ངག་བདུན་ལ་བློ་སྦྱངས་ཏེ༔
རྣམ་གཉིས་བྱང་ཆུབ་སེམས་དང་མི་འབྲལ་ཤོག༔

Even at the cost of our lives we will never abandon the unsurpassed three jewels who protect from fear. Training our minds with the seven-part practice of cause and effect, may we never be separated from relative and absolute altruistic openness.

This verse offers the orientation of the mahayana sutra path, a commitment to disciplined altruistic practice. We take refuge because we need refuge; we are lost, lonely, all at sea, even if, on a good day, it doesn't seem like that. The three jewels of buddha, dharma and sangha provide protection from fear by pointing to their illusory nature. Respecting the Buddha and aspiring to awaken like him, studying and practicing the dharma to gain direct experience, and communicating with the sangha in order to gain their support and stay on course, all help us to remove the basis of fear.

Fear arises from the felt sense of being a vulnerable entity. It is grounded in attachment to our body, to our social identity, to our thoughts – in fact to all the constituents of our usual sense of self. There are so many of these and they are all contextual, contingent and vulnerable. The buddha points towards our own true nature, relaxed, open, self-existing. When we awaken to this, fear vanishes as we no longer identify with transient moments as if they were who we actually are. We are not entities, we are flow. Moreover, we are not masters of that flow but participants in it – the flow of the energy of awareness inseparable from emptiness.

When we realise how valuable, how rare and precious those who offer refuge are, it becomes meaningful to say *even at the cost of our own lives we will never abandon the unsurpassed three jewels who protect from fear.* In western countries it is unlikely that people would be killed for practicing dharma, though this has happened to people in Tibet, China, Vietnam and so on. What this line refers to is a commitment to stay true to our practice even if that means not focusing on developing the factors that sustain our relative existence. This can arise if we do a long isolated retreat; we might get sick and no one would know. The great expression of this is the Four Vows of the Kadampa, an early buddhist school in Tibet:

> 'May I practice dharma all my life.
> May I practice dharma intensively in retreat.
> May I practice in retreat until I die.
> May I practice dharma alone in retreat, with no-one knowing when I die.'

What an incredible and inspiring commitment this is, placing dharma above everything else, which is then seen as a distraction from the chance of making good use of this rare opportunity.

So many things are invested with importance by us in the course of our lives. When we die our accumulated possessions are sorted out by others and much of it is thrown away as rubbish. Yet for us it was so important. It is always useful to review one's possessions and see what function they perform. Have they anything to do with our highest aspirations? Or are they merely reminders of the ties that bind us into the passing show of daily events? Looking at our lives in a clear way can help us to see how easily we put dharma in the second rank of our actual concerns. If we take practice seriously then this is a shocking fact. Our intentions are often better held in place when supported by vows and trainings. So the third line of this prayer points to the seven-part practice of cause and effect.

Training our minds with the seven-part practice of cause and effect, may we never be separated from relative and absolute altruistic openness. In this practice we start by focusing on all beings having at one time been our mother, so that we are not strangers but are in fact deeply connected. Their kindness to us was great so we generate a sense of gratitude. We then develop a resolve to repay that kindness by doing something for them. We will do this not just out of duty and obligation but out of love and warmth which create a willingness to do whatever it takes.

We focus on developing true compassion for all our mothers, a genuine concern and wish that their suffering will quickly end. In order to fulfil this wish we develop both the altruistic intention to help them, and the altruistic practice of actually helping them through our daily practice. We commit ourselves to this for countless lives, until the last sentient being has been saved, for only then will we ourselves move from the ceaseless activity of a bodhisattva to the spaciousness of full enlightenment.

This practice focuses on the nature of cause and effect. If we do not develop a clear sense of past causes and of how others have helped us, we will not develop the cause now that will lead to the enlightenment of all beings. Understanding how past, present and future link together we become careful about the causes we create and we see how much of our lives are the result of causes developed by others. This interweaving of self and other, cause and effect, awakens us to the flow of interdependence of all phenomena. We are already bound to all sentient beings, and so working for their benefit while simultaneously being aware of their inseparability from the natural state of purity becomes as easy breathing. Remembering how we are in the world with others, participants in the infinite universal unfolding, we find that helping others is not different from helping ourselves, as both activities arise effortlessly in the manner of a dream.

ཕྱི་སྣོད་འཇིག་རྟེན་རི་རབ་གླིང་བཞི་དང་༔

ནང་བཅུད་ཕུང་ཁམས་སྐྱེ་མཆེད་འདོད་ཡོན་ཚོགས༔

གསང་བ་རང་རིག་སྐྱེ་མེད་བྱང་ཆུབ་སེམས༔

ཡང་གསང་དགྱེས་རིག་བདེ་ཆེན་མ་ཧྲུལ་འདི༔

རྒྱལ་བའི་ཡབ་གཅིག་ཁྱོད་ལ་འབུལ་ནུས་ཤོག༔

The outer container of the world with Mt. Meru and the four continents, the inner contents of all beings with their constituent aspects and all desirable phenomena, the secret unborn bodhicitta, my own awareness, the joyful secret mandala of awareness and hospitable space, all this, sole father of the buddhas, may we have the power to offer it to you!

This is a verse of offerings. In the first line we offer *the outer container of the world with Mt. Meru and the four continents,* that is, the environment in which we live, our world and all that we encounter. It is described in terms of the traditional geography with Mt. Meru in the centre and four great continents in the four directions around it. We offer all that we know. If we really offer it we will be left with nothing. What could that mean? What we actually offer are names, descriptions, identifications which we take to be truly real. When these are offered we have no concepts left to rely on. This reveals the fresh immediacy of the moment. What we then respond to is shape and colour, the energetic resonance of appearance in its most simple form. These illusory forms have no real divisions between them since they are experienced as they are, devoid of any inherent self-nature or essence of entity-ness.

Then we offer *the inner contents of all beings with their constituent aspects and all desirable phenomena.* We are offering all the beings who inhabit the world and the functions which generate their habitual sense of self. These have all been described in an earlier verse. They give rise to all the objects of the world that evoke desire in any of the many different kinds of being. Thus we offer all possible manifestations.

We offer *the secret unborn bodhicitta, my own awareness, the joyful secret mandala of awareness and hospitable space,* an offering which is secret in the sense of not being available as an object for our usual state of consciousness. This is our own natural awareness, the unborn enlightened mind. It is not a thing, it is not a personal possession, and yet it is a very intimate offering to make. Then we offer the even more secret or ungraspable or inexpressible offering. This is the inseparability of infinite hospitable space that hosts all arisings, and the awareness that pervades it in the way the colour blue permeates the sky. The non-differentiation of these two constitutes the mandala of great happiness. This happiness is inseparable from emptiness. It has no substance or true existence yet it arises as a texture of ground spaciousness.

These are the inconceivable, wonderful offerings that we display, *all this, sole father of the buddhas, may we have the power to offer it to you!* He is their sole father because all the buddhas require a teacher; even Padmasambhava showed the form of having many different teachers. The guru is the one who opens the door to enlightenment. All beings require this function to be performed for them if they are to attain that state. When we offer to our guru, it is to the guru in this particular human form, but as the verse that comes shortly before this stated, the guru is Vajradhara. That is to say, the guru is unchanging but shows many forms. The guru is the presence of enlightenment itself. The guru is the unfolding of our own natural state which has been folded in on itself, disguising itself from itself. When we offer everything to the guru, the whole of samsara is offered to the presence of enlightenment; all limits are dissolved and the natural integration of the ground and its display is revealed. All that inhibits this is our own self-referential attachment – and this is the first and last offering we have to make.

ཆོས་དང་ཆོས་ཅན་རྣམ་པར་དབྱེ་བྱས་ནས༔

བདེན་པར་མ་གྲུབ་ཕྱི་ནང་སྒྱུ་མའི་ཆོས༔

སྣང་སྲིད་སེམས་སུ་ཡིན་པར་ཐག་ཆོད་ཅིང་༔

སྒྱུ་ལུས་ཟབ་མོའི་ཚོགས་འཁོར་བསྒྲུབ་བྱས་ནས༔

རྣམ་བཞིའི་མགྲོན་རྣམས་སོ་སོར་མཉེས་བྱེད་ཤོག༔

Distinguishing clearly between object and subject, and then recognising that there is no actual basis for this, all outer and inner phenomena are seen to be illusory. Clearly experiencing that all possible appearances are the play of the mind may we practise the profound offering assembly with our illusory bodies and thus make each of the four classes of guest happy.

Firstly we need to analyse our actual situation to see what it means to be a subject in contact with objects, hence *distinguishing clearly between object and subject.* At first our sense is often that we are just in our life, getting on with it. The outer interplay between ourselves and the world, and the inner interplay between our mind and our thoughts, is continuous. Something is always going on. So the first step is to slow down, and to start to put our habitual sense of things into question. We can begin to see the fleeting nature of our actual experience and observe how objects are held in place by our own abstract concepts. It is our own mind that develops these concepts and we can learn how to analyse their production and function. In this way we come to see how the mind and what arises for the mind are separate.

Further examination brings us to the point of *recognising that there is no actual basis for this, all outer and inner phenomena are seen to be illusory.* What we take to be the subject and what we take to be the object can be seen to be without any inherent, personal essence. They arise due to the interplay of diverse factors each of which in turn arises from and as the interplay of many different factors – and so on to infinity. All of these forces arise as the play or energy of emptiness and so are illusory, appearing yet without substance, like a mirage or like the reflection of the moon on water.

From this level of analysis we move to meditation and a deeper encounter with ourselves, directly, non-conceptually, observing how we function and what the actual nature of our awareness is. Looking for the mind we cannot find anything substantial or enduring. Awareness is inseparable from emptiness, yet we are 'here', vibrantly present to all that is arising with us, manifest yet ungraspable and without substance. From this experience we relax from our identifications, into the state where all that could possibly occur is like a drama, an effortless display, like a rainbow in the sky. Learning to play with the play of experience is the only work we have to do. With this we *clearly experience that all possible appearances are the play of the mind.*

With this awareness we offer up our ordinary bodies which carry so many hooks for reification. To do this we *practise the profound offering assembly with our illusory bodies.* With our awareness in the form of the red dakini, we take our ordinary illusory body and chop it up, feeling and dissolving the tension between our meditative experience that it is illusory and our habitual sense of attachment to it as something real. We offer the pieces in a vast cup made of our own skull. With this offering we *make each of the four classes of guest happy* as they each experience the offering as something fitting their taste. Thus there are rays of light for the buddhas; mandala palaces for the deities; medicines, dharma teachings and desirable objects for the worldly gods and human beings; and all kinds of sense gratification for the local gods, especially those who are usually left out. Each guest is satisfied by the radiance of our illusory body which we offer in the open state of awareness.

བླ་མ་རྡོ་རྗེ་སེམས་དཔའ་སྤྱི་བོར་བསྒོམ༔

གཉེན་པོ་སྟོབས་བཞིའི་བཤགས་སྡོམ་རབ་བྱས་ཏེ༔

ཕྱིན་བཅུན་ཀུན་འབྱུང་ཀུན་བཟང་ཧེ་རུ་ཀ༔

བཅོམ་ལྡན་འདས་མ་མཆོག་དང་དབྱེར་མེད་པའི༔

དཔལ་ལྡན་བླ་མའི་སྐུ་གསུང་ཐུགས་གསུམ་གྱི༔

གསང་བ་བསམ་མི་ཁྱབ་པའི་རྡོ་རྗེ་ཡི༔

རྣལ་འབྱོར་མཆོག་ཉིད་འབྱོང་བར་བྱིན་གྱིས་རློབས༔

Meditating on the guru as Vajrasattva on the crown of our heads may we confess with the four strong antidotes and keep our vows well. Glorious guru, you who are not different from Kunzang Heruka and Chomden Dema Chog, the source of all blessings − may we gain the blessing of the excellent yoga of the secret inconceivable vajras of your body, speech and mind.

Finally we practice guru yoga, experiencing our inseparability from the guru by firstly visualising him, *meditating on the guru as Vajrasattva on the crown of our heads.* His nature is the indestructible awareness which is the natural purity of all beings. With him as our witness *we confess with the four strong antidotes and keep our vows well.* We feel regret at all the unhelpful actions we have made, including being distracted whilst reciting this prayer. We confess, or bring into consciousness, all the actions we have done that have limited or harmed all beings including ourselves, and we form a clear intention never to repeat them. With this we also strengthen our vows and commitments. Although our nature has been pure from the beginning we use this practice to unfurl our energy which has developed the spin of turning in on itself. We then pray to our guru as the ultimate wrathful form, Kunzang Heruka united with his partner Chomden Dema Chog. *Glorious guru, you who are not different from Kunzang Heruka and Chomden Dema Chog.*

They are the supreme wrathful forms who overcome all obstacles. We pray that the enlightened presence of their body, speech and mind will flow into us, making us inseparable from them. We visualise rays of white light coming from their foreheads, rays of red light coming from their throats and rays of blue light coming from their hearts. We visualise each light in turn and then all together. By means of this we receive the four empowerments and become inseparable from the body, speech and mind, the three vajras, of the guru. *The source of all blessings – may we gain the blessing of the excellent yoga of the secret inconceivable vajras of your body, speech and mind.* Details of this practice can be found in the book *Being Guru Rinpoche* (see www.simplybeing. co.uk.) which provides a commentary on an important tantric practice revealed by Chimed Rigdzin's first manifestation.

We are not alone on the dharma path. These great allies are always willing and ready to help us by merging with us to reveal our own nature free of habitual obscuration. Praying is a way of working with energy. Blessing is energy; it is the availability of the radiance of the natural mode. By our conscious intention we can utilise this for the sake of ourselves and all sentient beings. The dynamic interplay of forces is always ready to respond. The function of the prayer is to help us enter into effortless participation in the flow of experience, through awakening to our unborn purity.

The prayer ends here and we can imagine our guru dissolving into light, and ourselves as the dakini dissolving in light. Then the light vanishes into space and we rest in openness, inseparable from the ground nature.

Then we can recite whatever dedication of merit we are familiar with, just as we would use our customary refuge and bodhisattva vow prayers at the beginning. Widely used versions of these prayers have been given before and after the recitation text, but readers can of course use the ones familiar to them. As Chimed Rigdzin says in the colophon, he has prepared the text so that it can be used by anyone from any of the four schools of Tibetan Buddhism.

The colophon clearly describes the circumstances of the composition of this prayer. Chimed Rigdzin Rinpoche encouraged all his students to recite it regularly and to participate in his annual offering of 100,000 butterlamps.

May the ceaseless radiance of his presence illuminate all beings.

Ingram Content Group UK Ltd.
Milton Keynes UK
UKHW020806010523
421007UK00013B/418